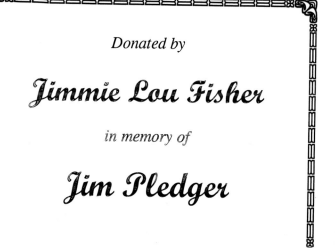

Donated by

Jimmie Lou Fisher

in memory of

Jim Pledger

THE ZEN *of* FISH

THE ZEN *of* FISH

The story of sushi,
from samurai
to supermarket

TREVOR CORSON

HarperCollins*Publishers*

HarperCollins books may be purchased for educational, business, or sales promotional use. For information, please write: Special Markets Department, Harper-Collins Publishers, 10 East 53rd Street, New York, NY 10022.

"I Am a Fish, Cuisine Is My Sea" calligraphy is reprinted with the permission of the calligrapher, Rokusaburo Michiba, and the owner, Toshi Sugiura.

Excerpts of dialogue from the Japanese comic book *Sushi Chef Kirara's Job* appeared in the Super Jump Comics series *Edomae-sushi Shokunin Kirara no Shigoto,* vol. 1, p. 206; vol. 4, pp. 80–81 and 188–190, by Hikari Hayakawa and Cozoh [Kozō] Hashimoto. Copyright © 2003–2006 by Hikari Hayakawa and Cozoh Hashimoto. Reprinted with permission.

FIRST EDITION

Designed by *Nancy Singer Olaguera, ISPN Publishing Services*

Library of Congress Cataloging-in-Publication Data is available upon request.

ISBN: 978-0-06-088350-8

ISBN-10: 0-06-088350-2

07 08 09 10 11 ISPN/RRD 10 9 8 7 6 5 4 3 2 1

AUTHOR'S NOTE

This book is a work of documentary nonfiction, and all names, people, places, and events in the book are real. All descriptions rely on extensive firsthand reporting; the author witnessed most of the scenes described in the book and took detailed notes at the time. All speech in quotation marks (" ") was recorded in person by the author in a notebook or on tape at the time it was spoken or immediately afterwards. (In a few cases, quotation marks also indicate material quoted from a secondary source; these cases are generally clear from context and are noted in the source notes at the end of the book.) Speech in single quotation marks (' ') represents speech that was not directly witnessed by the author but was described to the author as having occurred. Conversations between Japanese subjects in the story generally occurred in Japanese and were translated by the author. Japanese names are presented in Western format, with the given name first and the surname last. The author has no affiliation with the California Sushi Academy. He paid for all sushi consumed in the course of his research.

CONTENTS

Week 1

Week 2

Weeks 3, 4, and 5

*W*eeks 9 and 10

*W*eeks 11 and 12

*E*pilogue

I AM A FISH,

CUISINE IS MY SEA.

Calligraphy by the first Iron Chef Japanese, Rokusaburo Michiba, presented as a gift to Toshi Sugiura of the California Sushi Academy, June 2000.

Week 1

1

SUSHI SCHOOL

Kate Murray's alarm clock went off at 5:30 a.m. She forced her eyes open. Her college classes had never started before noon.

The day before—the Fourth of July 2005—Kate had loaded her Mustang and driven up the coast from San Diego to Los Angeles. Now unopened boxes sat scattered around the little house. She still had no furniture, and she missed her dog.

Kate dragged herself out of bed. In the bathroom mirror she looked skinny. The weeks leading up to sushi school had been stressful, and she'd stopped eating again.

On the drive to the academy she hit L.A. traffic. By the time she finally reached Hermosa Beach, she was running late. Fit-looking people on Rollerblades glided down the strip along the sandy beach, and several surfers were already out testing the waves. The Pacific Ocean stretched to the horizon. A block from the beach, Kate located the Hama Hermosa sushi restaurant and hurried inside.

She entered the foyer and saw a small dining room on her left with tables, a couple of booths, and a shiny red sushi bar. The restaurant appeared to be deserted, except for a gold Buddha sitting in an alcove.

Through a cutout in the hallway wall Kate glimpsed people. She followed the hall and stepped into a large space with a high ceiling and skylights. A second red sushi bar ran across the back wall. Down the center of the room stretched a stainless-steel table with sinks built into it, like in a chemistry lab.

All eyes turned and looked at Kate. Her classmates had already taken all the spots at the table, except for the one closest to the Japanese chef at the head of the table. *Crap,* Kate thought. She walked up to the remaining space. Everyone was standing. There were no chairs.

The chef was a short man with a shaved head. He introduced himself as Toshi Sugiura, chief executive officer (CEO) of the California Sushi Academy. He was also executive chef of the Hama Hermosa restaurant. The restaurant and the academy shared the building.

Toshi was a pioneer of American sushi. He had started serving sushi in Los Angeles in 1978, before most Americans had even heard of it. Throughout the 1980s and early 1990s, Toshi's sushi bar and restaurant—Hama Venice, in Venice Beach, just south of Santa Monica—had been one of the hottest sushi spots in all of L.A. Two years ago Toshi had shifted his efforts to the current restaurant, and it hadn't been long before Phil Jackson, coach of the L.A. Lakers, had stopped by to inscribe his signature on the wall.

Toshi had founded the California Sushi Academy in 1998. Opening a school for sushi chefs was unprecedented. For nearly 200 years, becoming a sushi chef had required a long apprenticeship—often five or more years. Toshi wanted to train people in a few months.

Toshi hired staff to manage the school and to teach. When the academy opened, three-quarters of the applicants were not even Asian. Toshi accepted them all. He couldn't be certain, but he assumed that many of his fellow Japanese sushi chefs considered him a traitor for welcoming outsiders into the world of sushi. The way Toshi saw it, Americans had already embraced sushi, and it would be foolish not to train American chefs. Since then, a few other sushi schools had opened in L.A., including the Sushi Chef Institute, run by a former instructor at Toshi's academy. So far, these were the only formal training programs for sushi chefs in the United States.

Anyone could apply to the California Sushi Academy. Toshi didn't require his students to have restaurant or kitchen experience. Hobbyists and home cooks had attended the school, along with experienced chefs, including seasoned veterans of some of America's best kitchens. Not all of the graduates went on to become professional sushi chefs. Over the years, the proportion of non-Asian students had remained high.

'*Ohaiyō gozaimasu!*' Toshi bellowed to the class. This meant "Good morning" in Japanese. But around the restaurant, the chefs said it whenever they arrived for work, even if it was afternoon or evening.

Toshi taught the class another word. '*Irasshaimase!*' That meant "Welcome." Sushi chefs yelled it whenever a customer walked in. Most Americans thought Japanese people were supposed to act quiet and dignified. But in old Tokyo, sushi chefs were loud and boisterous.

Kate liked Toshi immediately. He was cheerful and stern at the same time, like a monk who was also a kung-fu warrior. Toshi asked the nine students to introduce themselves. Kate looked around at the people who would be her classmates for the next twelve weeks. There were six men and two other women. It had never occurred to her that most of her classmates would be men. It hadn't occurred to her that there was anything unusual about a woman, or her in particular, wanting to become a sushi chef. Kate didn't see why a 20-year-old Irish-Italian girl with a pierced belly button and a nose stud couldn't make sushi.

The other students were also young, and a majority of them were white. They had come to the academy for a variety of reasons. Most of them had restaurant kitchen experience, and a few already had experience making sushi. Kate had neither.

One young man had made his start mass-producing sushi at a Whole Foods grocery store in North Carolina, and he wanted to move up to restaurant work. Another had seen how widespread sushi had become, and he hoped to purchase his own sushi restaurant in southern California. A man from El Paso, Texas, had been sent by his company, a real-estate and restaurant-development firm, because sushi was the hot new meal on the Mexican border.

Several of the students, including a woman from Barcelona, wanted to open their own catering businesses. A 17-year-old blond boy from Colorado thought working behind a sushi bar would be a great way to meet girls. There was one young woman, still in high school, who looked Japanese. She was from L.A.—her dad wanted her to learn Japanese food. There were two guys who looked Filipino or Indonesian, but they were both American.

At the far end of the table was a man from Japan. He introduced himself in broken English, in a quiet voice. Apparently, he'd come all the way from Japan to learn sushi in California. That seemed odd.

Toshi turned the class over to the academy's coordinator for student affairs, a Japanese-American man named Jay Terauchi. Jay would be keeping his eye on the students throughout the semester and would help them with whatever they needed.

Jay handed out their uniforms: black pants, white chef's jackets embroidered with the words "California Sushi Academy," and white pillbox-style chef's caps. Dressed in her street clothes, Kate had a slim and shapely figure. But her chef's jacket was too big, and when she put it on, she looked like a kitchen appliance.

Finally, Toshi introduced the academy's chief instructor, who would be teaching most of the classes. Kate was surprised to see that the instructor wasn't Japanese.

'My name is Zoran,' he said in an Australian accent. His full name was Zoran Lekic. The exotic-sounding name came from his Yugoslav ancestry. He'd grown up in Australia.

As if a Yugoslav-Australian sushi chef wasn't unusual enough, Zoran had served in the elite Royal Australian Air Force, had been a champion bodybuilder, and had worked as right-hand man to one of Australia's wealthiest entrepreneurs. In search of something new, he'd attended the California Sushi Academy and become a sushi prodigy. When he graduated in 2003, at the age of 31, Toshi had hired him on the spot.

Now Zoran taught at the academy during the day and worked behind the sushi bar in the restaurant at night. Zoran was well-proportioned, but there was nothing left of the bodybuilder's physique. He was wiry, with angular features, and he moved and spoke with speed and precision.

Zoran explained that each student would have to complete 100 intern hours to graduate. The students could earn intern hours by assisting the chefs in the restaurant, helping with catering jobs, and aiding Zoran or Jay when one of them taught the academy's basic, three-hour sushi-making class for civilians, usually on weekends.

While Zoran was talking, Toshi circled the table and handed out a black case to each student. One by one, the students flicked open the latches and raised the lids. Inside each case was $600 worth of knives. Japanese characters were etched into the blades. The knives had been hand-forged by Japanese craftsmen in a village famous for its samurai swords.

Kate stared. The biggest knife she'd ever held was a steak knife. The only thing she'd ever cooked with any confidence was scrambled eggs. When she'd signed up for sushi school, she'd imagined rolling up rice with a bamboo mat.

Japanese knives are among the sharpest in the world. After a powerful warlord unified Japan in 1600, a period of peace followed, and by the late 1800s, the samurai were no longer allowed to carry swords. The artisans who crafted swords turned their skills to forging kitchen knives from laminated, high-carbon steel. The blades hold a sharper edge than Western knives. The knives are beveled on only one side of the blade, instead of on both sides, like a Western knife. This extends the edge and makes Japanese knives sharper still. At banquets in medieval Japan for samurai and noblemen, chefs performed astonishing displays of knife work, slicing up fish and animals before the assembled guests. To this day, priests affiliated with the emperor wield knives in similar ceremonies at Shinto shrines.

Zoran held up the longest knife from his own case, a slim, 10-inch blade with a point like a stiletto.

'This is your *yanagi*,' Zoran said.

The name means "willow." The tapered blade is the shape of a willow leaf. This is the sushi chef's primary knife for work behind the sushi bar. Zoran held up two more knives for kitchen use: a rectangular blade for cutting vegetables, called a *usuba*, and a triangular blade for filleting fish, called a *deba*.

Zoran told the class they would have to sharpen their knives by hand—every day. The high-carbon blade allows for a very sharp edge, but the edge is also more fragile, and the metal rusts easily, so Japanese knives require daily care. Through sharpening, Zoran explained, a sushi chef trains his knife to his specific needs. A sushi chef shares his knives with no one, Zoran added, unless the sharing is between master and disciple.

Suddenly Zoran was handing out cucumbers.

'Okay, get out your *usuba!*' he yelled. Kate was already overwhelmed by all the Japanese words. She looked around. The other students pulled out their rectangular knives.

Zoran held a long chunk of cucumber in front of him vertically and spun it in his left hand. With the knife in his right, he peeled off a lengthy ribbon. Zoran's fingers moved in a blur beside the blade, which was pointed straight at his face.

'*Katsura-muki!*' Zoran shouted. The word meant "column peel." When the ribbon of cucumber dangled to his cutting board, Zoran stopped.

'Okay, your turn!' he yelled.

The other students picked up their chunks of cucumber and imitated Zoran. Kate lifted her rectangular knife. It felt awkward and dangerous in her small hand. It was a huge razor blade with a handle. Kate's mother and grandmother had always said, *Never cut toward yourself.*

Oh my God, Kate thought, *I don't have medical insurance.* The guy across from her was peeling off a long ribbon.

Zoran lay several sheets of cucumber ribbon on top of each other and chopped them at high speed—*thwack-thwack-thwack-thwack*—with a noise like a machine gun. He yelled out another Japanese word.

'*Sengiri!*' This was how to cut the little cucumber sticks that went inside sushi rolls.

Kate tried to cut like the others, but she managed only to destroy her cucumber. Zoran glowered at her misshapen slices. He handed her a couple of his ribbons.

'You're going to have to use these,' he said. None of the other students needed extra help.

When everyone had cut the cucumbers, Zoran made them do it all over again.

When the class finally ended at 12:30, the other students practiced sharpening their knives. They rubbed their blades carefully across blocks of volcanic stone, their fingertips pressed against the high-carbon steel. To Kate it looked dangerous. One slip, and she could slice the tip of her fingers right off. She shut her knife case without sharpening anything and slipped out of the building. When she arrived at her Mustang she found a parking ticket on the windshield.

On the drive back to her empty house, she kept thinking, *What have I done?*

The next morning in class Kate opened her knife case. Overnight the blades had rusted. Zoran glared from the head of the table.

'Kate,' he yelled, in front of the whole class, 'your knives are terrible!'

Everyone looked. Zoran handed her one of his knives.

'You're going to have to use this.'

The rest of the week was a disaster. Kate couldn't do anything right.

2

EATING TO LIVE

K ate had never been an adventurous eater. She grew up on chicken casseroles. Her family rarely ate fish; when they did, it was deep-fried. They didn't eat much rice, either. Kate's family ate potatoes.

But Kate had a stong appetite, and by the time she was in high school she'd become curvaceous. She was also pretty, but not in a delicate way—her strong chin made her look like she had an attitude.

At school Kate liked to hang out with guys more than girls. She liked the camaraderie, the joking and teasing. She was an athlete, and loved soccer. She pursued visual design, and took a video class. She produced short videos of herself performing stand-up comedy routines.

Kate was reasonably happy until partway into her senior year, when she broke her index finger. The injury prevented her from playing soccer. Without soccer, Kate got depressed. She stopped going to school. Then she got sick.

At first she thought it was the flu. When she ended up in the hospital, the doctors told her she had a kidney disease. They ran tests. She'd improve for a while and then relapse. No definitive diagnosis ever emerged. She lost a lot of weight. The doctors told her she needed a healthful diet with lots of protein and iron, and she needed to stay in good physical condition. But

Kate's energy and athleticism had deserted her. The depression worsened.

After leaving the hospital she didn't eat well. A glut of fast food made her feel terrible. She lost her appetite. She started to feel sick again. Then she'd worry about not having health insurance and would spiral deeper into depression.

A friend tried to talk her into eating sushi; after all, the fish and seaweed contained protein and iron. At first Kate scoffed at the idea of eating raw fish, but finally she relented. Her friend took her to a neighborhood sushi bar, where Kate tried something called pepper salmon *nigiri*. It tasted fresh and clean. She ordered more. Then she tried albacore tuna *nigiri,* and next something called a crunchy roll. She stuffed herself.

Soon Kate was eating sushi three or four times a week. She liked the food, but she also liked the fact that the sushi chefs were jocular and outgoing behind the sushi bar—just her style. She made friends with one of the chefs. She'd wait to get a seat in front of his position at the bar. She and the chef would joke with each other, and she would watch him work. He made her feel special, as if he were her buddy. Her health returned, and she gained weight.

In Japan, there is a famous short story called "Sushi," written in 1939 by a woman named Kanoko Okamoto, who was a poet and Buddhist scholar. It tells the story of a gentleman who eats regularly at his neighborhood sushi bar. The customers come to the sushi bar to escape themselves and the worries of their daily lives. The chef remembers what each one likes to eat and in what order, and recommends certain fish when they're in season and especially fresh. The atmosphere of the sushi bar is relaxed, sometimes rather silly.

The particular gentleman in the story had hated eating as a child. All foods repulsed him, especially fish. He would eat only a Japanese version of scrambled eggs. He was thin and sickly. In desperation, his mother set up an impromptu sushi bar in the house. She prepared sushi rice. As the boy sat across from her, she rolled up her sleeves and showed him her clean, empty hands. She flipped them like a magician and squeezed together a piece of sushi in her palms. She topped it with sweet fried egg cake—a common sushi topping not so different from scrambled eggs.

Seeing his mother squeeze the sushi together especially for him made the boy want to eat it. He liked the egg and the taste of the tart, lightly vinegared sushi rice. His mother squeezed out more sushi, adding new toppings of mild white fish—flounder, then snapper. Watching her, the boy ate happily. After that he moved on to clams and squid. He grew into a strong and handsome man, and ate sushi regularly for the rest of his life.

Kate credited sushi with her return to health. Some of her old sociability returned. She spent less time depressed and more time getting to know the people she encountered in her daily life. That made her feel better, though she still fell in and out of depression.

She didn't know what she wanted to do with her life. In the past she'd worked jobs in which she interacted with people—for example, as a receptionist at a hair salon, and as a hostess and cashier at a Chuck E. Cheese pizza parlor. Most recently she'd been working at a surf shop on the beach. She liked the social aspect of all these jobs, but none of them gave her the chance to get to know her customers. She wanted a career where she could build camaraderie with repeat customers over time. Better yet, one where she could joke and laugh with her customers, and help them enjoy themselves.

One day on her way to the L.A. airport she saw a sign for the California Sushi Academy. She keyed the telephone number into her cellphone. For a year she toyed with the idea.

Her family was skeptical. She had no cooking experience, and there was really no reason for her to leave San Diego. Her job at the surf shop was fine. She liked being near the beach, and she had started dating one of the guys who owned the shop. Still, Kate thought about it, and one day mentioned to her boyfriend that she was considering attending sushi school in L.A. He told her he didn't want her to go.

That didn't sit well with Kate. She called the academy and spoke with Jay Terauchi, the coordinator for student affairs. She talked her dad into covering half of the $5,500 tuition; she would cover the other half and her living expenses. She located a tiny house she could rent month-to-month in an industrial suburb of L.A. called Torrance, near Hermosa Beach. She quit her job at the surf shop.

A few weeks before the semester started, Kate realized she was taking a huge gamble. She stopped eating again. Right before she left, her boyfriend dumped her.

3

MOLD

*L*ater in the first week of school, Zoran piled the students into the restaurant's old van. They drove north for an hour on a ten-lane freeway, exited near a Home Depot, and stopped at a factory that made miso. Kate thought miso was a kind of soup. What did this have to do with sushi?

They walked through a large garage door. The company, Miyako Oriental Foods, could trace its roots back to the oldest miso-making operations in the United States, begun by Japanese immigrants in California before World War II. The factory currently made several brands of miso. A Japanese man showed the students a jar of green powder.

'This is mold,' he said.

Without this mold, sushi as we know it wouldn't exist. The mold's Japanese name was *kōji*.

Scientists call it *Aspergillus oryzae*. Like all molds, it's a form of fungus. Out in the wild, it has family who are killers. One of its closest cousins, a vicious carcinogen, doomed 100,000 turkeys and ducks in England in 1960, simply by sitting around on a pile of peanuts. Some of its other relatives are less exciting. They're known as mildew.

A handful of small shops in Japan are in charge of most of the good mold. Mold experts manage mold as though they are breeding racehorses. Some of the shops have been selling the best strains for centuries. They keep backup jars of mold in high-security vaults or hidden in caves. The green powder in the man's jar consisted of mold spores—around a trillion of them.

Mold has to eat. The spores are dormant, but when you give them something to munch on, they germinate and grow into white fuzz like the type you see on old bread.

The man led Kate and her classmates onto the factory floor. Kate saw machines two stories tall, with conveyor belts, catwalks, and pipes going everywhere. Once a week, the Japanese man said, he pours a little mold into a funnel on one of the big machines— just enough to infect a batch of 6,600 pounds of rice. Once the rice is properly infected, he shoots it through a high-pressure pipe into an incubator the size of a house.

The big incubator looked like a nuclear reactor. The man explained that inside, it was like a warm, moist cave. The machine cost several million dollars and was equipped with a control panel the size of a vending machine. In the old days, miso makers had simply used a box lined with a blanket.

In the incubator, the mold gobbles away at the rice and grows at tremendous speed, sending out feelers like ivy until it has ensnared every grain of the 6,600 pounds of rice in a web. The mold eats so fast that the incubator, like a nuclear reactor, would overheat if it weren't properly controlled. In two days, the fuzzy web has eaten so much rice that some 500 pounds of it has simply vanished.

At that point, the man cooks 5,000 pounds of soybeans. The moldy rice rides a conveyor belt into a computerized meat grinder that churns it up with the soybeans, along with a dose of sea salt, bacteria, and yeast.

Then the process turns low-tech. From the meat grinder, Mexican laborers shovel 1,300 pounds of the mush at a time into tubs the size of a Jacuzzi. They cover the tubs with tarps and drive them with a forklift into a temperature-controlled garage. Then the process gets really low-tech—the tubs just sit around. For months.

Molds don't have stomachs, but they do manufacture digestive enzymes. Enzymes are like robots in a chemical factory where the assembly line can run forward or backward; they put different molecules together or, just as often, take them apart. And they work fast. There's an enzyme that shortens a certain chemical reaction from 78 million years to 25 milliseconds. That's the kind of speed you want when you're a hungry mold.

From the mold's point of view, the rice and soybean plants have spent their lives soaking up sunlight and building it into giant molecules that are much too complicated. The digestive enzymes take those molecules apart. The enzymes split the proteins into useful building blocks called amino acids. They split the carbohydrates down into little energy bars in the form of simple sugars. In fact, this is just what you do with your food. Humans would not survive without the digestive assistance of enzymes. Mold and man think alike.

Which is what makes the subsequent betrayal so tragic. After the tarp goes over the Jacuzzi tubs, the mold in the miso suffocates and dies before it has even had a chance to have sex. Or rather, since mold produces spores asexually, before it has had a chance to have non-sex. The man wants the mold just for its enzymes. The mold might need air, but the enzymes don't. They keep right on digesting.

Soybeans contain a lot of protein, and most of that protein is a type called glycinin. The enzymes tear it apart, leaving behind an amino acid called glutamate. Humans love glutamate. It tastes fantastic. Glutamate is also crucial for human functioning. It is the most abundant fast excitatory neurotransmitter in our brains and spinal cords; it is believed to be important for thought and memory. In addition, it is the most frequently used building block in the proteins throughout our bodies.

The enzymes tear apart the carbohydrates in the rice as well, leaving behind glucose and other sugars—also yummy to humans.

The process still isn't finished. Next, the bacteria go to town. The same bacteria that make yogurt and cheese are the life of the party in miso. Cows never caught on in Japan; miso is, in a sense, Japan's cheese.

Like mold, the bacteria manufacture digestive enzymes, but their enzymes gobble up sugars. They leave behind lactic acid and acetic acid, some of the substances that give yogurt its pleasant tartness and prevent it—and miso—from spoiling.

Finally, the yeasts join the party. Put crudely, yeasts eat sugar and pee alcohol. In the miso, the alcohols produced by the yeasts then react with the acids made by the bacteria. The result is a group of fruity-smelling compounds called esters, which are also present in the complex aromas of fine wine.

When the contents of the Jacuzzi tubs have finished fermenting, the Mexican forklift operators move the tubs back out of the garage and into a refrigerated room for packaging. Now, the miso possesses just about every attribute you could want in a food: savory amino flavors, sugary sweetness, acidic tartness, salty tang, and fragrant smells, along with nutritious proteins, sugars, fats, helpful digestive enzymes, and friendly bacteria.

It's got something else as well. And that's where the connection to sushi comes in. Around the edges of the tarp, a brown liquid has oozed out. It contains many elements of the miso, especially the tasty glutamate.

Possibly as early as 1,200 years ago, discerning chefs who cooked for the Japanese aristocracy decided that plain miso, with its bumpy texture, wasn't refined enough for the delicate tongues of their lords and ladies. They noticed the brown liquid oozing out. Instead of flavoring their dinner with miso, they drizzled the new liquid over it.

Other, similar products were probably discovered in different places at different times in different ways, in both China and Japan. Historians don't agree on the details. But one thing is clear: soy sauce originated as a by-product of making miso.

Like miso and soy sauce, cured ham is rich in glutamate. Parmesan cheese is, too. So are tomatoes. Because of glutamate, a serving of sushi with soy sauce actually has taste elements in common with a plate of pasta covered with tomato sauce, anchovies, and Parmesan cheese.

Before soy sauce, the Japanese, like the Chinese and Southeast Asians, had preferred fermented fish sauce. Vegetarianism became popular when Buddhist monks arrived in Japan in the sixth century. As in America today, Buddhist food manufacturers in ancient Japan racked their brains for ways to make soybeans taste like meat. Miso and then soy sauce were the results.

For a long time, soy sauce remained a luxury. Japanese commoners made do with miso. Then, about 500 years ago, Japanese food companies built the first soy-sauce factories, and soy sauce became commonplace. About the same time, the makers of soy sauce added wheat to the mold fermentation process to make the sauce sweeter.

The man at the miso factory explained to the students that Japanese companies now use mold and incubators to make soy sauce in their modern manufacturing plants.

The same kind of mold and the same kind of incubator are also used to produce the initial stage of Japanese rice vinegar. In the case of rice vinegar, the fermentation process produces acetic acid, which is what gives vinegar its tangy sourness. And rice vinegar is what sushi chefs add to cooked rice, along with sugar and a little salt, to make it tangy and sweet.

Kate and her classmates had been under the impression that what made sushi delicious was the fresh ingredients. In fact, the fundamental flavors of sushi—soy sauce and rice vinegar—depend on infecting certain foods with fungus and letting them get moldy.

Kate enjoyed the field trip. It was a welcome diversion from the routine. Back in the classroom, Zoran made the students practice cutting cucumbers every day. Then he started them cutting giant white radishes using the same technique.

Zoran continued to yell at Kate, close beside him at the head of the table. When he wasn't yelling at her, he treated her like some sort of special-needs student, giving her extra help while the rest of the class watched or moved ahead. Kate had always prided herself on pulling her own weight in a group, on being "one of the guys." But here, she was certain her classmates had already written her off as a total flake. At the end of every day she considered quitting.

Week 2

4

TASTE OF THE SEA

'These are bonito flakes,' Zoran explained, showing the students a bag of fluffy beige flakes. He was teaching them to make a broth called *dashi*. Dashi is highly flavorful, and it is a cornerstone of Japanese cuisine. Dashi is the soup base to which miso is added to make miso soup. Like soy sauce, dashi plays a supporting role in sushi, but the method for making dashi is very different.

First, Zoran had simmered slabs of kelp, a type of seaweed with broad leaves. Now he switched off the heat and sprinkled the bonito flakes into the pot. Kate watched the flakes melt into the steaming water. She gathered that bonito was a kind of fish. She'd seen those flakes before, sprinkled on food at Japanese restaurants. She'd always thought they were bacon. After a few minutes, Zoran removed the kelp and bonito flakes with a strainer. The remaining broth was dashi.

Kelp—like miso, soy sauce, cured ham, Parmesan cheese, and tomatoes—is loaded with tasty glutamate. Called *konbu* in Japanese, kelp is the first half of what makes dashi delicious.

The second half of dashi's magic is the bonito flakes. Bonito are a type of tuna, also called skipjack tuna. Like their larger tuna cousins, they swim fast, sometimes in bursts that reach 40 miles an hour. They accomplish this feat by loading their muscles with high-energy power pellets that provide fuel to their cells. These power pellets are called ATP—adenosine triphosphate.

The manufacturers of bonito flakes simmer fillets of bonito

before smoking the fish for ten or twenty days. Like the makers of miso, they infect the fish with mold and lock up the fillets in a box. After two weeks they pull out the moldy fillets and lay them in the sun. They scrape off the old mold, add new mold, and lock them back in the box. They repeat this procedure three or four times.

Just as with miso and soy sauce, digestive enzymes break down the proteins in the fish into tasty amino acids. The ATP gets broken down into a series of other molecules, resulting in a delicious compound called inosine monophosphate, or IMP, which the human tongue savors nearly as much as glutamate.

After a few months of molding and drying, the bonito fillets are hard, like pieces of wood. To make the flakes, the fillets are shaved with a tool like a carpenter's plane.

Dashi's role in sushi usually goes unnoticed, particularly in the United States. Most Americans think they are supposed to dunk all their sushi in soy sauce. But full-strength soy sauce overpowers the delicate flavors of raw fish. A good sushi chef adds all the flavoring the sushi needs before he hands it to the customer. He mixes his own sauce and uses it behind the sushi bar. This sauce is called *nikiri*. Each chef has his own secret formula. Most are a variation on a standard recipe, and dashi is a key supporting actor. To 100 parts soy sauce, the chef adds twenty parts dashi, ten parts sake, and ten parts mirin, a sweet rice liquor used in cooking. The mixture is heated and reduced briefly, and is then ready to use. *Nikiri* is a kinder, gentler, and more complex soy sauce, with a broad array of flavor compounds appropriate for enhancing sushi.

The Hama Hermosa restaurant attached to the California Sushi Academy provided its customers with straight soy sauce. But at the sushi bar, Toshi and the other chefs frequently painted a sheen of *nikiri* across the top of pieces of sushi with a basting brush. This was the traditional method of seasoning sushi. The chefs were forever handing sushi to customers and admonishing them, "No soy sauce!" Most sushi chefs in America don't make this effort.

The deliciousness of dashi and soy sauce intrigued a Japanese chemist named Kikunae Ikeda, who in 1908 figured out that glutamate is what makes kelp broth so delicious. He realized that the stuff could be manufactured. The product was called monosodium glutamate, or MSG.

A few years later, a colleague figured out what made bonito broth so tasty. It was the IMP. Much of what makes all fish delicious is IMP, created when the ATP in the fish's muscles breaks down after the fish's death. Scientists discovered that IMP could be manufactured, too, and like MSG used as a flavor additive.

Western scientists believed that the human tongue could taste only four fundamental flavors: sweet, salty, sour, and bitter. The Japanese scientists argued that there was a fifth fundamental flavor, triggered by amino acids like glutamate and compounds like IMP, and epitomized by foods such as dashi and *nikiri*. They called this fifth flavor "tastiness," or in Japanese, *umami*.

For decades, Western scientists were skeptical that *umami* was a fundamental flavor. Finally, in the past few years, scientists at the University of California, San Diego, have demonstrated that the tongues of humans and other animals possess specific receptors for *umami*.

Today, MSG is manufactured by the ton and added to all varieties of processed foods. Most Americans associate MSG with Chinese food, but it is also added to canned foods, soups, salad dressings, chips, and fast food. On product labels it is usually disguised as "hydrolyzed vegetable protein." It is even added to much of our processed meat and poultry because modern industrial production has robbed animal flesh of its own flavor. The Buddhist vegetarian condiments of ancient Japan are now used to make American factory meat palatable.

After class, Kate drove to McDonald's, as she'd been doing every day after class. She bought a Big Mac. She drove home. She sat on the one chair in her lonely little house in Torrance, surrounded by her unpacked boxes. She stared at the floor and slowly chewed her Big Mac.

After two weeks at the academy, Kate was afraid her family had been right to be skeptical. During the second week, the classes had covered more basics of Japanese cuisine. None of it had much to do with sushi. Every day she wondered what she was doing there. She had given up everything in her life that she knew and entered a world where she didn't belong.

At least the Big Mac felt familiar and comforting. One of the ingredients of its "special sauce" was hydrolyzed vegetable protein.

Friday morning, at the end of the second week, Kate dragged herself back to class. Zoran announced that they were going to make sushi—finally. He gave the students a crash course in *nigiri* and *te-maki,* or "hand rolls."

Nigiri are the little rectangles of rice topped with slices of fish and other toppings that sushi chefs squeeze together with their fingers. Hand rolls are an informal sushi roll that don't require a bamboo mat to make. The chef places half a sheet of nori—the crisp, dark-green Japanese seaweed paper—on his palm, presses on a blob of sushi rice and a piece of fish, and rolls it up like a waffle cone. The *nigiri* and hand rolls that Kate made looked ragged and fell apart.

Then Zoran told the students why he was teaching them to make *nigiri* and hand rolls. The next day—Saturday—Toshi, Zoran, Jay, and all the students would load the restaurant's catering equipment into a truck and drive to Hollywood, to the studio lot at Paramount Pictures, to serve sushi at a party for 3,000 people.

5

LIKE THE VOMIT
OF A DRUNKARD

Jay wasn't just the academy's coordinator for student affairs. He also handled myriad other tasks for Toshi's restaurant and school. On Friday afternoon at the end of the second week of the semester, Jay loaded eight blue insulated bins into the academy's old van. Imported from Japan, the bins were labeled "Sanitation Listed Food Equipment." They were designed for keeping rice at body temperature—the ideal temperature for serving sushi.

Jay drove along a wide boulevard lined with the strip malls characteristic of Los Angeles. He knew that many of the generic storefronts hid hole-in-the-wall eateries that served authentic ethnic cuisine, often next to restaurants serving fast food or Americanized imitations. Some of the best sushi in America was hidden in L.A.'s strip malls—along with some of the worst.

Food fascinated Jay. He was the kind of guy who, if he heard that the best Mexican tacos in L.A. were being served from a truck in a distant suburb, would drive out and try them. During college, Jay had worked in the kitchen of a Japanese restaurant. If he didn't prepare a dish perfectly, the chef would scream and throw the dish back at him.

Jay's interest in sushi had begun only about five years ago. He attended the California Sushi Academy, then worked for Toshi in the kitchen. Next, he worked behind the sushi bar and then taught at the academy. Now, he served part-time as the academy's coordinator for student affairs and filled in around the restaurant. The rest of the time he ran his own consulting business, giving advice to restaurateurs who wanted to open sushi bars.

Jay was American, but his ancestors were Japanese. As he'd learned more about sushi, he'd become worried about the state of sushi in the United States. He would sit at a sushi bar and see people stirring globs of green wasabi paste into their soy sauce to make a thick gray goo. They'd slather their fish with the goo, eat it, and exclaim, 'Oh, that's such good fish!' Jay himself used to do the same thing.

But now Jay knew that this behavior was distressing to the chef. Wasabi is a type of horseradish, and in the quantities required to make that thick gray goo, the spiciness of wasabi overwhelms the human capacity for taste and smell. The chef might have risen at 4:30 that morning to go to the fish market and haggle over the best fish, only to see his customers slather it with wasabi so they couldn't even taste it. Jay believed chefs were becoming disillusioned and customers were missing out. Americans liked food that was hot and spicy, but there was so much more to sushi than that.

Jay had learned that in Japan, sushi chefs might put a touch of wasabi inside a *nigiri*, using a larger dab of wasabi with fatty fish, and a smaller one with lean. But they never served extra wasabi on the side. They would serve a pinch on the side with sashimi—plain raw fish, without rice. But diners certainly weren't supposed to mix the wasabi into their soy sauce and apply it indiscriminately.

Another thing Jay noticed was people gobbling up the pickled ginger as an appetizer. But the point of the ginger was to cleanse the palate between servings of different kinds of fish. Not eating a slice of ginger between each type of fish, Jay felt, was like mixing five different wines and trying to taste the Chardonnay.

He'd also see diners dunk the rice side of their *nigiri* in the soy sauce, instead of the fish side. Or they'd eat the *nigiri* in two bites instead of one. Or they'd force themselves to use chopsticks, when in fact most Japanese people just use their fingers to eat sushi.

Jay noticed, too, that people automatically assumed sushi was good for them. But in the United States, the most popular form of sushi was big sushi rolls, loaded with carbs, sugar, fat, and sodium. A sushi takeout box at an American supermarket could easily contain as many calories as two slices of pizza, and the rolls served in restaurants are often worse.

At the sushi academy, Jay would watch each new batch of students with interest. Most of the students were American in one way or another—sometimes Asian American, sometimes Caucasian. A few African Americans had attended the school. One woman had come from Barbados. Some of the students came from Europe. Some were global citizens, others were local in their outlook. Almost none was in any sense traditionally Japanese.

As Jay observed the waves of students coming through the school, he came to think that people who were not traditional Japanese chefs might communicate better with American customers. This new generation was more familiar with American culture and the English language. The trick was to teach them Japanese traditions so they could master authentic sushi.

Jay's thoughts returned to the eight blue insulated bins sitting in the back of the van. He had arrived at his destination. He parked the van next to a nondescript one-story warehouse of red brick and stepped through an unmarked side door into a hallway. Rows of shoes sat on shelves, neatly arranged in pairs. Workers in white aprons and white rubber boots shuffled along the hall, their hair tucked into bouffant caps and their faces hidden behind sanitary masks. This was the California Rice Center, a hub of L.A. sushi. Down the hall was a cavernous factory that produced sushi rice on an industrial scale.

The modern term "sushi" refers not to fish, but to rice—rice seasoned with rice vinegar, sugar, and salt. Any food made with this seasoned rice can be called sushi, whether it involves fish or not.

Traditionally, sushi apprentices in Japan spend up to two years simply learning to cook and season the rice before they're allowed near the fish. Master sushi chefs agonize over their sushi rice, perfecting secret recipes. In the old days, the larger sushi shops in Japan employed full-time specialist chefs whose only job was to prepare the rice.

This is ironic, because the original sushi chefs threw the sushi rice away.

About 140,000 years ago, people in what is now Japan probably ate a lot of roasted elephant. After the earth's climate shifted, they switched to acorns, which was surely a step down. To supplement the acorn diet, they hunted wild boar. They also dug in the coastal mud for clams and rowed out into the ocean in dugout canoes to harpoon bluefin tuna and catch bonito with wooden hooks. They dried the red fillets in the sun to make jerky. In those days, the closest thing a Japanese person had to sushi was a strip of tuna jerky wrapped around an acorn.

Even after the Japanese learned to grow rice—probably around 400 or 300 BC—early sushi didn't involve tuna or any other ocean fish. Sushi began inland. Historians think it was first invented along the Mekong River, in what is now landlocked southern China, Laos, and northern Thailand. No one knows just when, but it was after rice cultivation began in the region; remains of rice have been located in northern Thailand dating back to 3500 BC.

The people along the Mekong River caught freshwater fish. During monsoon season, the rivers would flood into the rice paddies, and fish would swim into the rice fields. Soon the farmers were raising fish in the paddies along with the rice. But the supply of fish came and went, and the farmed fish had to be harvested at the end of the rainy season, before the rice paddies dried up. The dilemma was how to store fish for later consumption. Near the ocean this wasn't a problem because people could catch fish all year.

The inland folk packed the whole fish, including its guts, in a large amount of salt. Guts contain digestive enzymes. These enzymes, along with other enzymes in the fish's flesh, broke the proteins of the fish down into amino acids. The salt prevented harmful bacteria from growing. The result was fermented fish paste. This was how Asian fish sauce got its start.

But large amounts of salt could be hard to come by. This technique also obliterated the fish itself, creating a slimy, stinky mush. In Japan, a version of it is still eaten today, called *shiokara*. People who try it for the first time usually want to throw up; that said, fermented fish paste has enjoyed surprising global popularity. A nearly identical product, called *garum,* was one of the most popular cooking ingredients throughout the Roman Empire.

The inland rice farmers along the Mekong River discovered a second way to keep their fish edible for long periods. This method kept the fish in one piece and left it much less stinky. First, they gutted and cleaned the fish. Then, they packed it in cooked rice and sealed it inside a jar. They cooked the rice first because they wanted it to decay.

Inside the jar, mold quickly digested the carbohydrates in the rice, breaking it down into sugars, just as in the making of miso. Then yeasts ate the sugars, creating alcohol. The alcohol protected the remaining sugars from the bacteria in the air inside the jar.

With the notable exception of botulism, many nasty bacteria—the ones that spoil food—need oxygen. Many benign bacteria don't; they probably first evolved inside piles of rotting vegetation. In the rice in the jar, these nicer bacteria digested the sugars. They gave off lactic acid and acetic acid as waste. By now the rice was horribly sour. A Japanese source from the twelfth century describes it as "no different from the vomit of a drunkard."

But acids do prevent food from spoiling. When a bacterium runs afoul of an acid like lactic acid or acetic acid, the acid shoots hydrogen ions into the bacterium. The ions disable the cell's machinery and wreak other havoc, and the bacterium dies. Inside the jar, the fish was surrounded by acids in which very few bacteria could survive, and there was no oxygen for them, anyway.

The fish didn't stay perfectly fresh, of course. Digestive enzymes broke down most of the proteins. But the fish would keep, and stay in one piece, for as long as a year.

When the inland farmers wanted to eat the fish, they opened the jar, cleaned off the gooey, vomit-smelling rice, and threw it away. The fish tasted pretty good—today it would strike us as a bit like a pungent aged cheese, with butter and vinegar overtones.

This original form of sushi spread to China, and then to Japan. Apparently the Japanese considered it a very special meal. By the year AD 718, a Japanese government document said people could use sushi to pay their taxes.

No one is certain where the Japanese word *sushi* comes from. One of the Chinese words for preserved fish was probably pronouced something like *chee*. In Japanese, that sound could have become *shee*, supplying the second syllable of the word *sushi*. The first syllable might have come from the Japanese word for "sour," *suppai*, making *su-shi* to be "sour preserved fish."

In Japan, people gave this original form of sushi its own name— *nare-zushi*, which means "aged sushi."

The Japanese began to use shellfish from the ocean to make *nare-zushi*, too, including abalone and mussels. But until the end of the ninth century, most of the fish in sushi continued to be freshwater fish from lakes and rivers rather than ocean fish.

While sushi was adopted in Japan, it disappeared in China. Possibly this was because Genghis Khan and the Mongols conquered China, and they preferred red meat to fish. But the original form of sushi is still eaten today in Thailand, as well as on the island of Taiwan off the southern Chinese coast.

It is also still eaten in Japan. The Japanese make the original form of sushi from freshwater fish—in particular, a species of carp related to goldfish. The fish are called *funa. Funa-zushi* remains on the menu to this day at restaurants and shops around Lake Biwa, near Japan's ancient capital city of Kyoto.

Lake Biwa, closer to Kyoto than to the sea, is Japan's largest lake and throughout history probably provided a steady supply of fish. Gradually, people who could command the luxury of regular deliveries of fish—probably aristocrats in the capital—began to eat *nare-zushi* sooner and sooner in the fermentation process. They didn't have to worry about preserving the fish for long periods.

By the 1400s or so, these people were eating *nare-zushi* so early in the process that the interior of the fish's flesh remained relatively fresh. They discovered that the rice itself, though fermented, was still edible and quite tasty at the earlier stage. The flavors of this food were different: tart, slightly acidic rice, and fish that tasted fresher and less cheesy.

By 1600, people were calling this lightly fermented mixture of fish and rice *nama-nari* (or *nama-nare*), which translates roughly as "ready raw" (or "raw aged"). For *nama-nari*, the fish and rice were aged for a month or less, and sometimes as briefly as a few days.

The original form of sushi had been a side dish. Now it became a self-contained meal of fish and tart rice. This form of sushi was a luxury, not a necessity. Sushi makers began to entertain their aristocratic customers with new ingredients, including ocean fish.

A dramatic new development took place around 1600. People fermenting sake figured out how to age the dregs from the rice liquor, add new bacteria, and ferment it further to produce acetic acid. This is when rice vinegar was born, and it was delicious. In addition to acetic acid, it contained some seventy other flavor components—amino acids, organic acids, sugars, and esters. In the second half of the 1600s, a doctor for the shogun tried adding vinegar to sushi rice. He discovered that the uniquely tart taste of sushi rice no longer required fermentation at all. Instead of packing fish in rice and letting it sit around until bacteria produced lactic acid, sushi makers could just splash on the convenient new liquid. They achieved a similar taste instantly, with the acetic acid in the vinegar. The acids in the vinegar helped to prevent the rice from fermenting in the first place because they killed bacteria. The purpose of the rice in sushi had been completely reversed. The new sushi, fresh instead of preserved, grew popular. People called it *haya-zushi* — "quick sushi."

In modern-day Japan and in Los Angeles, the quests for ease and speed have resulted in factories that mass-produce sushi rice. At the California Rice Center, tons of rice and gallons of sweetened vinegar churn through vast steamers and vats and mixing machines. Trucks deliver the product to locations throughout Los Angeles. Supermarkets, hotels, catering companies, and takeout stands buy sushi rice in 17-pound tubs for $18. It can even be purchased in pre-squeezed rectangles, ready to be paired with slices of fish.

Jay placed his order and unloaded the eight insulated bins from the van. Tomorrow he would retrieve them, full of 150 pounds of factory sushi rice. It would sit for seven or eight hours at body temperature in the bins. During that time, a dramatic battle would occur within the bins. Spores of a toxic bacterium almost always present in raw rice would wake up, germinate, and discover a paradise of warmth and delicious food. The acetic acid in the vinegar would bombard the bacteria with hydrogen ions, warping their enzymes. It is a war waged daily behind every sushi bar in the world.

On the drive back to Hama Hermosa, Jay pondered the new class of students. The party in Hollywood tomorrow evening would be an annual fund-raiser. This year was at least the sixth year that Toshi would be taking the students to Paramount Pictures to make sushi.

Every year, the students' hands trembled when they stood in front of an audience for the first time and tried to put fish on rice.

6

SEVEN GODS IN EVERY GRAIN

The factory sushi rice that Jay had ordered from the California Rice Center was only for the catering job. At the Hama Hermosa restaurant, the staff cooked and seasoned their own high-quality rice every day. When Jay arrived back at the restaurant, Takumi Nishio, the one Japanese student in the class, was preparing the rice for that night's dinner service.

Takumi leaned over the row of sinks against one wall of the kitchen and rinsed 10 pounds of rice in an oversize metal mixing bowl. He was unshaven and had bags under his eyes. Jay had noticed that Takumi worked far harder than any of the American students. He was always studying in the classroom or busy in the kitchen. Takumi stirred the grains of rice in cold water until the water turned milky white. He glanced at the clock. There wasn't much time left before the restaurant opened for business.

Until recently, rice producers coated rice with white talc powder to protect it during shipment. But talc is inedible and may even cause cancer, so cooks had to wash the rice thoroughly before use. Most rice is now talc free. In the United States, the FDA encourages producers to powder white rice with vitamins instead, and some states require it. Health authorities discourage people from washing rice because it sends the vitamins down the drain. But it's hard to tell the good white powder from the bad, so people have continued to wash their rice.

As if in an arms race, rice enrichers have developed rinse-proof technologies. They lacquer vitamins onto 0.5 percent of the rice grains with elaborate coating processes and stealthily mix them in with the rest of the rice. One company has even developed man-made vitamin pellets that look exactly like grains of rice, intended to trick people into eating their vitamins.

In Japan, producers do not usually add vitamins to white rice, and in the United States, the rapid spread of sushi has created a whole new industry: premium Japanese rice, grown in America and often sold under Japanese brand names. A few of the mass-market brands are enriched with vitamins; most are not. However, there is another reason rice still ends up covered with white powder and why it needs to be rinsed.

No rice starts out white. The rice plant is a kind of grass, and each grain of rice is actually a tiny fruit—which is to say, the plant version of an egg. The hull is the egg's shell, made mostly of the same hard silica found in rocks. Under the hull is the brown inner husk, or bran, and under that a super-thin layer of oils, enzymes, and vitamins. Inside is the egg's food supply.

In the modern world, rice is run through high-tech milling machines after harvest. First, steel rollers encased in rubber are used to break off the hull. At this point, all rice is brown. Next, to make the rice white, fine wire brushes scrape off the inner husk, or bran, along with the oils and enzymes. After polishing, there's a dent in the end of each grain. That's where the embryo used to live.

The milling process leaves behind a bit of starch as a fine powder on the rice. This leftover starch creates too much stickiness in cooked rice, which is why sushi chefs rinse it off. A few brands of rice go through an additional step, a process trademarked Kapika. A special Japanese machine rubs the grains together so they polish each other clean. Kapika rice keeps longer and doesn't require as much rinsing.

The problem with all this processing is that removing the inner husk, or bran layer, also removes the vitamins. That is why health officials have advocated re-enriching white rice. An alternative would be to encourage people just to eat brown rice.

Most health-conscious people assume that brown rice was the form of rice that humans originally consumed, but that's not the case. Throughout most of rice-growing history, people pounded rice grains in a wooden mortar with a mallet to break open the shell. The Japanese built oversize mallets that looked like seesaws with a heavy pounding head at one end. A person stood on the other end, leveraging the mallet up and down with his body weight.

In practice, the effort required to break open the hull of the rice grains also broke off most of the inner husk, so eating brown rice wasn't even an option until the invention of modern milling. That, and not a preference for luxury or purity, is why white rice has been eaten for most of history. Fortunately, traditional pounding techniques left a bit of the bran on. Average "white" rice was actually "slightly beige" rice, and it retained some vitamins.

That said, rich people in Japan and other countries preferred the taste of bright white rice, and so they paid extra to have their rice polished. Sadly for them, the Japanese diet contained little besides rice bran to supply vitamin B_1. People who ate polished rice condemned themselves to emotional disturbances, impaired sensory perception, weight loss, heart failure, and even death—the results of beriberi, or vitamin B_1 deficiency. About 350 years ago, as more Japanese acquired wealth and moved from the countryside to cities, the consumption of highly polished rice increased. So did recorded incidences of beriberi. One food historian reports that for a time, it was considered Japan's national disease.

But aside from the lack of vitamins and certain minerals, white rice can provide all the basic protein and starch that a human needs to survive, and it beats out wheat handily. A person who weighs 150 pounds would have to eat five or six small bowls of rice three times a day in order to survive on rice alone. That's a lot. But if he tried to survive on bread, he'd have to eat 72 slices of it a day.

Takumi dumped the rinse water and added fresh water for another rinsing. Eight or nine rinses later the milling starch had washed away and the water ran clear.

At this stage, some sushi chefs soak their rice in cold water for as long as 30 to 60 minutes. The chefs at Hama Hermosa preferred to run cold water from the tap over the rice for just ten minutes or so. This achieved both a quick soak and a thorough rinse. Then the chefs would pour the rice into a colander to drain. Each grain of rice continued to absorb the moisture on its surface, like a tiny sponge.

Takumi's hands had turned red from the frigid rinse water. Anything but cold water would cause the rice to soften too much before cooking. A sushi chef in L.A. named Katsuo Niiyama remembered the first two years of his apprenticeship in Japan as nothing but frigid water and freezing hands. Every morning at 6:00 a.m. he fetched buckets of cold water and scrubbed everything in the restaurant. Then he rinsed nine batches of rice, each batch requiring multiple rinses in cold water. On most days he did something wrong, which earned him a slap in the face from the chef. Some days the chef chased him with a stick.

Takumi looked at the clock again. Barely two hours remained before customers would start to arrive. Today was a Friday and the restaurant might be busy. Takumi would have to prepare two full batches of sushi rice. Nearby, Zoran rushed around doing prep work. Takumi could tell that Zoran, out of the corner of his eye, was watching him.

Japan's native religion, Shinto, starts with the belief that everything—trees, foxes, fish, samurai swords—possesses its own spirit. Takumi abided by this belief. For example, he lavished care on his sushi knives because a skilled craftsman had poured his heart and soul into their creation, and so they had acquired spirits of their own.

Rice seems especially sacred because it is Japan's staple food. Sushi chefs call it *shari,* a Buddhist term that refers to tiny pieces of the Buddha's bones. According to Japanese folk tradition, each grain of rice contains not just one spirit but seven. In his two batches of sushi rice, totaling roughly 20 pounds, Takumi was currently responsible for the fate of some three and a half million tiny gods.

All rice, whether it houses deities or not, belongs to a single species of plant, with the sole exception of one other species eaten only in West Africa. The primary species has more than 100,000 varieties, but these fall into two categories, Indica and Japonica. Japonica rices are shorter and stickier, and include sushi rice.

Sushi rice is sticky because it's hopelessly disorganized. Most plants store solar energy inside seeds and grains, as little energy bars of sugar—glucose. They pack these energy bars inside the seed or grain in one of two ways. The first way is neat and orderly, and results in nice, straight strands of starch, each strand containing 1,000 pieces of sugar.

The second way is to fling the energy bars into tangled, irregular, prickly heaps of starch, each containing anywhere from 5,000 to 20,000 pieces of sugar. Sushi rice contains more of this second, disorganized type of starch than do most other kinds of rice. The prickly heaps make the rice stick together.

Average sushi restaurants use a medium-grain version of Japonica. Each grain is oblong, two or three times longer than it is wide. Because of its shape, medium-grain rice does not form itself into sushi quite so willingly. But it is less expensive. The California Sushi Academy stocked medium-grain rice for the students in the classroom.

High-end sushi restaurants pay extra for short-grain rice. Each grain is more round than oblong. Hama Hermosa purchased its premium Japanese short-grain rice from American farmers who grew it just 400 miles away, in the Sacramento Valley of northern California.

Takumi draped a Teflon net inside the bowl of a large commercial rice cooker. The Teflon mesh was to prevent the rice from sticking to the bowl. Then he poured in the short-grain rice he'd washed. It sounded like rain.

Sushi apprentices in Japan spend a couple of years on rice alone because preparing it is so tricky. Traditional chefs consider the rice more important than the fish. The goal is grains that are firm, plump, and sticky. Myriad factors affect the results.

Although each grain of rice originally contained a living embryo and skin, the part that remains after polishing—the embryo's food supply—is a mass of dead cells containing stored starches embedded in a grid of proteins. Good growing seasons can be bad for sushi chefs because high-starch grains can break open during cooking, resulting in mush.

The most favored sushi rice in Japan is a variety called Koshihikari. The starch in the core of the grain is more condensed than in other varieties, and the walls of its storage cells are thicker. Both factors contribute to a firmer and denser texture, qualities that sushi connoisseurs consider crucial. Koshihikari grains also contain aromatic fatty acids, providing flavor and a moister sensation in the mouth.

In Japan alone, farmers have cultivated at least 2,000 varieties of rice. Like winemakers and coffee sellers, serious sushi chefs often blend different varieties, and different harvests, to achieve a unique texture and flavor. At Hama Hermosa, the rice that Takumi was preparing for dinner was a blend of Koshihikari and one other variety.

Regardless of the type of rice, sushi chefs generally prefer rice that has aged for a few months after harvest because it's drier. To sushi purists, perhaps the most important factor is not the type of sushi rice but how it was dried. Most Japanese rice today is force-dried with hot air before milling. The purists complain that this causes the surface of the grains to become pasty. When vinegar is added to force-dried rice after cooking, the pasty surface of the grains can form a membrane, blocking absorption of the vinegar. The very best rice is left to dry naturally in the sun.

After letting the rice drain, Takumi's next step was to add water for cooking. But before adding the water, Takumi did something that might be considered cheating.

Traditionally, sushi chefs cook their sushi rice with a splash of sake and a strip of kelp to add flavor. Instead, Takumi reached for a maroon can of white powder manufactured by the Otsuka Chemical Industry Corporation. This substance, known by its trade name Miora, came into commercial use as a rice additive in Japan after World War II. When labeled for sale in the United States, a sticker on the can declares in English that the ingredients are simply "potato starch and glucose." But the Japanese ingredients list includes other items—enzymes called amylase and protease, plus "kelp flavor."

Amylase breaks starch down into glucose. Protease breaks protein down into amino acids. Cooking with Miora creates rice with unnaturally high levels of glucose and amino acids, which makes the rice sweeter and gives it more of the tasty flavor of *umami*. As for "kelp flavor," that's usually just code for MSG.

Rice cooked with Miora makes people want to return to their favorite sushi restaurants again and again. Because of all the glucose, some doctors worry that the body will convert more of this rice to fat. In using the Miora, Takumi was simply following standard practice at Hama Hermosa. It's likely that more sushi restaurants use Miora than anyone would like to admit.

Takumi measured the proper amount of water and poured it into the cooker bowl. Sushi chefs cook their rice with less water than if they were cooking rice for regular use. Too much moisture softens the grains, makes them too sticky, and prevents them from absorbing the vinegar mixture the chef adds after cooking. But too little water also prevents the rice from absorbing the vinegar because the starches in the core of the grain will reharden before the vinegar gets a chance to penetrate.

Takumi switched on the rice cooker. While the first batch of rice began to boil, he set out a low-sided cypress tub. He poured in enough water to cover the bottom and left it to soak. The cypress had to be wet before he dumped in the cooked rice. Otherwise, the absorbent wood would suck the moisture from the rice. He checked the clock again. Time was running out.

When the rice had finished cooking Takumi emptied the water from the cypress tub. Then he yanked the rice out of the cooker by the edges of the Teflon net and lugged it toward the tub. Steam billowed around his forearms. He flipped the mesh bag upside down into the tub in a huge cloud of steam.

Small clumps of rice still stuck to the Teflon net. Tens of thousands of tiny rice gods were in peril of not making it into the tub. Takumi started to pick the grains of rice off one by one.

Zoran dove in and snatched the net from Takumi's hands.

"Come on, don't worry about it!" Zoran barked. Zoran tossed the net in the sink. Takumi glanced at the clock. There was other work to be done.

He washed the second batch of rice while the first batch cooled. If he added the vinegar too soon after cooking, the rice wouldn't soak it up. But if he let the rice sit too long, it would start to harden and wouldn't absorb the vinegar, either. At the right moment, he returned and poured Hama Hermosa's recipe of sushi vinegar over the cooling rice. In a tiny office off the kitchen, the recipe was taped to the wall: seven parts rice vinegar, five parts sugar, one part salt.

In the 1600s, in the area around Kyoto, the recipe for "quick sushi" came to include not just vinegar in the rice but sugar as well. It tasted good, and along with the vinegar, the sugar helped prevent the rice from spoiling for a few days. Sugar molecules love water. When water is in short supply, they suck it right out of the bodies of bacteria and the bacteria die. That's why fruit jellied with lots of sugar is called "preserves."

In Japan, the sweetness of sushi rice has varied by region and era. When sushi spread to what is now Tokyo in the eighteenth and nineteenth centuries, the people there preferred their sushi rice tart and tangy.

After years of wartime deprivation during and after World War II, most Japanese developed more of a sweet tooth, and even Tokyo sushi became sweeter. But as prosperity returned, so did the preference for tart sushi. Nowadays, as you travel from Tokyo toward Kyoto, the sushi is sweeter and sweeter. When you reach Kyoto, the sushi rice is about three times sweeter than it is back in Tokyo.

One of the most venerated Tokyo sushi chefs today, Jirō Ono, ads almost no sugar to his sushi rice. The sugar, he says, makes people feel full too quickly, before they've had a chance to sample a sufficient variety of fish. Too much sugar can also overwhelm the delicate flavors of some of the best fish for sushi.

In general, Tokyo sushi chefs take tartness seriously. Like a martial-arts dojo or a school of tea ceremony, each sushi bar follows techniques handed down from the founding masters of the lineage to which it belongs. The most closely guarded secret is usually the ratio of vinegar to salt in the sushi rice. It's said that a master chef can tell the lineage of a sushi bar simply by tasting its rice.

In the United States, sushi has Kyoto-style sweetness. Sushi chefs have noticed that when they add more sugar they get extra compliments. In a sense, the fundamental taste of sushi is no different from the fundamental taste of America's other favorite Asian food. Chinese restaurants serve sweet-and-sour pork; sushi restaurants essentially serve sweet-and-sour rice.

Takumi folded the sweet vinegar mix into the rice with a bamboo paddle. Zoran swooped in again.

"Okay, okay," Zoran said, "now, *shari-kiri!*" Literally, it meant "cutting the Buddha's bones." Zoran motioned with his hand.

Takumi nodded and sliced through the rice with the edge of the paddle, breaking up clumps. When he stopped to let the rice cool further, Zoran snatched up the paddle. He arched his body around the tub, grasping the edge with his free hand, and flipped patches of the cooling rice upside down with brisk twists of his wrist, circling the tub as he worked. That way the underside of the rice could cool and release excess moisture as well.

Takumi wandered about the kitchen, a quizzical expression on his face. He couldn't find the maroon can of magic white powder. He turned to Zoran.

"Do you know where," he asked in his broken English, "is Miora?"

"You should have put it back where it belonged!" Zoran yelled, his back hunched over his work. "Get some sleep!"

Zoran himself rarely slept more than four hours a night. He flew to a shelf and grabbed the can. "Is this what you were looking for?"

Takumi half-nodded, half-bowed. "Thank you."

Takumi readied the second batch of rice for cooking and checked the clock. He packed the first batch of sushi rice into a couple of insulated canisters, laid damp kitchen towels over the rice, tightened the heavy lids, and lugged them to the front sushi bar. The second batch of rice would be used at the longer sushi bar in the back room. Most nights, Toshi opened only the sushi bar in the front dining room for business. On Thursday, Friday, and Saturday, he opened up the back sushi bar as well.

When the second batch of rice had cooked, Takumi repeated the seasoning procedure, racing the clock. By the time he'd finished and washed the wooden tub, a wad of discarded rice had accumulated in the basket drain under the row of sinks. Takumi didn't want to think about how many divinities lay there dying. He pulled on his chef jacket and hurried to the front dining room.

The entire restaurant staff had convened for the daily staff meeting. Several of the chefs were Japanese. There was a Korean trainee. Next to Zoran stood a young white woman. Her name was Fie Kruse.

Fie was a Danish supermodel and movie star. Or rather, Fie was *not* a Danish supermodel and movie star. She had cut short her film career and turned down offers from modeling agencies, and had come to L.A. to pursue her dream of becoming a sushi chef. She had graduated from the California Sushi Academy in March and was now a chef in training.

After the chefs had reviewed the night's specials, Toshi took over.

"All right!" he bellowed in Japanese, his face stern. "You're all going to work hard tonight!" He looked around the room. "Got it?"

There were nods, a few sharp utterances of *"Hai!"*

The restaurant manager shouted out the universal welcome. *"Irasshaimase!"*

The staff yelled back in unison, *"Irasshaimase!"*

The chefs and waitresses dispersed, and the manager propped the front door open for business.

For two decades, Toshi's restaurant in Venice Beach had been packed every night of the week. Movie stars had stopped in for dinner all the time, and they treated him like a buddy. Now, in Hermosa Beach, Toshi's fortunes had taken a dramatic turn for the worse. Every day there seemed to be fewer customers, and the restaurant was hemorrhaging money.

Toshi stared out the open door, his face impassive.

7

L.A. STORY

The first Japanese restaurant in Los Angeles opened about 1855, in the neighborhood that would become Little Tokyo. By the early 1900s, Little Tokyo bustled with shoppers, who patronized a number of Japanese food establishments.

But few of America's Japanese immigrants ate in Japanese restaurants. By 1910, more than 40,000 Japanese migrant laborers were toiling on American farms, along with another 10,000 on railroads and several thousand more in canneries. The farm workers often survived by drinking the water in the irrigation ditches and eating the grapes and strawberries in the fields, perhaps supplemented by a dinner of flour dumplings in salt soup if they were lucky. The closest the railroad workers got to fine dining was a monthly visit to town to buy a bottle of bourbon, a can of salmon, and some rice. Nostalgic for home, they'd squeeze together what they considered "extravagant" rice balls and cover them with slices of fish.

By 1940, Japanese immigrant farmers were growing 95 percent of California's snap beans and celery, nearly 70 percent of its tomatoes, and around 40 percent of its onions and green peas. They owned many of the produce stalls in L.A.'s city market.

But discrimination against the Japanese made it difficult for them to enter other businesses. One option was importing Japanese foodstuffs and selling them to other Japanese in the United

States. People called this the "homesickness trade." In L.A., a group of these importers formed an organization called the Mutual Trading Company.

Japan's attack on Pearl Harbor interrupted the homesickness trade. The U.S. government locked up Japanese Americans in internment camps. A group of Catholic nuns in downtown L.A. protected the Mutual Trading Company's warehouse stock until the end of the war.

After the war, a man named Noritoshi Kanai joined Mutual Trading and decided that to survive as a business, the company would have to sell products that average Americans would buy.

In the early 1960s, Kanai traveled back and forth between Japan and America in search of products to sell to Americans. He tried importing canned snake meat, chocolate-covered ants, and a type of biscuit. The last went over well, but was immediately imitated. On one of his trips to Japan, Kanai took along an American business partner named Harry Wolf. After an unsuccessful day of scouting, Kanai was hungry for a meal at a traditional sushi bar. Wolf tagged along.

Wolf told Kanai he'd never experienced anything so delicious. Every day for the next week, Wolf returned to the same sushi bar. For Kanai, it was an epiphany. He decided to make "the East Asian food that most disgusted white people," as he put it later, the core of his new business.

Back in L.A., Kanai did everything in his power to launch proper, Tokyo-style *nigiri* sushi in the United States. He partnered with a Japanese restaurant in Little Tokyo called Kawafuku and brought an authentic sushi chef and his wife from Japan to America. They opened a sushi bar inside Kawafuku in 1966.

Acquiring the fresh seafood specific to sushi was a problem. At the time, the idea of flying in fish packed in ice on airplanes was considered ludicrous because the cost was so exorbitant. But Kanai ordered fresh seafood from Tokyo anyway. Hearing that fishmongers in Boston were throwing away the fatty belly meat of tuna, he boarded a plane for the East Coast and arranged to buy the bellies. When he learned that good sea urchins lived in the waters near L.A., he hired a diver to harvest them.

The sushi bar at Kawafuku prospered. Another sushi bar opened in Little Tokyo in a restaurant called Eigiku. Yet another opened down the street in a fancy restaurant called Tokyo Kaikan, which had been built in the style of a traditional Japanese inn.

But the customers at the new sushi bars were Japanese—mostly businessmen and expatriates. Kanai had succeeded in launching sushi, but he had failed to sell it to Americans.

Then two things happened.

The Japanese businessmen introduced their American colleagues to the sushi bar. Eating sushi quickly became an exciting novelty and a badge of courage for these Americans.

And, after a few years, the first sushi chef at Kawafuku returned to Japan and opened a lavish sushi bar in the Ginza in Tokyo. Word spread that he'd made a fortune in L.A. Young sushi chefs frustrated by long apprenticeships and rigid hierarchies in Japan had a new option—America.

But in L.A., sushi was still confined to Little Tokyo. The first sushi bar outside Little Tokyo opened in 1970, in L.A.'s Century City near Beverly Hills. Its target wasn't ordinary Americans. It was Hollywood stars.

The sushi bar was called Osho, and it was located next to the Twentieth Century Fox movie studio. The actor Yul Brynner became a lunchtime regular, and the transformation of sushi into an American meal began in earnest.

Over the next few years Hollywood embraced sushi. It was an exotic meal. Sushi's new customers had a lot to learn. Many of them were surprised to discover that tuna meat was red, not white, as it came in the can.

Sushi arrived in New York City and Chicago, too. In New York, a Japanese restaurant called Nippon began serving raw fish; and in 1975, the city's first full-fledged sushi restaurant, Takezushi, opened for business. In Chicago, a restaurant called Kamehachi opened in 1967 and began serving sushi. The restaurant was across the street from The Second City comedy club, and a performer named John Belushi was a regular customer. A few years later Belushi was in New York, playing a Japanese samurai deli chef on *Saturday Night Live.*

In response to the new interest in sushi, a wave of Japanese men arrived in Los Angeles and opened so many sushi bars that

Wilshire Boulevard in West L.A. earned the nickname "Sushi Row." Kanai's vision had become reality. His Mutual Trading Company finally prospered as it became the primary sushi restaurant supplier in the United States.

The timing was fortuitous. In 1977, the U.S. Senate issued a report called *Dietary Goals for the United States,* that blamed fatty, high-cholesterol foods for the increasing incidence of disease. The report recommended greater consumption of fish and grains. Around the same time, health experts also began to promote the benefits of omega-3 fatty acids, abundant in fish. Many Americans discovered sushi as a healthful alternative.

In L.A., some of the Japanese men who arrived to open sushi restaurants were trained sushi chefs. Many were not. One of the untrained was the future executive chef of Hama Hermosa restaurant and CEO of the California Sushi Academy, Toshi Sugiura.

Toshi had grown up in Japan in the seaside town of Hayama, just south of Tokyo, where fresh fish were abundant. His mother owned a small restaurant, but Toshi had shown no interest in the family business. By the age of 15, all he could think about was leaving Japan and traveling to Europe and America. When he failed the college entrance exams, he found his excuse.

In the mid-1970s, Toshi hitchhiked throughout Europe for three years, sometimes living on water and bananas. He was good with his hands, and he earned money practicing the art of *kirie*— elaborate paper cutout pictures. He'd walk door to door around dinnertime selling his cutouts. Often he'd receive a free bowl of food. In medieval Japan, it would have been the lifestyle of a wandering Buddhist monk. In Europe in the 1970s, Toshi called it the lifestyle of a hippie.

In 1978, he borrowed $400 for a ticket to Los Angeles. When he arrived, he asked an acquaintance what was trendy in L.A. His friend said sushi. Toshi figured since he was good with his hands, he could make sushi, even though he'd hardly ever eaten the stuff. Running a restaurant would be easy—if his mother had done it, so could he.

Most of the new sushi bars in L.A. were traditional in style. But Toshi found a Jewish doctor who had just installed a sushi bar in his non-Japanese restaurant in Malibu. The first sushi chef to work there had quit. Toshi talked his way behind the sushi bar. He had no idea what he was doing. The restaurant was called Something's Fishy.

Toshi quickly taught himself the bare basics: he mixed sweet vinegar with rice, squeezed it into rectangles, and topped it with slices of fish. Whenever he could get away, Toshi visited the sushi bar of a traditionally trained Japanese chef in L.A. named Katsu Michite. Katsu was becoming one of the most respected sushi chefs on the West Coast. Toshi would sit at Katsu's sushi bar, order food, and memorize every move the elder chef made. Soon Toshi was spending a third of his salary on sushi at Katsu's bar. Everything he saw Katsu do, he would return to Something's Fishy and imitate.

What Toshi lacked in experience he made up for with charisma. Malibu in 1978 was crazy. Americans would sit at Toshi's bar, and he would joke and drink with them while he served them sushi, and pretty soon the sushi bar turned into a wild party. Toshi laughed, screamed, and got hammered right along with his customers.

Toshi had no idea who these people were. He just knew they were fun. He gradually learned their names. There was one pretty customer named Olivia Newton-John. There was a guy named Robin Williams, one named Neil Diamond, and some lady named Linda Ronstadt. One night Toshi was serving Barbra Streisand sushi. She asked Toshi if he knew who she was. 'No idea!' he yelled, moving on to the next customer. He'd been hitchhiking across Europe making paper cutouts and eating bananas, and before that he'd been a kid in Japan. Hollywood might as well have been on another planet.

After a year, Toshi was hired away from Something's Fishy to run a place in Venice Beach called Hama Venice—the word *hama* means "beach" in Japanese. Venice Beach was an edgy town, full of artists, hippies, and film and music industry types who wanted something gritty and authentic. And like Malibu, it was wild.

At Hama Venice, Toshi was able to define the style of the restaurant from the start. Most Japanese chefs filled their restaurants with shoji screens and quiet shamisen music. Toshi blared rock 'n' roll and acted crazy behind the sushi bar. Customers loved it. The priesthood of Japanese sushi chefs in L.A. hated it.

But Toshi wasn't simply a rebel. From watching Katsu, Toshi had learned to be a stickler for cleanliness and quality. At his new restaurant, he insisted on strict hygiene and high-quality ingredients and fish.

More important, Toshi served traditional Japanese sushi, but not in a traditional style. He had no problem serving his customers bland, American-style sushi: rolls filled with salmon and cream cheese, "burrito" rolls, and the like. But he also made them weird, exotic, Japanese sushi, whether they ordered it or not.

First, he would serve them what they'd ordered; then, he'd start handing them *nigiri* topped with bizarre fish and the sex organs of sea urchins. He'd pour them more beer or sake and yell at them— 'Just eat it!'—until they swallowed the stuff. If they liked it, he'd give them more. If they didn't, he'd try something else on them. 'Just eat it!' He was like a Nike commercial, for sushi.

Toshi's restaurant was both wildly exotic and utterly approachable. It was a formula for success. The restaurant was packed every night. Celebrities came—old friends from Something's Fishy, then Tom Hanks, Brooke Shields, and others. Hama Venice became one of the go-to sushi spots in L.A.

In 1980, NBC aired a TV miniseries based on James Clavell's novel *Shōgun*. Richard Chamberlain played a British ship captain who arrives in Japan around 1600 and learns the ways of the samurai. *Shōgun* was one of the highest-rated programs in NBC's history. It sparked a nationwide interest in all things Japanese, including sushi.

The owner of Hama Venice retired in 1983 and sold the restaurant to Toshi. He acquired other restaurants. In 1989, Toshi married a Japanese woman who was a fashion consultant to Japanese celebrities. They had a daughter and then a son. They bought a BMW, a Mercedes, and a condo with a view of Marina del Rey.

The world of sushi was changing. By the 1990s, sushi restaurants were everywhere. At Hama Venice, most of the celebrities stopped coming. Still, Toshi's business continued at a brisk pace and he never ceased his antics behind the bar, carousing with his customers. Many mornings he woke with a hangover. Some nights he stumbled home and fell asleep on the carpet. His wife worried about him.

In 2003, Toshi's world crashed down around him. He'd been having too much fun to pay much attention to business management. He was cited for twenty-four years of tax evasion. Toshi's bank accounts were stripped bare and Hama Venice was put up for sale. Unlike citizens in Japan in AD 718, Toshi could not use sushi to pay his taxes.

In Hermosa Beach, a few miles from Venice, a friend of Toshi's owned a restaurant called California Beach. Once a legend, it had lost ground to an invasion of cheap, generic sushi places. The owner wanted to relaunch the restaurant with a new look. Hama Hermosa was born.

Building a new clientele for the new restaurant from scratch was difficult and competition was stiff. Toshi was still responsible for the fate of several other restaurants and a small army of chefs and staff, not to mention his wife, 14-year-old daughter, and 13-year-old son. As soon as he put money in the bank, the authorities removed it to pay off his debt. The stresses mounted.

In April 2005, on a Friday night during dinner service, Toshi was slicing scallops behind the sushi bar when he put down his knife. He couldn't move or speak properly. He nearly collapsed, but steadied himself. He rested for a few minutes, then forced himself to keep making sushi, until his customers had all gone home. He tried to work in his office the next day, but gave up. Finally he saw a doctor. He'd had a stroke.

Toshi gradually improved, and soon he was back at work. He was lucky to be functioning at all. But try as he might, most of his energy and charisma had deserted him. For Toshi, that was like losing his soul.

Hama Hermosa started losing customers, and now it was losing money.

The one bright spot was the academy. Toshi loved seeing new students arrive to begin their training. The beginning of a semester always held a sense of anticipation and possibility.

This was the academy's thirtieth class, and he'd already grown fond of the students. Most of them would do well, he thought. But he was worried about Kate. It was obvious that she lacked confidence. A number of women had come through his sushi academy, and the ones who'd succeeded were the ones who'd believed in themselves. Given the challenges that female sushi chefs faced, if Kate was going to survive in the world of sushi, somehow she'd have to find confidence.

8

BATTLE OF THE SEXES

In Japan, a popular comic book series called *Sushi Chef Kirara's Job* tells the fictional tale of a young female sushi chef. Kirara's father deserts her mother, and her mother dies when Kirara is young. A kindly old sushi chef of great fame adopts Kirara and raises her in his small neighborhood sushi shop. When the old chef gets sick, he must close the shop. Out of love for the old man, Kirara decides to reopen his famous shop herself.

The old man is the last chef to have been taught the secret techniques of the most renowned sushi establishment of old Tokyo. Kirara is his only protege, and she struggles to keep the lineage alive. To prove that his old style of traditional sushi is still the best, Kirara goes on a television show called *Sushi Battle 21*, in which sushi chefs compete for the title of national champion.

Kirara is a skinny girl with a pretty face. The male sushi chefs are muscle-bound athletes. They practice sushi making as if it were a martial art, and challenge each other to duels of skill and endurance, like samurai defending their honor. Kirara's chief rival, a man named Sakamaki, pumps iron at the gym as part of his sushi training.

Prior to the battle, Sakamaki visits Kirara's little shop and orders sushi at the bar. While waiting for his food he lights a cigarette. When the sushi comes, he taps his cigarette ash onto the fish. "You don't understand this world," Sakamaki growls at Kirara, "because you are a woman."

Later, Kirara meets the only other woman chef in the contest. The woman is a hardened veteran. She tells Kirara she has suffered all manner of discrimination and humiliation, from both customers and other chefs. To survive, she has cut her hair short and obliterated any hint of femininity in her appearance and personality. "I have become both physically and mentally a man," she says.

The comic book tale isn't far from the truth. In real-life Japan, sushi is a man's world. Male chefs use all manner of excuses to defend their sushi bars against women who want to work there. Women can't be sushi chefs, they say, because makeup, body lotion, and perfume destroy the flavor of the fish and rice. Some male chefs claim that the area behind the sushi bar is sacred space and would be defiled by the presence of a woman. Others say women don't have the reflexes necessary for the knife work. Until 1999, Japan had a law prohibiting women from working later than 10:00 p.m. at any job, which made employment at most sushi bars impossible. A writer in Tokyo asked her friends if they would eat sushi made by a female chef, and even the women said no.

The most common argument against female sushi chefs is that a woman's hands are warmer than a man's. A woman chef, people claim, will cook the raw fish simply by handling it. In fact, a study published in *The Lancet* in 1998 demonstrated that women are likely to have colder hands than men.

Sushi is a man's world on the customer side of the sushi bar, too. At a traditional, high-end sushi bar in Japan, a Japanese woman who walks in to eat by herself is likely to feel just as intimidated and unwelcome as an American tourist. In the mid-1990s, Reiko Yuyama, a Japanese publishing executive, stopped by a famous sushi bar for a meal. She was alone. Most of the other customers were men. The chef chatted amiably with the other customers but ignored Yuyama. She managed to order several pieces of sushi, but after only her fourth piece a cup of green tea appeared in front of her. Since green tea is often served at the end of the meal, she took this as a request that she leave. She stayed for an hour, continuing to order. When she asked for the bill, it was obviously for more than she'd been served.

Spurred by this incident, Yuyama visited many of the best sushi bars in Tokyo and around Japan, always alone, and described her experiences in a book called *One Woman Sushi*. Traditional sushi bars are like exclusive clubs, Yuyama found—difficult for single women and the uninitiated to enter, especially since there are no menus.

The other women Yuyama encountered in the sushi bars were almost always accompanied by men, and the men used the opportunity to impress their dates with ostentatious displays of sushi knowledge. She watched the women play along, deferring to the men in everything from ordering to eating techniques. When Yuyama ordered sushi herself, the other women glared at her. Yuyama concluded that traditional sushi bars are the last place in Japan where men still feel completely superior to women.

The invention and spread of "conveyor-belt sushi," or *kaiten-zushi*, has helped democratize low-end sushi in Japan. Small plates of sushi ride around on a conveyor belt and the customer picks whichever he or she wants to try. Interaction with the chef is eliminated. In a survey, Japanese housewives said that while they were intimidated by the price and formality of traditional sushi bars, they frequented conveyor-belt sushi restaurants.

By the end of the 1990s, revenue at traditional sushi bars in Japan had declined, while revenue at conveyor-belt sushi restaurants had increased. Afraid of losing more business, some traditional sushi bars have become more open to women dining on their own.

In recent years in Japan, another new style of sushi bar has appeared as well. Inspired by the popularity of sushi in America and Europe, as well as by the culture of women's rights in the West, these new sushi bars have Western-style interiors, play jazz over the sound system, and sometimes have televisions displaying international news. The sushi they serve borrows many ingredients from Western cuisine. Young women dining on their own or with other young women are their best customers.

Despite the obstacles facing female sushi chefs, in recent years women in Japan have, like Kirara of the comic book, gradually fought their way into jobs behind the sushi bar. But many Japanese women trying to become sushi chefs simply leave Japan for America.

As sushi restaurants proliferated in the United States, Toshi watched standards of quality and hygiene deteriorate. A traditional apprenticeship required at least five years to complete, and demand for chefs in the United States had outstripped supply. Like Toshi, many chefs were jumping into the business with little or no training. Toshi worried that sooner or later someone would die after consuming improperly prepared sushi. Opening the academy was his attempt to prevent that, and to help people like him—chefs who hadn't completed a traditional apprenticeship—learn proper technique.

Toshi expected most of the students to be Asian. To his surprise, a majority of the applicants were American, and some were women. One of the first women to attend the California Sushi Academy was the actress Tracy Griffith, half-sister of Melanie Griffith. A feisty redhead, Tracy had gotten to the point in her film career where she no longer wanted to wear the things the directors wanted her to wear or say the things they wanted her to say. She saw an ad in *Gourmet* magazine for the sushi academy.

At the age of 12, Tracy had accompanied Melanie to the sushi bar in Malibu called Something's Fishy, where Toshi would begin his career. Tracy had fallen in love with sushi. She loved to cook, and at the age of 18 she worked as a private chef. She signed up to attend the sushi academy.

Within five minutes of Tracy's arrival, the Japanese instructor at Toshi's new academy started yelling at her.

'You should not be here!' he screamed. He glared at her fingernail polish and her long red hair. 'You unnatural! No such thing sushi woman!'

He spent the rest of the class trying to intimidate Tracy into quitting. When she returned for the next class he was irate.

'What did I say?!' he screamed. 'What are doing here? You should not be here!'

Tracy complained to Toshi. The things the instructor was saying were illegal in America. Toshi shrugged and said there was nothing he could do—the instructor was a typical Japanese sushi chef; that's the way they were. Tracy would just have to deal with it.

Nearly every day, the man yelled at her. 'You should not be here!' He told Tracy that his reputation would be ruined if anyone found out he was teaching a woman. He brought her to tears regularly. But she kept coming to class, and she learned a lot from him.

After graduation, Tracy walked into one Beverly Hills sushi restaurant after another, asking for a job. Everyone laughed at her. 'There is no such thing,' they said. 'Get out!'

Tracy heard from a friend about a new Asian-themed nightclub about to open in Beverly Hills, called Tsunami. It would have a sushi bar. But it wasn't a Japanese-run operation. The man in charge was Mark Fleischman, a slick nightclub owner who had run Studio 54 in New York. Tracy arranged a meeting with Fleischman. He looked her up and down.

'So, you want to be a sushi chef,' he said. 'Okay, that's going to be great. We'll put you in a little number, put you by the window. See this hot chick with the knife?'

'No, no,' Tracy said, 'I'm a *real* sushi chef.' She had left acting to escape all that.

But competition was stiff and gimmicks were in vogue—tap-dancing sushi chefs, chefs who sang cabaret and performed line dances behind the sushi bar, even sushi served atop naked women.

A week later Fleischman introduced Tracy to the Japanese chef he'd hired. The Japanese chef looked at Tracy, then at Fleischman.

'What do you mean she's going to work here?'

'Yes,' Fleischman said, 'she's going to work with you. She's going to be our star!'

'I quit,' the chef said. He walked out.

Fleischman talked him into staying.

Tracy had a conversation with the chef. 'I don't know what the hell is with this female sushi chef thing,' Tracy said, 'but if I'm horrible and you can't deal with me in a month, I'll leave.'

He glared her. 'Okay.'

When Tsunami opened for business, Tracy refused to wear the suggestive outfit that Fleischman wanted her to wear. That didn't stop Fleischman from stirring up a media frenzy.

'We have the only female sushi chef in the world!' she remembers him saying, as news reporters snapped her picture. The Japanese chef stood aside and glowered.

Every night the club was packed. Tracy made sushi like a madwoman. At first she asked the Japanese chef questions, but he told her to shut up and just watch him. So she did—for a year. And she learned a lot. Tracy went on to run her own sushi bar, at a restaurant called Rika's on the Sunset Strip, and publish her own sushi cookbook.

Other women graduated from the California Sushi Academy and went on to successful careers in sushi. A Venice Beach native named Nikki Gilbert lived in Japan and returned to L.A. to found a sushi catering and teaching company called Sushi Girl. A tough Israeli named Tali Sever endured discrimination during a short sushi apprenticeship in Japan, then returned to L.A. and helped develop an American-style sushi cafe—a sort of Starbucks of sushi—called Sushi Central. An African-American woman named Marisa Baggett graduated and became head chef of a sushi bar called Do in Memphis, Tennessee.

Then, in January 2005, a woman arrived at the academy unlike any Toshi or his chefs had ever encountered.

Fie Kruse was one of the most beautiful women Toshi and his chefs had ever met, and her beauty could not have been more un-Japanese. She was Danish—shapely and tall, with large blue eyes and shockingly blond hair. And yet she seemed to act entirely Japanese. Fie was sweet, soft-spoken, and deferential. The Japanese chefs didn't know what to make of her. Most of them simply fell in love.

In Denmark, Fie had performed her first major film role by the age of 13, and at 16 she'd been recruited by four different modeling agencies. But Fie chose to work in her stepfather's takeout sushi shop.

During the Japanese economic bubble of the 1980s, Japanese restaurants had proliferated in Europe. In Paris, for example, Japanese businessmen took their French counterparts out for sushi, and the meal developed a following. In 1984, even conveyor-belt sushi appeared in Paris.

When Japan's bubble burst, many of these restaurants closed. But in 1991 in London, a sushi chef opened a takeout counter called Noto Sushi. It quickly caught the attention of Harrods department store. Harrods began selling Noto Sushi takeout boxes in 1993, and installed a Noto Sushi counter in the store the next year. In the ensuing years, sushi spread throughout Europe's most cosmopolitan cities. Conveyor-belt sushi restaurants were especially popular.

Fie's stepfather traveled frequently and saw sushi everywhere. He opened the first sushi shop in Fie's hometown of Aarhus, in Denmark. Fie worked there throughout her high school years. The shop was full of books on Japanese culture, food, and Buddhism, and Fie read voraciously. She took a class on Asian religion.

At 19 she traveled to Asia and ate her way across Thailand, Vietnam, and Cambodia. She returned to Europe, attended cooking school in Denmark, and saved her money. In Europe, sushi continued to soar in popularity. When Fie felt ready, she flew 5,600 miles to L.A. and spent her savings at the California Sushi Academy.

She quickly attracted attention in Hermosa Beach. Luke Walton, forward for the L.A. Lakers—and son of the NBA's great Bill Walton—saw her at a yoga class and asked her out. She turned him down.

After Fie graduated, Toshi let her stay and continue her training behind the sushi bar at Hama Hermosa. Fie had a different problem from the women who'd preceded her. The Japanese chefs bent over backwards to compliment her and help her out. Customers adored her. Sometimes Fie couldn't tell if the sushi she was making was good, or if everyone was just being nice to her because she was beautiful.

The night before the party at Paramount Pictures, a bigmouthed Caucasian man came to Hama Hermosa for dinner. He sat at the bar, near Fie, and drank sake and ate. One of the staff asked the man how he'd liked his meal.

"Well, actually," he boomed, drowning out the music on the sound system, "I don't like women chefs. I want a Japanese man to serve my sushi."

It was just as well that Kate hadn't been hanging around the restaurant that night. She was having enough trouble in class, feeling like the flaky girl who couldn't do anything right. She'd always been a tomboy, but at sushi school her male classmates were leaving her way behind. Zoran was still babying her. It had become clear that he held her to a lower standard than the rest of the class.

To keep up her spirits, Kate had been doodling love hearts in her notebook. Zoran saw them and laughed at her.

9

HOLLYWOOD SHOWDOWN

On the morning of the Hollywood party at Paramount Pictures, Toshi arrived at the restaurant well ahead of his staff. By 10:00 a.m. he was hard at work in the kitchen. The party would begin in eight hours.

Toshi stood at a stainless-steel table that would look at home in a morgue. The table was 12 feet long and ran diagonally across the kitchen. On its surface was a cutting board of high-density polyethylene, chemically fused to repel bacteria, fat, and blood, but soft enough that Toshi could wield his high-carbon blade for several hours without dulling its razor-sharp edge.

Toshi bent over a big block of blood-red flesh. When sushi first became popular in the early 1800s, a high-class chef like Toshi would have been run out of town for serving tuna. The bloody meat of fresh tuna and other red-fleshed fish spoils easily and the Japanese considered it smelly. The fatty belly meat of the tuna was especially despised.

But with the advent of refrigeration, the fish could be kept fresh, and in the years after World War II the Japanese learned from Americans to love red meat, including tuna.

Takumi, the Japanese student, stood across the table and watched. On his cutting board sat a similar but smaller slab of tuna.

Toshi carved through the block of flesh like a sculptor, scrutinizing the muscle, turning and trimming. He tossed scraps into a bowl.

"We'll use these for spicy tuna," he said. He was speaking Japanese, but the words "spicy tuna" were in English. There isn't even a name for it in Japanese. In the early days of American sushi, Japanese chefs in L.A. had realized they could take the worst parts of the fish—the fibrous scraps, the flesh left on the skin, and meat past its prime—and chop them up with chili sauce. The taste of the fish was lost, but Americans loved it.

"The Mexican influence here is strong," Toshi told Takumi. "Americans like spicy food more than Japanese people do."

Takumi nodded. In a few minutes, he would scrape shreds of meat off the skin with a spoon, chop them up with other scraps, and squirt the mixture full of hot sauce. But now he tried his hand at trimming his slab of tuna. When he started to cut, Toshi stopped him.

"No, not like that. You're cutting in the same direction as the fiber." With his finger Toshi traced the parallel lines of connective tissue that ran through the tuna's flesh like the grain in a piece of wood. "See? You've got to cut against the fiber." Toshi flipped the slab of meat over so Takumi could slice into it from the other side. "Cut them thinner than you would for the restaurant," he added. "For a catering job like this, we go for volume."

Other restaurant staff trickled in to help prepare for the party. Toshi's office assistant dumped a 2-pound bag of bright green powder labeled "wasabi" into a mixing bowl. Like most wasabi served in restaurants, there wasn't a shred of wasabi in it. Real wasabi is a rare plant that is notoriously difficult to grow and tastes quite different. This was a mix of horseradish and mustard powder. She added water and stirred. The powder jelled into a green blob, which emitted fumes. Toshi wheezed.

"Get the hell out of the kitchen with that thing!" he bellowed. "It's going to drive us all crazy."

The woman bowed, hugged the bowl to her chest, and left, her eyes watering.

Soon Kate and the other students trickled in and loaded the catering equipment into a rented truck. Jay shouted out instructions.

"Bring a minimal amount of stuff with you!" Jay said. "Do not bring big bags! Otherwise, you're not going to get through security!"

But, of course, they took their knives.

The students would ride in the restaurant's old van. Kate hopped into the front passenger seat and pulled the door shut with a bang. They cruised down the freeway. In the distance the glass towers of downtown L.A. rose through the haze. Soon they were driving straight toward the gigantic white "HOLLYWOOD" letters on the hill. They pulled alongside a vast, high-walled compound. Security cameras monitored the van's arrival.

At the security checkpoint there were men with guns—big guns. Some rested Winchester rifles on their shoulders. Others carried six-shooters on their hips. Most of them wore ten-gallon hats and chaps. They were actors. The real guards wore windbreakers and carried walkie-talkies. The actors passed their guns to the guards and walked through the metal detector. When the guards saw Kate's chef's jacket, they found her name on a list and waved her through, along with her case of knives.

Inside the compound Kate followed her classmates past a row of hangars and emerged onto the edge of an American frontier town of a hundred years ago, bustling with inhabitants of the Old West. The sushi students wandered into the town like a gang of lost samurai. Around them cowboys twirled lassos. The smell of grilled beef swirled through the streets.

The town continued for blocks. In the distance a pointy white water tower perched on stilts. Painted on its side was a snowy mountain under the word "Paramount." Kate shambled through the streets clutching her knife case. Ahead she saw Toshi and some of the staff setting up their sushi stall on a street corner.

More than sixty restaurants would be hawking food from colorful stalls, most of it seared or baked or fried, all of it smelling delicious. Some of those restaurants were legends. Pink's and its "famous hot dogs" had started in the 1930s. The stall neighboring the sushi stall was belching smoke. It was called "The Pig." When Toshi found a chance to slip away for a few minutes, he'd make a beeline for Lawry's roast beef.

Now he buttoned up his chef's jacket and surveyed the equipment—the 25-gallon coolers filled with fish, the insulated containers of rice, the cases of knives, the soy-sauce bottles, the blocks of disposable chopsticks.

Then he surveyed the students. Some were helping set up, but others stood around, not sure what to do. His eye lingered on Kate.

"We need backup," he said to himself.

Toshi rooted in the pile of equipment for his secret weapon: the Suzumo SSG-GTO. He located the black padded case and carried it to the back of the stall.

The Suzumo SSG-GTO looked like a wooden tub with a lid. Sushi chefs had been keeping rice in wooden tubs for nearly 200 years. This tub was different. Toshi tugged an electrical cord out of the back and searched for an outlet. He froze. This was the Old West. There were no outlets.

Toshi scowled and scanned the street for a grip. He'd been around Hollywood long enough to know that anywhere movies were made there was electricity. You just needed a grip to show you where it was. He spotted a man bristling with tools, gadgets, and brackets hanging off belts. Toshi dragged the fellow over to the sushi stall. The grip knelt and unscrewed a steel plate in the ground. Inside was an array of heavy-duty sockets. Toshi powered up the GTO.

Like the town around him, the wood on Toshi's wooden tub was fake. He lifted off the plastic lid and dumped in cooked rice. He pressed a button. A drawer slid out. He typed instructions on a keypad and the GTO hummed to life.

Toshi's wife and children had arrived. His son Daisuke rushed over to the GTO. The Japanese student, Takumi, joined them and the three of them leaned over the machine, hands on their knees, and peered inside.

Like the robots that build cars in the factories of Toyota and Honda, sushi-making robots have become commonplace in Japan, laboring tirelessly behind the scenes at mass-market sushi establishments. In Europe, owners of conveyor-belt sushi restaurants have been known to install elaborate, stainless-steel sushi robots in plain view, where customers admire their high-tech wizardry. But in the United States, sushi robots are a well-kept secret. Most restaurant owners keep them out of sight, and use them for takeout and delivery orders.

Toshi pressed a button on the GTO. Gears clicked and motors whirred. The GTO could crank out professional-grade rectangles of pressed sushi rice at speeds approaching 1,800 per hour. But it jammed. Toshi cursed.

"It's not working!"

Sushi as the world knows it today began with street stalls similar to Toshi's, except without any robots.

By the 1600s, people in the Japanese capital of Kyoto and the nearby city of Osaka were eating "quick sushi"—fish on vinegared rice. It looked quite different from today's sushi. It was made by spreading vinegared rice in a box, laying whole fillets of fish on top, and compressing it with heavy stones for a few days. After pressing, it was cut into pieces like a cake.

Around 1600, the new shogun moved the capital away from Kyoto, the seat of a thousand years of Japanese tradition and courtly culture, to a remote, unknown castle town called Edo. *Edo* meant "door to the bay," and it sat directly on the edge of a vast ocean inlet. Edo would become the city of Tokyo.

About fifty years after the move, a terrible fire destroyed most of the city. Workers swarmed into Edo to rebuild it. They needed something to eat, and a new kind of business sprang up: stands and shops selling quick meals on the street. Hot noodle soup was especially popular. Sushi might never have caught on, but in 1686, to prevent another fire, the authorities outlawed hot noodle stands during the busy dinner hours. As a result, stands switched to serving "quick sushi," which didn't require heat.

Edo grew rapidly. Regional lords set up part-time residences in the new capital and brought along their retinues of warriors and servants. By the second half of the 1700s, Edo had become the largest city in the world, a bustling metropolis crawling with samurai, construction workers, craftsmen, and merchants. Many of them lived in the provinces but stayed in Edo for extended periods on business, so an entire industry of food stalls and restaurants was created to serve them. Throughout this period, street stands selling sushi were the McDonald's drive-thrus of old Tokyo. Modern sushi began as fast food.

But "quick sushi" still wasn't fast enough. The cakes of fish and rice had to be pressed together beforehand with heavy stones. Around 1818, some sushi chef came up with the idea of using his hands to squeeze each piece as it was ordered. The hand-squeezed pieces of sushi were called *nigiri,* from the Japanese verb *nigiru,* "to grasp" or "squeeze."

A sushi shop owner named Yohei Hanaya is usually credited with inventing *nigiri.* But historians think that when Hanaya opened his shop in 1810 he was still selling the old "quick sushi." What Hanaya did, it seems, was bring the marketing skills of an entrepreneur to the new product. A poem from the time gives an indication of his success:

Crowded together, weary with waiting
Customers squeeze their hands
As Yohei squeezes sushi.

Hand-squeezed sushi was the hot new trend, and it spread throughout Edo. Soon men sold *nigiri* on street corners from portable stalls. It was more of a snack than a meal, and the situation was the reverse of today's sushi bars: the vendor sat behind his wheeled cart and squeezed together *nigiri* while his customers stood and ate. Some vendors walked around town selling sushi out of boxes on their backs. *Nigiri* were especially popular among idle samurai on their way home after an evening at the bathhouse, and takeout boxes of *nigiri* became a popular snack at the theater.

At the street stalls, people ate with their fingers. Some vendors nailed sheets of newspaper on a pole for customers to wipe their hands after eating. Fancier stalls hung a strip of cloth across the front of the stand. Sushi bars today still hang a sectioned piece of cloth across their entrances, but these have lost their utility—in nineteenth-century Tokyo, a person could judge the popularity of a sushi vendor by how dirty his cloth was. Meanwhile, at the theater, people acted more civilized, eating their *nigiri* by spearing them with long toothpicks.

As the new style of sushi took root, people began to identify it by the name *Edomae-zushi,* to distinguish it from older styles in other regions. The word *Edomae* literally means "in front of Edo."

Eel sellers first used the term to advertise their eels as having been caught in the rivers that ran through the city. When sushi sellers adopted the term, it probably referred to the bay in front of the city, where most of their sushi toppings were harvested.

Since *nigiri* was a street food, the toppings were modest. Boiled clam, abalone, and saltwater eel were common, as were small, light-fleshed fish that could be caught in the bay. The most delicious fish for sushi was considered to be *kohada,* which in English has the unappetizing name gizzard shad. Another popular topping—one that would make most sushi-goers nowadays gag—was *shirauo,* or whitebait. It had been a favorite of the shogun Ieyasu Tokugawa, who conquered and unified all of Japan in 1600. Sushi aficionados today still sometimes eat these tiny, translucent, wormlike fish, in bundles atop rectangles of rice.

When *nigiri* sushi was invented, the Japanese considered tuna such a low-class fish that not even street vendors would touch it. Around 1840, fishermen in the region hauled in a bumper catch of tuna. With so much of the fish available, a sushi stall owner marinated some of it in soy sauce and talked his customers into trying it. Vendors began serving tuna on sushi rice, but only as cheap food for the proletariat. Most people, commoners and aristocrats alike, would continue to disdain tuna for many more decades.

Nigiri might never have spread to the rest of Japan, and might never have become the form of sushi the world knows today, if it hadn't been for two cataclysmic events. Beginning with the Great Kanto Earthquake of 1923 and continuing on through World War II, much of the city of Edo—by then called Tokyo—was reduced to burnt ruins yet again. Sushi chefs left the city in droves. Most returned to their hometowns and opened *Edomae-zushi* shops in the provinces, serving *nigiri.*

As the war dragged on, food became scarce. The military authorities imposed strict rationing on rice, and one by one the provincial sushi shops shut down. Even after the war, sushi shops could not acquire enough rice to do business. Seafood was strictly controlled as well. Edo-style sushi, it seemed, was dead.

After the war, General Douglas MacArthur's American occupation forces controlled the country. As part of the plan to revive Japan's economy, the Americans wanted to restart the restaurant industry, but food was still rationed. They drew up regulations for what they called a "consignment processing system" and tested it in Tokyo.

The system allowed customers to bring their own supply of rationed rice to a sushi shop and pay the chef to make it into sushi. To prevent foul play, the regulations were very specific. Because the predominant style of sushi in Tokyo was *nigiri*, the regulations specified that a certain number of *nigiri* be made for a certain amount of rice.

Many Tokyo sushi chefs were skeptical, but in trials the system proved popular with customers. Soon sushi shops were reopening and doing a brisk business. The police clamped down on shops that used rationed fish, so chefs had to be creative with their sushi toppings. Instead of the usual fish, they used mullet, toxic puffer fish, clams, and even snakehead—a fish capable of dragging itself onto land and living out of water for three or four days at a time, hence easy to keep fresh. For variety, or when they couldn't get any seafood, the chefs used mushrooms, gourd shavings, and vegetables pickled in sake as sushi ingredients. Some of these ingredients have been used in sushi ever since.

With the success of the "consignment processing system" in Tokyo, the Americans instituted the system nationwide. As a result, sushi shops throughout Japan were able to reopen for business much sooner than other restaurants, ensuring that sushi became ubiquitous in postwar Japan.

Because the Americans had originally drafted the regulations for Tokyo, the consignment processing system continued to specify that chefs throughout the country make Tokyo-style *nigiri* rather than the other, local styles of sushi common in the provinces. Today, a great many regional varieties of sushi remain throughout Japan. But thanks to the American occupation forces, the Japanese meal that the world has come to know simply as "sushi" is *Edomae-zushi*—the street-stall fast food of old Tokyo.

At Paramount Pictures, the GTO robot was supposed to be cranking out Tokyo-style *nigiri*. Toshi jiggled the cutters. The robot didn't budge.

Toshi's son spoke in English. "Dad, you should have tested it beforehand." Daisuke's name means "Big Help."

Toshi peered into the rice chamber. "Let's take out the liner."

Takumi, eager to assist, grabbed the funnel-shaped insert and yanked it out, causing gobs of sticky rice to tumble into the machine's gears. Toshi cleared out the gears and fiddled with the cutters. Suddenly the machine started up again, and out popped a perfect rectangle of rice.

Toshi programmed the GTO for size and firmness. He plucked the first rectangle of rice from the bay. The machine ejected another one. Daisuke stuffed it in his mouth. The GTO produced another. Toshi nodded.

"*Yosh,*" he said. The sushi robot was working.

The late-afternoon sun beat down. Toshi wiped his brow and sat down with his wife in the shade at the back of the stall. He sank his teeth into a Krispy Kreme donut. Zoran sat nearby on a box, leaning against a wall, fast asleep.

A cowboy sauntered past, spurs scraping the asphalt. He squinted at the sushi bar, then at Toshi.

"What time do you guys kick into gear?" the cowboy asked.

Toshi roused himself. "Five forty-five."

The cowboy nodded. "I'll be here at five forty-four."

Later, after the cowboy had returned for sushi and strolled away satisfied, the town filled with tan and shiny Angelenos, and country-and-western bands played music. The line of people waiting for sushi snaked sideways down the street.

Behind the sushi bar, three academy students squeezed together sloppy sushi as fast as they could. Zoran, who worked beside them, quickly produced sushi that was tight and neat. The mesmerized Angelenos crowded up to the bar and stared. They never got this close to the chefs at the sit-down sushi bars.

Marcos Wisner was loving it. He'd come to the sushi academy at the age of 17, from Durango, Colorado—one of the youngest students ever to attend. He was a good-looking boy, tall, blond, and freckled. He thought of himself as a player. But he bumbled toward coolness in ways that weren't always successful.

Tonight Marcos liked having the tan and shiny Angelenos watch him. He figured it was a great way to meet hot girls. He'd just stand there behind the sushi bar, and they'd come to him—the sushi was bait. He'd worked in restaurants in Durango, but from behind the scenes in the kitchen he'd had few opportunities to meet hot girls. Plus, this was *sushi*—way cooler than regular food. Hot girls liked sushi.

Two attractive young ladies stepped up to Marcos's station.

'Can I have a hand roll?' one of them asked. He caught her smiling at him. She eyed him a few times while he worked, and he chatted with her. She devoured his roll, and gyrated to the music. Then she and her friend walked away.

More cute girls asked Marcos for sushi.

'Are you going to be around later?' one of them asked.

'Ah, I think I'm going to be stuck here until the sushi's gone,' Marcos said. He had just realized the problem.

Kate hung back, watching, hands clasped behind her. She had plastered a brave smile on her face, but she hadn't made any sushi yet, and it was nearly her turn to rotate in.

Kate was not normally shy. She'd been in the limelight as a high-school soccer player. At Chuck E. Cheese, she'd been the only employee willing to climb into the mouse costume and perform for birthday parties. In fact, she'd nearly been fired for dancing the Robot in the mouse suit at a kid's party. 'Kate,' the manager had scolded, 'Chuck E. does not do the Robot.' But Kate didn't feel like dancing now.

Takumi, the Japanese student, demonstrated a simple hand roll for her, in the shape of a waffle cone. He held the roll up and smiled reassuringly.

Gunfire erupted in the street. The Angelenos spun and a few ducked for cover. A man on a second-story fire escape was squeezing off rounds. Someone returned fire from a window across the street. It was the sheriff, aiming his Winchester at the outlaw. The Angelenos laughed and turned back to their sushi. There were now more people in line for sushi than for any other food, except for Mr. Cecil's California Ribs.

Zoran stepped away from the sushi bar. Kate found herself in his place. She was now the lead sushi chef, the one the hungry Angelenos first encountered after their long wait in line. Toshi watched from the back of the stall.

'Spicy tuna, please.' The customers pressed in. 'I'll take salmon.'
Kate had no time to think.

'Can I have extra wasabi?'

Her hands started to move.

'What's that fish there?'

She wasn't sure—albacore? yellowtail? It didn't matter. She pressed rice and fish on seaweed, rolled, and handed it off.

'Give me one of those shrimp—no, make it two.'

There were several perfect rectangles of rice on a blue plastic plate at her hip. She grabbed one, laid the shrimp on top, and squeezed it into a *nigiri* in her fingers. She tried to look as if she knew what she was doing.

The customers smiled. 'Hey, thanks!'

'Two tuna, please.'

Kate looked down. Another blue plate of perfect rice rectangles had appeared. She grabbed them, slapped on more fish, squeezed, and handed it off.

'That looks great! Thank you!'

She smiled. 'You're welcome.'

The line of customers was endless. But they were nice. They liked her sushi. And the blue plates of rice rectangles kept appearing.

Soon Kate was chatting with the Angelenos while she worked. They laughed. She laughed. She told them things about sushi that they didn't know. They thanked her. A press photographer came by and took a picture of Kate. A man with a video camera filmed her working. Marcos surprised her by getting in line and asking her to make sushi for him. Toshi reclined on an ice chest, watching Kate and grinning.

Daisuke was wearing his father's chef's jacket, draped over his tiny frame like a dress. The boy was running back and forth, snatching rice rectangles from the GTO as fast as the robot could spit them out. He loaded them onto a blue plate, ran them to the front of the stall, and slipped them onto the table by Kate. Then he ran back with an empty plate. He repeated this routine again and again.

Across the street people danced to the music. Daisuke planted his hands on top of the sushi robot, gyrated his hips, and sang along.

"Country roads," he crooned, "take me home, to the place where I belong."

By the time the sushi stall shut down, the staff estimated that the students had served close to 4,000 pieces of sushi. Takumi gave one of his American classmates a high five.

On the ride home, Kate sat in the backseat of the van. She couldn't stop smiling. She remembered the sushi chef she'd gotten to know at her favorite sushi bar, the one who joked with her and made her feel special. Tonight, for the first time, she felt like *she* could do what he'd done. She wanted to stand behind the sushi bar and joke with her customers, and make them feel special.

The van bumped back down the alley and pulled into the parking lot behind the restaurant. It was nearly 11:00 p.m. Kate climbed out and stretched her legs. There was a huge cleanup job ahead. Toshi dumped leftover rice in the trash. In the storeroom, Zoran threw boxes onto the shelves. Afraid he would start yelling, Kate hurried past.

The kitchen was crowded. Along with the students, the regular restaurant staff was cleaning up as well. Kate washed dishes at the row of sinks. Someone sidled up to her. She looked up and saw that it was Toshi.

"I was surprised at your confidence!" Toshi said.

A huge smile spread across Kate's face. "Thank you."

Weeks 3, 4, and 5

1 0

CHEF'S CHOICE

On Monday morning, Zoran pulled the attendance clipboard off the wall and barked out each student's name, as he did every morning.

"*Hai!*" each student responded.

Zoran stood at the head of the long classroom table and surveyed his students.

"You far exceeded my expectations on Saturday," he said. He paused. "But if your uniform is dirty, I will not let you in the class."

It was obvious that he was referring to Marcos, who probably hadn't washed his chef's jacket even once.

"Hygiene!" Zoran yelled. "Adjust your hats!"

Kate was riding high after the party at Paramount. For the first time since she'd arrived at sushi school she'd actually believed it was possible she could graduate and become a sushi chef. Maybe her lack of kitchen skills didn't matter. She'd proved to herself that she could interact with customers while squeezing together raw fish and rice. If she kept practicing, she wouldn't even need help from the robot.

Zoran interrupted Kate's reverie. He was telling the class that if they wanted to be sushi chefs, they couldn't just squeeze together raw fish and rice. They had to have kitchen skills, and they had to know how to cook. And not just cook, but to cook the multi-course courtly cuisine of Japan. A good sushi chef could toss out several fancy appetizers from a repertoire of traditional cuisine before he even started serving sushi. This was part of the craft of *omakase*.

The word *omakase* means "I leave it up to you." It's what the sophisticated customer says to the chef when settling down at the sushi bar. Sushi connoisseurs seldom order off a menu. Traditionally, sushi bars in Japan didn't even have menus. *Omakase* is an invitation to the chef—not just to serve what he thinks are the freshest ingredients of the day but also to show off his skills. And for any serious sushi chef, that includes cooking.

Zoran explained that courtly Japanese cuisine was called *kaiseki*. "*Kaiseki* cuisine originated from the traditional Japanese tea ceremony," Zoran said. "It was the meal eaten at the end of the ceremony."

Kaiseki is a meal of many small dishes served one after another, Zoran told them. Sushi at the sushi bar is the same way: a meal of many small servings of different fish. In modern American terms, *kaiseki* and sushi are both a sort of chef's tasting menu.

"Open your textbooks!" Zoran yelled. "Kate! Please read!"

Kate scrambled to get her book open, then cleared her throat and began in a monotone. The goal of the book, the author had written, was not to teach recipes. "The real purpose," Kate read, "is to teach you how to cook in the spirit of Japan, whose pure and restrained effects with food constitute an art."

Her classmates could barely hear her over the hum of refrigerators and freezers. Zoran interrupted Kate to add commentary.

"A Japanese person doesn't feel he's eaten dinner until he's eaten rice," Zoran said. "And miso soup should be at the end of the meal. When a Westerner sits down and orders miso soup to start, you know he doesn't know anything about Japanese food."

Zoran took over the reading in a loud voice. He jumped to a paragraph about drinking sake, the age-old Japanese rice liquor. Sake was a good accompaniment to *kaiseki*-style appetizers. But according to centuries of Japanese thinking, sake clashes with food that contains rice because the flavors of rice and rice liquor are too similar. Traditionally, sake and rice were never served together. Today, however, sushi restaurants serve as much sake as they can.

Sushi restaurants have high food costs. Pushing expensive sake is one way to make money.

Zoran moved on to a note about chopsticks. It seems that the Japanese have always had a thing about contamination. The textbook stated that at home, many Japanese use only their own personal pair of chopsticks, which are often small works of art, lacquered and decorated with inlay. But for a formal meal in a restaurant, people eat with cheap disposable chopsticks of unfinished cedar or bamboo. That way, they can be sure no one else's lips have tainted their eating implements. The cost of purity is stiff. Japan's Ministry of Agriculture estimates that the Japanese discard 25 billion pairs of chopsticks a year. Deforestation is leading some restaurants in Japan to switch to plastic. Many Americans believe it's proper etiquette to rub their disposable chopsticks together before eating, to remove splinters. In Japan this is considered impolite.

"For *omakase*," Zoran said, "you might start with three *kaiseki*-style appetizers." The appetizers could be small simmered or grilled dishes that use any number of ingredients. Then the chef would serve fish. "You want to move from light to heavy, and be seasonal," Zoran said. "For example, white fish, followed by scallops, followed by octopus. Those are all light, clean flavors. Then serve salmon or tuna, the heavier-flavored fish."

Zoran grabbed a thick photo album off the shelf. "Okay, gather round."

The pictures showed *kaiseki*-style appetizers that previous classes at the academy had cooked. "Some of these were absolutely terrible," Zoran said. "But it gives you a sense of the variety."

The elaborate sushi meals Zoran was describing seemed a far cry from modern sushi's humble origins as fast food, served from stalls in old Tokyo.

In the decades after *nigiri* first appeared on the streets of Edo in the early 1800s, the shogun's authority was undercut by political maneuvering. Behind the scenes, a noble named Sekiō Nakano amassed enormous power. As it happened, his mansion was close to Yohei Sushi, the shop that belonged to Yohei Hanaya, the man who first marketed *nigiri* successfully. That section of the city was, in a sense, "sushi central." After Yohei Sushi's success, a second large sushi shop had opened nearby, Pine Sushi.

Lords and officials seeking to influence Nakano passed by the sushi shops on their way to the mansion. Pine Sushi started to display extraordinary boxes of takeout sushi, involving a variety of different toppings on *nigiri,* many of them prepared with elaborate cooking or pickling methods. Yohei Sushi quickly followed suit. These fancy sushi boxes became the gift of choice for winning Nakano's favor, and grew more and more elaborate as visitors strove to outdo each other with their presents.

The idea spread, and shops sprang up around the city for selling elaborate sushi gift boxes. The extravagance of these shops and the prices paid for their sushi surpassed even the most exclusive and expensive sushi bars of the fabled Ginza district in contemporary Tokyo.

The appearance of extravagant sushi matched a general trend in the city of Edo, as merchants and artisans with disposable income became epicures and used gourmet food as a fashion statement. The samurai forgot their military skills and fell into lives of indulgence and idle luxury.

Soon the political winds shifted. In the early 1840s, a group of conservative bureaucrats decided to clamp down. The government issued prohibitions against extravagance. Nakano was stripped of power, and soldiers swept through the city, rounding up prostitutes, pornographers—and sushi chefs. Pine Sushi and Yohei Sushi were shut down, and over 200 employees of fancy sushi shops were arrested.

Lucky for sushi, the reforms didn't last, and the ringleader of the bureaucrats was ousted. Within a year or two, the high-end sushi shops were back in business, and even average citizens began to treat themselves to an occasional box of fancy sushi.

The stores prepared sushi to go or delivered it to the customer at his home or business. When the chefs packed the sushi to go, they separated the *nigiri* with decorative bamboo leaves. The leaves prevented the flavors from contaminating each other and added a mild antibacterial function. For their customers who were aristocrats, they even carved the family's crest from a bamboo leaf and used it to decorate the sushi. The green pieces of decorative plastic that are still served with takeout sushi are a carryover from these early practices. Some brands of plastic leaf are even coated with antibacterial chemicals.

Over time, some of the fancy to-go shops installed counters out front, similar to the street stalls, where pedestrians could stand and eat. A few shops added counters inside the shops or even tatami-mat rooms where diners could sit. Either way, the chef generally knelt on his heels on a raised platform behind the counter, usually behind a latticework barrier.

After World War II, the American occupation authorities banned outdoor food stalls as a health hazard. So when sushi chefs started up their businesses again after the war, sushi moved indoors. Chefs retained the spirit of a stand-up stall by building high counters with rows of stools. Now the chefs stood while they made sushi instead of sitting. The twentieth-century sushi bar was born.

With cheap sushi no longer available on the street, people of modest means could not afford it. Working-class Japanese would have to wait decades until inexpensive conveyor-belt sushi restaurants appeared, returning sushi to its humbler roots. In the meantime, sushi chefs at the fancier sushi bars added elements of *kaiseki* cooking to the elaborate, multicourse meals they served, taking the high end of sushi further into the realm of extravagance.

Zoran led the students past the long sushi bar at the back of the classroom and into the kitchen. He pulled two large metal trays from the restaurant's walk-in cooler.

The sushi toppings from which the chefs would pick while working at the sushi bar sat arrayed on small ceramic trays, each tightly wrapped in plastic wrap. There were slabs of tuna, salmon, yellowtail, flounder, and egg omelet; fillets of mackerel and grilled eel; pieces of octopus and squid; containers of spicy tuna mix, shredded snow crab, capelin roe, flying fish roe, and sea urchin roe.

"I want you to make one dish," Zoran said. "Everything has to be from scratch. You have fifteen minutes to read from your book. Then you have one hour to make it."

Kate looked at Zoran, not comprehending. The other students stared at the trays of ingredients.

Zoran snatched up some ingredients for himself. He grabbed a stainless-steel mixing bowl and pulled a stockpot from a shelf. Within seconds he was slicing and dicing and cooking.

The students stood still, in shock.

"See," Zoran barked, "this is what happens when you're at the sushi bar doing *omakase*. You get put on the spot!"

1 1

INSIDE THE ROLL

The students swung into action, assembling cooked appetizers. Kate froze. An hour and a half later, she'd managed to cut only a few pieces of vegetables and fish, and she hadn't figured out how to cook any of them. Zoran critiqued the other students' steaming hot dishes. He pretended not to notice Kate's cold plate.

The next morning he moved on to a new lesson.

"Set up your sushi stations!" Zoran barked.

For the party at Paramount, he'd taught the students to make hand rolls. Now it was time for them to make proper sushi rolls, using a bamboo mat.

In Japan, sushi rolls are an afterthought. A sushi chef might squeeze together a simple roll at the end of the meal, just to make sure his customer leaves with a full stomach. But in America, sushi is all about rolls. And most of the sushi rolls in America have never been served in Japan. For starters, American rolls are inside out.

The California roll is considered the key innovation that made sushi accessible to Americans. The roll was invented in L.A.'s Little Tokyo in the late 1960s, at Tokyo Kaikan, one of the first restaurants to open a sushi bar, and the premier Japanese eatery in L.A. The California roll's inventor was a chef there named Ichirō Mashita.

The California roll has come to be seen as a stroke of genius: the chef who devised it must have read the American mind, the thinking goes, and adapted sushi to American tastes.

In fact, the California roll wasn't primarily invented for the American palate at all. At first, the sushi bar at Tokyo Kaikan was patronized by a mostly Japanese clientele. The chefs there simply had difficulty obtaining fresh fatty tuna belly—called *toro* in Japanese—on a regular basis.

But truckloads of avocados were readily available in California. An avocado is nearly a third fat, equivalent to well-marbled meat. Avocado melts in the mouth sort of like fatty tuna.

First, Mashita tried mixing avocado with shrimp to give it a reddish color and the flavor of seafood. Later, he settled on crab meat. He served the mixture inside a traditional sushi roll—to his Japanese customers—to remind them of the fatty tuna back home. According to one report, three months passed before someone came up with the name "California roll."

It wasn't until later, as sushi spread beyond Little Tokyo and chefs started to appeal to American customers, that someone hatched the idea of making an inside-out roll. The point of the inside-out roll was to hide the seaweed.

According to an oft-told tale, in the late 1800s, the first Americans to visit Japan saw people eating the thin, crisp sheets of seaweed called nori and reported with shock that the Japanese ate black paper. In a sense, that wasn't far off. Nori was invented in Asakusa, a district of Tokyo famous for its paper making. The first nori manufacturers borrowed traditional Japanese paper-making techniques and applied them to seaweed.

The Japanese have been eating seaweed for more than two thousand years. By contrast, the Greeks and Romans disliked seaweed and fed it only to livestock, and only in emergencies. Yet the ancestors of many Americans enjoyed a version of nori. In the British Isles, coastal residents simmer the same type of seaweed, called laver, to make a paste that can be formed into patties, rolled in oatmeal, and fried to make laverbread, a breakfast treat accompanied by bacon.

Nori is simply dried laver. Laver is actually a kind of red algae that turns dark green when dried. The best nori, sushi chefs say, is so dark it's nearly black. Sheets of nori are so common today that it's hard to imagine that nori was once a luxury in Japan. Japan alone now produces around seven billion sheets a year. Much of the nori in the United States is produced in China and some of it in Korea.

But nori started out as a rare commodity. It was precious because harvesters were limited to what they could pull from the rocks at low tide. In the 1600s, people began to cultivate nori on nets in the water, but still yields were low. It was hard to grow because no one could figure out where laver came from. There didn't seem to be any seeds.

Through the first half of the twentieth century, laver growers relied on luck. Some harvests were good, some were bad, and nori remained expensive. Sushi rolls weren't common. Most sushi was *nigiri*.

The nori mystery was solved in 1949. The sleuth was not Japanese. It was a pioneering botanist in Britain named Kathleen Drew-Baker.

One of the first women to graduate from Manchester University, Drew-Baker was fired from her teaching job after marrying a fellow scientist in 1928—married women weren't allowed to teach. She dedicated her life to the study of seaweed and began collecting samples in old jam jars.

Drew-Baker gathered tiny, wormlike algae that bored into clamshells and oyster shells and grew them at home on eggshells. She discovered that one of these shell-boring algae was actually not a separate species, but in fact was the "parent" of the seaweed laver.

It turned out that the large red "leaves" of laver that people eat are basically sex organs designed to produce eggs and sperm—simply an intervening stage in the life of the microscopic shell borers.

The tiny shell borers send out spores from their hiding places. The spores grow into the red leaves. But the leaves have only half the chromosomes of the tiny parent. Some of the leaves produce clusters of male sex cells and some produce clusters of female cells. The female leaves build little bridges through the water to the male leaves, so the male leaves can fertilize them. If humans did the same thing, men would hide under rocks and ejaculate out sperm, which would grow into flags the size of skyscrapers. Women would do something similar with their eggs. Having sex would involve constructing bridges between the skyscrapers.

Drew-Baker's discovery meant that laver farmers in Japan could finally seed their nets instead of relying on luck. Today, nori manufacturing is efficient and predictable. In long rooms a bit like greenhouses, employees sprinkle tiny shell-boring algae from watering cans onto oystershells. The workers hang the shells on ropes in pools and let the algae bore and grow for about five months. After the borers release their spores, the workers wrap nets around big drums and roll the drums in the pools like water wheels. The spores catch on the nets and take root.

Laver farmers can then freeze the seeded nets and use them later, or they can transport the nets directly to a quiet bay and string them on frames in the seawater. The male and female leaves grow for forty or fifty days, until the harvesters trim them off the nets, shred them into flakes, and dry them so that they form sheets. A sheet of nori is basically a nightclub orgy of boy and girl seaweed, pressed into an edible piece of paper. As it happens, the orgy is loaded with glutamate and inosinic acid, or IMP, the delicious double whammy of *umami* taste that makes both dashi and nori so pleasant to the human palate. Old-fashioned sushi chefs still toast their own sheets of nori, preferably over charcoal, to make them extra crisp.

Kathleen Drew-Baker died in 1957, unaware that she had single-handedly laid a foundation for Asia's modern nori industry. In the process, she paved the way for sushi rolls to conquer the West.

But she was not forgotten. In southern Japan, a group of nori farmers collected donations for the construction of a granite pillar on a wooded promontory overlooking the Ariake Sea, where much of Japan's nori is grown. On the pillar is a portrait of Kathleen Drew-Baker in bas-relief, with a short English inscription that says "Mother of the Sea."

Japanese people still mostly eat *nigiri* sushi. Without Americans, who are crazy for rolls, the nori business might still be languishing, even decades after Drew-Baker's discovery.

"Today," Zoran said, "I'm going to show you *ura-maki*"—American-style inside-out rolls.

Zoran covered his bamboo rolling mat in plastic wrap so it wouldn't stick to the rice. People often asked Zoran what sushi chefs in Japan had used before wrap. Zoran would laugh because Japanese sushi chefs had never wrapped their rolling mats in anything. Traditionally, they didn't make inside-out rolls.

Zoran told the students to watch while he constructed a California roll. He set out half a sheet of nori. He wet his fingers so the rice wouldn't stick to them, clapped his hands together to knock off any excess water, and spread a fistful of sushi rice across the nori. After a sprinkling of sesame seeds he flipped the pad of rice and seaweed over. The layer of sticky rice remained attached to the seaweed and was now underneath. He tapped his fingers in a line across the center of the nori to create a valley where he would load the filling.

Next Zoran sliced an avocado. He laid a couple of wedges of the green fruit in the valley across the center of the nori. He tossed on crabmeat and cucumber. He lifted the edge of the rice and nori pad, pushed it over the filling, tucked it into the far side of the valley, and rolled it just a quarter turn to form a loose log. The nori had disappeared. The outside of the roll was rice, scattered with sesame seeds.

Zoran dropped his wrap-covered mat over the log of rice and gave it a quick squeeze, his fingers and thumbs tapping it flat on the sides and top. Inside-out rolls aren't so much rolls as squished rectangles.

Zoran dipped the tip of his long willow-leaf knife in his dish of water. He tilted the knife toward the ceiling and tapped the back of the handle on the cutting board. A drop of water rolled down the blade. A wet blade has the advantage of not sticking to the rice.

Zoran swept his knife horizontally across the cutting board. The blade passed under the roll and out the other side, severing the sticky rice from the wood. He swiped his blade down with another quick cut through the middle of the roll, spun half the roll around so it was side-to-side with the other half, and executed two more quick cuts through both halves at once. He turned the six slices on their sides, revealing the colorful cross sections.

"Your turn," he said.

They tried. Mostly they piled on too much filling. Avocado and cucumber spurted out of the ends.

At the party at Paramount, Kate had made so many hand rolls for customers that she'd gotten pretty good at them. Now she managed to construct a California roll, and it held together.

Slicing it was another matter. She was still afraid of cutting herself. She handled her willow-leaf knife gingerly. Her slices came out slanted, and the pieces were all different lengths. Her California roll looked like a miniature obstacle course.

"Okay," Zoran ordered, "now, *kappa-maki.*" It was time to master Japanese tradition—the basic cucumber roll.

The basic cucumber roll is a type of *hoso-maki,* or "thin roll." For the most part, thin rolls are the only rolls eaten in traditional Japanese sushi. There are only a few types of thin rolls, and the fillings are always simple. The two main kinds are cucumber and tuna.

Thin rolls have the seaweed on the outside—usually half a sheet. But the earliest record of a rolled form of sushi is from a 1776 Japanese cookbook, and the recipe calls for a more exotic wrapping than seaweed. It says to lay the skin of a poisonous blowfish on a bamboo window blind, spread rice across it, and lay fish along the center. Then roll the window blind up tightly, squeeze it into the shape of a square, and press it with something heavy. Today's bamboo mats for rolling sushi look like miniature window blinds because that's precisely what they are.

The cucumber roll gets its Japanese name, *kappa-maki,* from a mythical water sprite called a *kappa,* believed to inhabit lakes and rivers. *Kappa* are known for gobbling up children and generally causing trouble by farting and looking up women's kimonos. In old Japanese paintings, these ugly green water sprites look rather like Teenage Mutant Ninja Turtles. In fact, in one of the *Teenage Mutant Ninja Turtles* films, the turtles travel back in time to medieval Japan and get mistaken for *kappa*. The only food *kappa* prefer over human children is cucumbers. Thus, the name of the cucumber roll.

The other common thin roll, the tuna roll, is called a *tekka-maki*. Most Japanese people think the name comes from the slang term for a gambling den. The gamblers wanted to eat sushi without getting their fingers sticky—so the story goes. But the name more likely comes from the original meaning of *tekka,* a red-hot shaft of iron. The red strip of tuna in the center looks like a red shaft, and the wasabi creates a burning sensation. And some would say that the raw, iron-rich tuna flesh tastes metallic.

Cucumbers are a lot cheaper than tuna, and Zoran liked to brag that he still practiced ten cucumber rolls a day, the way a concert pianist practices scales. He took pleasure in making his students do the same. Regardless of the scheduled lesson on any given day, without warning Zoran was liable to instruct the students to set aside their work and begin practicing cucumber rolls. He would stroll around the room and say, "I'll tell you the secret of mastering these." The students would all look up, expectant. Zoran would grin. "Practice."

As the students practiced cucumber rolls, the room filled with the smell of sushi. Mostly it was the scent of the seashore, which comes from compounds called bromophenols. Bromophenols are not actually the smell of the sea. They are the smell of the algae that live in the sea—algae such as laver, used for nori.

Zoran paced around the room, his arms folded across his chest. Some of the students' rolls looked perfect. Others didn't. "Marcos," Zoran said, "too much rice."

Kate looked down at her rolls in dismay. Like the slices of her California roll, the slices of her thin rolls had come out all different shapes. But she had an additional problem. Her thin rolls were popping open. Zoran glanced at them, but said nothing.

The next morning Zoran began by demonstrating a popular piece of American sushi called a crunchy roll. But he was emphatic that this was not Japanese food.

"Anything that's greasy or oily isn't part of traditional sushi," Zoran warned. "That's all Western influence."

The funny thing was, sometimes Japanese tourists would come into Hama Hermosa and order the American rolls. The California roll and a few other American rolls had been adopted at low-brow, or "American-style," sushi shops in Japan, and people had taken to calling avocado "the *toro* of the fields," because of its similarity to fatty tuna. But many other American rolls weren't available in Japan. The tourists from Japan loved them.

Most American sushi rolls are built on a basic inside-out roll foundation, like a California roll. But as soon as Zoran flipped over his pad of nori and rice, things took a dramatic new turn.

Onto the nori, Zoran squirted a glob of mayonnaise laced with red chile. On that he laid two straight shrimp that had been deep-fried in heavy batter. Next was cucumber. The only thing that was Japanese was the bright orange stick of pickled burdock root for extra crunch; it was loaded with dye and MSG. Zoran squeezed the roll closed. He tossed it around in a tray of "crunchies"—bits of deep-fried batter—until it was covered. He sliced it, squirted on some sugary sauce, and held it up on a plate.

"The customer has to pay ten bucks for this!" He laughed. "Crazy! Would you pay for this?" Zoran shook his head in disbelief. "One shrimp costs, what, twenty cents? This is a *big* moneymaker. I guarantee you guys will have to make these."

1 2

PUTTING ON
THE SQUEEZE

"Stop what you're doing!" Zoran yelled.

The students looked up, surprised, some of them still in the middle of practicing their American rolls.

"All food off your cutting board," Zoran ordered. It was time to make *nigiri*.

The students gathered around Zoran. He hefted a plastic tub onto the table. Inside lay slabs of fish. He pulled one out and laid it on his cutting board.

"When we cut *neta* for sushi," Zoran said, "we cut slices two fingers wide, four fingers long."

The word *neta* comes from the word *tane* (pronounced *ta-né*), which literally means "seed." In old Japan, laborers frequently reversed the syllables of common words as a form of slang. They reversed the syllables of *tane* and used the word *neta* to refer to things that were the seed or source for something. *Neta* can refer to the topics of newspaper articles, evidence against criminals, or material for jokes and comedy routines. Young people in Japan today use the word *neta* in conversation, and on their blogs, to refer to a person or to events that are a source of amusement. Sushi chefs use the word as slang to refer to toppings for *nigiri* and fillings for rolls. The glass case at the sushi bar is the *neta* case, and the trays inside are *neta* trays.

More specifically, for a sushi chef, *neta* refers to the particular pieces of fish that he has cut down to the size of a *neta* tray. It was in this sense that Zoran was now using the term.

The *neta* tray is one of the fundamental size units of sushi. The average *neta* tray is about 9 inches long and 4 or 5 inches wide—or, as many sushi chefs prefer to measure it, about twelve finger widths long. Sushi chefs like to measure everything in fingers.

Aside from preparing rice, a true sushi chef's most crucial skills involve converting each creature of the sea into a useful piece of *neta,* ready to be cut into small slices for *nigiri.* The process often begins early in the morning with a chef's purchases at the fish markets and continues during the afternoon in the kitchen. By the time the customer shows up for dinner, the chef has already been hard at work for many hours. The chef saves the final slicing of small pieces for *nigiri* until the last minute, when the customer places an order. That way, the meat will spend only a short time exposed to the degrading effects of oxygen.

Zoran slapped a *neta*-size block of salmon onto his cutting board and expertly sliced off a small rectangle. He held his hand over the little slice of salmon, first one way, then the other. Just as he'd said, it was two fingers wide and four fingers long.

"When you cut, each slice should be one motion. No back and forth." He set the heel of his blade against the block of salmon and pointed the tip upwards. He drew the handle back and up, letting the blade trace a single smooth arc down through the fish. "Don't push hard. Let the knife do the work."

He carved more slices and laid them in a neat row, overlapping, across the top of his cutting board.

"After the cut, lay the slice presentation-side down." Generally, the prettier side of the fillet was the presentation side. "That way, when you pick it up, the presentation side will be in your palm, away from the rice. Okay, now you guys try. Everybody get a fillet."

The students chose different types of fish and hunched over their cutting boards, drawing their blades down through the *neta.* Because of the various shapes of fish, blocks of *neta* are seldom exactly the right size. The chef must cut with his blade on an angle to create a slice that is the right length and width, as well as the appropriate thickness. Soon there was a row of *nigiri*-size slices across the top of each cutting board.

Kate had tried to imitate Zoran's cut, but her willow-leaf blade scared her and it wouldn't cooperate. Her slices came out in random shapes, and all of them were too thick.

Next she tried to remember the routine Zoran had taught them for squeezing *nigiri*.

Different lineages of sushi chefs employ different techniques for squeezing *nigiri*. The students at the California Sushi Academy learned a basic nine-step process.

First—if the sushi chef is right-handed—he reaches his right hand into his canister of rice and gathers together a cylinder of rice the size and shape of a wine cork. With his left hand, he plucks a piece of fish with his thumb and index finger and dangles it inside his cupped hand. He rotates his hand outward so that the slice of fish settles flat across the palm. Since he has already laid the slices of fish presentation-side down on his cutting board, the presentation side of the slice now lies against his fingers, and the underside is exposed. He cups his left hand into a *U*, with the slice of fish lying in the trough at the bottom. Then he presses the clump of rice lightly down into the *U*, on top of the fish.

Step two is simple. Keeping his left hand tightly cupped, he pinches the top and bottom of the wine cork of rice with his right thumb and index finger, squeezing the rice from an oblong shape into a triangle that points upward toward his face, sitting on the slice of fish.

Step three seems surprising. The chef holds his right index finger flat and presses down the point of the triangle, pushing it back into an oblong shape against the slice of fish. This appears to have accomplished nothing, but actually it serves a purpose. It forces the grains into alignment.

A sushi chef wants the grains lined up along the length of the finished rectangle. That way the grains will stick to each other without lots of extra squeezing. A tightly packed *nigiri* is bad. The chef's goal is a piece of sushi just firm enough to stay in one piece while the customer handles it, but loose enough that it will immediately disintegrate in the mouth. When a perfect *nigiri* crumbles apart on the tongue, the grains of rice mingle instantly with the fish, combining tastes and textures. The sensation some diners feel is gratitude because the chef has calibrated the sushi so perfectly that they hardly have to chew.

Researchers have conducted MRI scans of *nigiri* made by master sushi chefs. The scans reveal that a master chef's *nigiri* disintegrates easily on the tongue because it contains more empty space than a *nigiri* made by a novice. Scans of *nigiri* made by sushi robots showed a product tightly compressed, with almost no empty space on the interior at all.

Now, on to step four of the *nigiri*-making process. The chef opens up the *U* of the left hand and rolls the oblong cylinder of rice, along with its attached slice of fish, from the palm onto the base of the fingers. The *nigiri* has now turned right side up, with the fish on top.

Step five is to press the top of the *nigiri* lightly with the left thumb, holding the fish down onto the rice, while using the thumb and index finger of the right hand to flatten the long sides of the rice cylinder, shaping it into more of a rectangle.

At step six, the chef again cups his left hand into a *U*. With the index and middle fingers of his right hand held out flat, he presses along the length of the fish, squeezing the *nigiri* down into the trough of the *U*. This presses out any air between the fish and the rice. The warmth in the chef's fingers also warms the fish slightly. Minutes ago the fish was refrigerated. By the time it's served, it should approach the warmth of the rice, which is at body temperature. At the same time, the chef uses his left thumb to press down the upper end of the *nigiri*, using a motion similar to that of holding down the button on a cigarette lighter. This squares off the end of the rectangle.

At step seven the chef opens up the left hand again. With the right hand, he rotates the *nigiri* clockwise 180 degrees.

Step eight repeats step six, further shaping the *nigiri* into a rectangle and squaring off the remaining end.

Finally, step nine is to repeat step five, to put the finishing touches on the shape. The *nigiri* is complete.

A master sushi chef will adjust the height of his *nigiri* to account for the fact that he cuts firmer fish in thin slices and softer fish in thick slices. When he's finished, the different types of *nigiri* should be a uniform height, despite different thicknesses of fish.

Different lineages of chefs create different shapes of *nigiri*. The most common shape is not, strictly speaking, a rectangle. The top of the *nigiri* is arched slightly like a dome so that the slice of fish drapes over it. Sushi chefs call this the comb style because the shape resembles a traditional Japanese hair comb. Other shapes include box, fan, boat, and rice-bale styles.

Kate's clumps of rice fit in what could charitably be called ball style, and they were all different sizes. One of her slices of fish was so narrow that she laid it across the rice on a diagonal. Some of the other students' *nigiri* looked nearly perfect. Again, Zoran glanced at Kate's sushi and said nothing.

Kate knew that the sushi she'd made this week had been terrible. Unlike the young female chef Kirara, in the comic book *Sushi Chef Kirara's Job,* Kate hadn't been raised by a master sushi chef. She had some of Kirara's spunk, but none of her skills. It was hard for Kate not to feel that she was once again losing her own personal battle with sushi. She turned her back on her block of fish. No more slicing. She hunted in the refrigerator until she found some shrimp tails already prepared by the restaurant chefs. She made the rest of her *nigiri* with those.

After class Marcos carried his *nigiri* into the kitchen. He peeled the slices of fish off his *nigiri* and tossed the fish in a sauté pan on the stove. It was premium sushi-grade fish, flown over fresh from Japan. It sizzled and turned brown and greasy.

"I'm getting kinda sick of eating raw meat," he muttered.

13

FAST FOOD

*B*efore Zoran took roll the next morning, he stepped out of the classroom to fill his plastic travel mug with coffee. Upon his return, he noticed one of the students rubbing her knife on a pumice stone at her cutting board. She was trying to get off a few spots of rust. Zoran almost dropped his mug.

"Never!" Zoran screamed. "Never! Never!"

The woman jumped, and nearly cut herself.

"Never, ever, do that over your cutting board," Zoran shouted. "You're going to get little bits of rust in your food!"

He shook his head and strode to the head of the table. He took a sip of coffee. "Today," he announced, "you're going to make sushi rolls for the vegetable deliveryman. Make it professional. You're making it for a customer." He scribbled a list of sushi rolls and *nigiri* on the whiteboard. "You have an order on the board."

Zoran squinted and peered down the table. The Japanese student, Takumi, had already gotten to work.

"Stop! Stop!" Zoran cried. "Don't make your sushi yet!" He pointed to the list of items on the whiteboard. "What order do you make these in?"

The students stared at the board. The list of sushi Zoran had written on the board began with Japanese-style thin rolls: two cucumber rolls (*kappa-maki*). Next were American-style inside-out rolls (*ura-maki*): one California roll, one spicy tuna roll. There was one other type of roll: a "big roll" (*futo-maki*)—this is a larger sushi roll that uses not a half sheet of nori but an entire sheet. Zoran had ended the list with four *nigiri*.

He repeated his question. "What order?"

The students stared at him, their faces blank.

"I'll tell you," Zoran said. "You want to make your *ura-maki* first." He pointed to the two inside-out rolls—the California roll and the spicy tuna roll. "The nori is on the *inside*." He shook his finger and laughed. "The customer won't be able to tell if it gets soggy."

Crisp nori is a hallmark of a good sushi roll—at least, in Japan. Traditional sushi rolls—the ones with nori wrapped around a thin filling of rice and cucumber or tuna—should be eaten right away, while the nori is still dry and crackly. If a customer is sitting at a table in a restaurant, there's no point in ordering a traditional sushi roll. By the time the waiter delivers it, the nori on the outside will be damp from touching the rice. Traditional thin rolls are supposed to be eaten at the sushi bar, within seconds of leaving the chef's hands. But with inside-out rolls, the nori is on the inside, where it goes instantly soggy anyway.

Zoran jotted the number 1 next to the spicy tuna and California rolls on his list. Next he pointed to the "big roll," or *futo-maki*.

"The second thing you want to make is your *futo-maki*. They don't have to be super crispy." The diameter of a big roll is nearly twice that of standard inside-out rolls, so it must be sliced thin enough for the customer to eat each piece in one mouthful. The filling dominates, so the crispness of the nori is less crucial. Zoran wrote a number 2 next to the *futo-maki*.

"Now, your *kappa-maki* should be the most crispy, so you want to make those last." Zoran scribbled a number 3 next to the cucumber rolls, and a number 4 next to the *nigiri*. *Nigiri* were quick to make, and saving them for last ensured that the fish toppings would be as fresh as possible.

"You must choose your own plates to display your sushi," he added. "Remember, in Japanese presentation, use no more than seventy percent of the plate." He glanced at the clock. "Commence! You have twenty minutes."

Kate stared at the block of fish on her cutting board. Twenty minutes! This was crazy.

"If you make it in the wrong order," Zoran yelled, "you're doing the dishes!"

Right out of the gate, Kate screwed up. She panicked and started cutting her block of fish first simply because the fish was sitting right in front of her. It was a bad move, because now her slices of fish would sit exposed to the air while she made the rest of her sushi.

Zoran, having started a race, appeared set on winning it. Kate glanced at him and her mouth fell open. He was making three rolls *at the same time.* His hands flew around the cutting board in a blur, tossing ingredients onto different pads of rice and nori as though he were dealing a hand of cards. In under five minutes he'd completed all five of the rolls in his list. After that he started making extra rolls. It wasn't clear how fifty sushi rolls and forty *nigiri* were going to be eaten by one vegetable deliveryman.

The entire history of sushi has been a quest for speed. More than a thousand years ago, when people made sushi they had to wait for a year before they could eat it. In the 1600s, they shortened the fermentation time to a month. After the invention of vinegar, they pressed sushi under stones for just a couple of days. With the invention of hand-squeezed sushi in the 1800s, it could be eaten immediately. Sushi had evolved into a meal of instant gratification.

But chefs in America have taken the speed of sushi to a new level. In 2000, a Japanese essayist named Toyoo Tamamura visited sushi restaurants around L.A., including Hama Hermosa, which at the time was called California Beach Sushi. He was startled to see that sushi restaurants in the United States were larger and had more tables than the small sushi bars he was used to in Japan.

When he sat down to eat, he was also startled to see people ordering as many as six *nigiri* all topped with the same kind of fish. To an American, it makes perfect sense to choose only his favorite items on the menu, as he would in any other restaurant. In Japan, Tamamura was accustomed to asking the chef for a series of small surprises, one or two *nigiri* at a time, each topped with a different item.

But Tamamura was most surprised by the volume of rolls that

Americans ordered. Rolls are far more labor-intensive than *nigiri*. The chefs worked as if they were under siege, squeezing out roll after roll for table orders at a furious pace, their hands never at rest. Tamamura wrote that "there are even tough guys who make three or four rolls at once." He decided that sushi chefs back in Japan had it easy.

Zoran's cutting board was now piled with rolls. One by one the students completed their sushi plates. One of the women in the class had plated her slices of roll in blocks that formed an asymmetric sunburst around her four *nigiri*. It was precisely the sort of display Zoran was looking for. He nodded his approval.

But he steamed around the table declaring the other presentations dismal failures. He rearranged the sushi on most of the plates.

Kate had struggled through the exercise. Her *nigiri* looked terrible, and her roll slices were still popping open.

Zoran arrived at Kate's station. For once, he didn't ignore her, nor did he criticize her in front of the whole class.

"Here, I'm going to show you something," Zoran said, his voice quiet. His hands whirred and assembled the foundation of an inside-out roll. He stacked an impossibly high pile of cucumber and avocado on the nori. "Watch this."

Zoran arched his hands and lifted the edge of the rice and nori pad. His thumbs and fingers gathered the pad up and hauled it over the filling like a pair of industrious spiders.

"You want to curl the near edge up, over, and down, and *tuck* it in." With the tips of his fingers he pressed the curled edge of the pad down into the cavity of filling, then held the position and looked at Kate. "You've got to really *tuck* it in, *tuck* it tight." He squeezed. "Like this."

Kate watched. Something in her head clicked. She nodded.

Perhaps it was just as well that the vegetable deliveryman hadn't arrived. Zoran told the students to pack up their sushi and take it home.

"Thank you, everybody, for a good day today," he said. He turned to go. "I think we learned something."

AMERICAN STYLE

The next day Zoran taught the students another style of Japanese cooking that sushi chefs used in *omakase*—simmering in broth. Near the end of class, Toshi appeared and reviewed the results. He was horrified. The students had used small appetizer bowls, but they'd filled them to the brim. It was so American.

"Small portions!" Toshi yelled. Everything a sushi chef served at the sushi bar ought to be tiny, Toshi explained—lots of little courses, each one beautifully arranged. "You gotta eat with your eyes," Toshi said. Kate liked that. She was glad to have Toshi back in the classroom, if only for a few minutes. Toshi showed the students how to arrange a miniscule serving into an elegant pyramid. He chuckled. "Like little Mount Fuji!"

As the students cleaned up around noon, Jay, the coordinator for student affairs, slipped through the classroom carrying takeout containers of Chinese dim sum. He'd found a fabulous hole-in-the-wall in a nearby mall. Jay had been eating too much raw fish and rice lately, and he was looking forward to a lunch of steaming-hot pork dumplings.

He carried the dim sum into one of the private dining rooms. Hama Hermosa only served dinner, so the place was deserted. He arranged five or six containers of fragrant food on the table.

Today Jay had invited a man named Jeffrey Nitta to lunch. Like Jay, Jeff was a Japanese American and a restaurant consultant who worked in the sushi business. Jay had come to his serious interest in sushi about five years ago, but Jeff had been analyzing Japanese food trends in the United States for decades.

Jeff arrived, and the two men oohed and aahed over the dumplings. Right away, they started talking about the early days of American sushi, when sushi was first catching on in L.A.

"I remember hearing about the headaches," Jeff said, laughing. "Restaurant owners were saying, 'Sushi chefs are worse than regular chefs!' The Japanese chefs were stubborn, and they thought Americans were too stupid to understand sushi."

Jeff had been raised in Los Angeles. At school, most of his friends were white. But at home, he lived in a world that was partly Japanese. His father had come to the United States from Japan as an adult; his mother had grown up in America but was in many ways a traditional Japanese woman. Jeff had spent his childhood with a foot in both cultures.

As a young adult, Jeff had eaten in sushi restaurants frequently during the period when sushi first took root in the United States. It was an exciting time. Freed from tradition, Japanese chefs innovated, adapting the cuisine to American tastes and experience. Ambitious chefs like Nobu Matsuhisa—championed by Robert De Niro—invented a new hybrid cuisine for the Western palate. But Jeff also saw Japanese chefs dumbing sushi down for Americans. It frustrated him that the chefs didn't make the effort to educate their customers.

Toshi had been an exception. Jeff remembered visiting Hama Venice and thinking that Toshi's approach was brilliant. Toshi didn't try to adhere to tradition or even to explain anything to his customers. He acted like a crazy American. But he stocked high-quality fish and authentic Japanese ingredients, and he used his charisma to challenge his customers to try real sushi.

Jeff recounted a meeting of members of the Japanese food industry back in the 1980s. "I said, 'Americans are ready if you educate them. It may take some time. But they will know what good fish is, *if* you educate them. You're not educating them, you're just writing them off.'"

At the time, Jeff would sit down at a sushi bar in L.A., and some-times a real Japanese customer—from Japan—would be there. The Japanese chef would serve the Japanese customer authentic sushi, Japanese style. The Americans at the bar would look up from their American-style rolls and peer over at what the Japanese was eating. 'Wow,' they'd say, 'I want to eat that!' The Japanese chef would say, 'No, you don't want to eat that. *You* can't eat that.'" Jeff looked at Jay and threw up his hands. "That's what they said!"

It was easier just to serve the Americans inside-out rolls full of mayonnaise and chili pepper. The chefs were guaranteed to make money that way. They built big restaurants. The restaurants had lots of tables and they had menus, with lists of American-style rolls. They were sushi-roll factories.

As more and more sushi chefs jumped on the bandwagon, they competed with each other to appeal to American tastes. Non-Japanese joined the fray, too—Koreans, Chinese, Latinos, and others. Restaurants undercut each other with cheaper prices.

"You're seeing them in a rut now," Jeff said. "The all-you-can-eat places started coming in, and now the customers are like, 'I'm not going back to my old sushi place because it's half price across the street.' And so the Japanese sushi chefs are saying, 'Well, we're going to do that, too.' They start joining in with the fifty percent–off specials, and they've shot themselves in the foot. They didn't educate." Jeff shook his head. "They were greedy with the econom-ics. And that's what's sad. Now you're jeopardizing your Japanese culture, you're selling out, you're commercializing your product that was, you know, your history."

As Japanese Americans, Jeff and Jay wondered how best to pre-serve Japanese culture in the United States. Jay's father, an architect, had designed the restaurant Tokyo Kaikan, where the California roll had been invented. Tokyo Kaikan had been a showcase for tra-ditional Japanese architecture. But the building had since been torn down to make room for a parking lot.

"The purists are still holding on," Jeff said. He was thinking of the minority of Japanese chefs who still made authentic Japanese sushi. There were some in L.A. There were a good number in New York City. "But it's only the high-level American customers who under-stand that, people who already know about Japanese culture."

As a result, many of the purist chefs had jacked their prices up so high that an average American would never set foot in the door just to try it out, especially in New York. In Manhattan, the chef Masayoshi Takayama—popularly known simply as Masa—wouldn't even consider serving you lunch or dinner unless you handed him $350. Thanks to him, America's most expensive restaurant is, astonishingly, a sushi bar.

To Jeff, Masa and his prices were as much an affront to Japanese sushi as were inside-out rolls loaded with mayonnaise and chile— maybe worse. In Japan, the sushi experience was a matter of getting to know the chef at your neighborhood sushi bar, visiting frequently, and letting him choose what he thought you would like from the freshest ingredients that day.

Jay nodded. People were always asking him for the inside scoop on where to get the best sushi. He'd shrug and tell them to find a neighborhood place where they liked the chef.

Jeff smiled. "When my father introduced me to sushi, the sushi bar he took me to was in a bowling alley."

"Holiday Bowl," Jay said, nodding.

"Right," Jeff said, "Holiday Bowl. And I remember as a little kid, he put me up on a stool, and we'd sit around eating sushi. The Japanese chefs were very traditional. They knew my dad. They knew that he liked his beer in a small glass instead of a big mug. My dad would never even have to order. He would just sit down and they'd make him sushi. It was *omakase,* automatically, you know?"

Jeff wanted most American sushi diners to be able to have a similar experience.

Toshi had done what he could. But times had changed. With competition from low-end sushi everywhere, even Toshi couldn't draw the crowds any longer.

15

SHOW TIME

*T*hursday evening, the back sushi bar at Hama Hermosa opened up to customers along with the front bar. Zoran and the gorgeous Dane, Fie, set up for business. Takumi helped out. He would be on hand in case things got busy.

The hostess cranked up disco music in the back room and set out stools and place settings around the classroom table, converting it into extra dining space—again, just in case it got busy.

But the back room languished for two hours. Zoran disappeared.

Finally, around 7:30 p.m. the manager ushered in a Caucasian couple and sat them at the back bar. Fie greeted them and offered to make them something.

"We're here for Zoran," they said.

"Ah, for Zoran." Fie dipped her head and retreated.

Seconds later Zoran appeared in his chef's whites.

"Hey!" Zoran bellowed, all smiles. "How've you been?" He sat in a chair next to the couple and chatted. The man slapped Zoran on the back. They laughed.

Zoran excused himself and disappeared into the kitchen. As soon as he was out of sight he dashed madly from one refrigerator to another, grabbing the special ingredients, garnishes, and sauces that underpinned his *omakase* arsenal. Every sushi chef who practiced *omakase* had secret weapons, and now Zoran installed himself behind the back sushi bar armed with his.

The couple had been coming to Hama Hermosa for Zoran's *omakase* nearly every Thursday for the past year and a half. Zoran adored them. But every week, as Thursday rolled around, Zoran would feel anxious. *Omakase* customers always expect the sushi chef to surprise them. That meant Zoran had to come up with new ideas for eight to ten little dishes every week.

Jay, the academy's coordinator for student affairs, wandered into the dining room, fresh from his lunchtime conversation with Jeff earlier in the day. Seeing Zoran about to serve *omakase*, Jay strolled over to an unobtrusive corner of the bar and sat down to watch.

Zoran delivered his opening shot right away—little blocks of egg tofu in small bowls. That bought him a few minutes to engage the couple in conversation, and he used the opportunity to probe their current preferences. The trick for Zoran was to expand their horizons in a way they'd enjoy. He spooned something out of a Tupperware container. The man peered at it.

"Oh, man, green stuff," the man said.

Zoran smiled.

The man frowned. "What *is* that?"

Zoran kept smiling. "If I told you, you wouldn't want to eat it!"

Jay sipped on a soda, amused. Part of the difficulty in encouraging Americans to appreciate the sushi experience was getting them to relinquish control. In America, you were considered a sophisticated eater if you insisted on having things a certain way. To really experience sushi, you had to let the chef decide what was best for you. It was hard for Americans to do. That was why the most uncompromising Japanese sushi chef in L.A.—a man named Kazunori Nozawa, more popularly known as "the sushi Nazi"—had a big sign hanging over his sushi bar. It said, "Today's Special: Trust Me."

Jay glanced at Takumi, who was standing behind the sushi bar watching Zoran work. By now it was clear to Jay that Takumi had talent in the kitchen. Judging from the food he made, he was a creative spirit, respectful of Japanese tradition but not constrained by it. He was capable of thinking outside the box without dumbing the food down. Yet Takumi was so shy and reserved that it was difficult to imagine him ever being the sort of sociable sushi chef that Zoran was tonight.

Zoran enjoyed displaying himself in front of customers while he worked. He used his charisma to enliven their meal and convince them to try new things. Kitchen skills were important, but a sushi chef needed more than kitchen skills. He had to be a performer.

Takumi caught Jay's eye and ambled over to say hello. They chatted quietly across the bar, Takumi speaking slowly in his broken English. Takumi pointed at the empty space in front of Jay.

"You don't want to eat?" he asked.

Jay chuckled. "I've eaten too much sushi lately." He sighed. "I keep thinking about that fantastic bolognese sauce you made."

Takumi's eyebrows shot up. The previous week he'd cooked spaghetti for the staff. Jay had been raving about it ever since. Now Jay drew an imaginary fence around his seat at the bar, marking it off from the rest of the restaurant. "Italian section!" he laughed.

Takumi laughed, too, as he headed to the kitchen.

Zoran was handing his customers a pair of rectangular plates, each with three small bowls indented in the surface. Each bowl contained a small pyramid of something mysterious. Zoran proudly described the contents to the couple; squid marinated in rice vinegar and sesame oil, seaweed sprouts marinated the same way and sprinkled with sesame seeds, and strips of scallop and tiny rice noodles marinated in sweetened sake. The seaweed sprouts were the "green stuff."

They were delighted. "Hey," the man said, "let's have a round of drinks for the chefs!"

The hostess fetched the biggest bottle of beer she could find and added it to their tab.

"Thank you!" Zoran smiled and bowed. Zoran's customers knew he didn't drink, but buying beer for the chefs was still the proper thing to do. "I'll be right back," Zoran shouted, "with some Diet Coke!"

Takumi had vanished, so the only person for whom the hostess could pour beer was Fie. Zoran returned with his Diet Coke. They all clinked glasses across the fish case and bellowed out a toast in Japanese.

"*Kanpai!*"

Fie pretended to sip her beer. Later she would pour it down the sink. Zoran went right back to work.

Takumi slipped back into the bar from the kitchen. He snuck over to Jay, reached across the fish case, and placed a tall shot glass in front of him. It contained half a dozen olives on a skewer. Takumi glanced around, like a spy, then tipped his upper body in a quick bow.

"First course," he said. He disappeared back into the kitchen.

Takumi's full name, Takumi Nishio, meant nothing to Americans. Takumi liked it that way. Unlike in Japan, here he could putter in the classroom at Hama Hermosa, or back in the kitchen, and no one except the Japanese chefs had any idea who he was.

There had been an awkward moment when one of the Japanese chefs had taken him out to a Japanese hostess club in Torrance. Toyota and Honda both had their American headquarters in Torrance, and it was full of Japanese people. At the hostess club that night somebody had recognized him. He'd taken it graciously.

None of Takumi's classmates at the academy had a clue that he'd been a rock star. In the late 1980s and early 1990s, during the go-go years of Japan's economic bubble, Takumi had been a member of a Japanese boy band called CHA-CHA. They had released five albums and ten singles. On stage they were known for their choreographed dance routines and their humorous banter. Takumi had traveled all over Japan, singing, dancing, and joking on stage for crowds of fans.

At the height of his career Takumi had married Tomomi Nishimura—more popularly known by her stage name Tororin—one of Japan's biggest female pop idols during the bubble years. As many pop stars do in Japan, Takumi and his wife had transitioned out of their singing careers and become popular television personalities. They appeared frequently on quiz and talk shows. In 2002, they were named Japan's "Ideal Couple of the Year."

But Takumi had grown weary of celebrity, and he'd discovered that his true passion was cooking. His wife had continued her television work, but Takumi had withdrawn from show business into the kitchen.

First he'd dedicated himself to Italian cuisine. When he'd mastered making pasta by hand, he tested salt-to-water ratios from 0.5 percent to 2 percent for cooking it, and settled on 1.34 percent. He and a friend, a famous folk singer, opened a little Italian restaurant called Monpetquoi in the trendy Shibuya district of Tokyo. Takumi installed himself as the head chef. Off the stage and in the kitchen, out of sight, Takumi would be judged solely on the quality of his food.

But it didn't turn out that way. People came to the restaurant and ate his handmade pasta, but they were really there just to get his autograph. Restaurant critics made fun of him—how could a Japanese pop star be taken seriously as an Italian chef? In the fall of 2004, the restaurant shut down.

The experience left Takumi feeling that people in Japan were closed-minded. He saw how Westerners had welcomed sushi, embracing Japanese food and altering it at the same time. He liked that. He didn't think most Japanese appreciated the global reach of their traditions.

If his fellow Japanese weren't going to take him seriously at home, he would go out and explore the larger world. Now, at the age of 38, he puttered happily in solitude in the kitchen at Hama Hermosa, sautéing garlic chips in olive oil for Jay.

Out at the sushi bar, on display, Zoran continued his performance. He prepared an octopus ceviche—a South American style of raw seafood—and delivered it across the fish case with a flourish, much to his customers' delight. Next Zoran wowed them with something he called "herb *toro.*"

Jay chuckled. Even at their best, sushi chefs weren't above serving old fish. "Herb *toro*" was fatty tuna that had been left in the walk-in refrigerator too long. It had changed color, from pink to gray, and could no longer be served raw. Marinating it with onion and herbs, tossing it in a sauté pan, and drizzling it with miso dressing had camouflaged its age. Zoran had served it with an additional dose of charm, and the couple loved it.

Takumi reappeared. He snuck over and placed a small bowl in front of Jay on the sushi bar, *omakase*-style. Its contents were arranged in an elegant pyramid—a little Mount Fuji, just as Toshi had instructed that morning. But it wasn't Japanese food. The bowl contained five mushroom ravioli, sprinkled with fried garlic chips and drizzled with olive oil. Jay waved the aromatic steam toward his nose.

Zoran sliced fish with samurai bravado. His hands flew around a wide dish of black lacquer with red and gold inlay. Slices of sashimi fell into place. Some slices became a staircase, others a fan, and still others petals in a flower.

Zoran handed the dish of sashimi across the bar. The couple was awestruck. "Wow."

Takumi emerged from the kitchen a third time, holding something below the level of the sushi bar.

"Main course," Takumi whispered to Jay.

It was another little Mount Fuji. Jay gazed down and inhaled deeply through his nose. Takumi had sautéed cubes of beef with fresh rosemary and more fried garlic. Jay tucked a morsel in his mouth. He closed his eyes and moaned. Takumi smiled and slipped back into the kitchen.

It was past ten o'clock when Zoran's couple finally left. Zoran flew into a frenzy of cleaning. He stowed ingredients and sauces, returned trays of *neta* to the walk-in, and scrubbed countertops. He still had to prepare the following day's lesson. He got to bed after 1:00 a.m. His alarm clock would go off at 4:30 a.m., for his weekly trip to the fish markets.

1 6

FRUITS OF THE SEA

A little before 5:00 a.m. the fax machine spit out the day's price lists from the area fish markets. Zoran snatched it up and glanced down the rows of data—bluefin tuna from Spain, Croatia, and Australia; bigeye from Hawaii and Fiji; yellowfin from Florida and Vietnam; and nearly a hundred other items.

He burst out the back door clutching two bags of trash, which he tossed in the dumpster on his way to the old van. He fired up the engine, breaking the silence in the dark alley. Soon he was cruising down a deserted boulevard. Twenty minutes later the sky was brightening. Zoran removed one hand from the steering wheel and placed a call on his cellphone.

"*Ohaiyō gozaimasu!*" he yelled into the phone.

He pulled up to an apartment complex to pick up Tetsuya Tsumoto, the head chef at Hama Hermosa. Tetsu padded outside, moving like a sleepy bear. He was a stocky man with puffy eyes and droopy cheeks. He was wearing a jacket even though the morning was already warm. Tetsu had come to the United States as a language student thirteen years ago and worked for Toshi as a busboy. Toshi had turned him into a first-rate sushi chef.

Zoran gunned the van and headed for the Santa Monica freeway. Tetsu's chin dropped to his chest and he fell asleep. The sun rose over the mountains, ushering in the beginning of a hot July day.

They left the freeway and entered the seedy garment district downtown, glass skyscrapers looming overhead. They drove down an avenue a few blocks south of Skid Row. Shafts of sunlight slanted through cracks between buildings. Homeless men lay in sleeping bags or stood in clutches on the corners. Zoran turned into a warehouse lot crammed with cars and trucks. He double-parked and hopped out. Tetsu rolled out of the passenger seat and trundled after him.

The two men walked through streams of cold air falling from the open backs of refrigerated trucks. As they walked through a loading door into the warehouse, they felt the chill of the huge refrigerated space. The smell of the ocean assailed their nostrils. Their shoes squished over a film of frigid water on the concrete floor. Under a high ceiling, long tables were covered with plastic bins and Styrofoam boxes full of ice. Zoran nodded to Tetsu and the two men split up.

Shouts in Spanish and Japanese filled the room. Everywhere men were in motion—most of them rugged-looking Hispanics with mustaches. They were dressed in work boots, heavy jackets, overalls, and hardhats. One man, wrapped in an insulated winter work suit and wearing a wool cap, drove a forklift around the room as if he were behind the wheel of a sports car. He came and went with frost-covered boxes on wooden palettes.

Zoran eyed the bins. There were sardines, squid, and barracuda from the waters of California. There were butterfish, tilefish, skate, and live Maine lobster from the East Coast. There were amberjack, grouper, and trevally from Australia and New Zealand. From Japan there were Pacific saury, blue snapper, red gurnard, largehead hairtail, chicken grunt, and many other fish that didn't even have English names.

There were night smelt, ling cod, Dover sole, and *loup de mer*. There were king crabs, conches, mussels, and sea urchins. And, of course, there were salmon, yellowtail, and tuna—cuts of big tuna, graded and priced. The belly meat from bluefin that had been fattened in pens in Malta was going for $63.50 a pound.

This was L.A.'s oldest Japanese fish market—International Marine Products, opened in 1968 by the same company that built the Tokyo Kaikan restaurant. The showroom was about the size of a basketball court. In the back, behind a heavy curtain of clear plastic strips hung across a wide doorway, was a cavernous storage freezer.

This place was tiny compared with the central fish market in Japan. On a trip to Tokyo with Toshi the previous year, Zoran had visited the famous Tsukiji Fish Market, Japan's main seafood clearinghouse. He'd walked through the maze of Tsukiji's twisting alleys in awe. Tsukiji is easily the world's largest fish market. It sprawls across a slab of wet concrete the size of forty football fields, and is home to the equivalent of thirty New York Fulton Fish Markets, with more than 1,600 seafood vendors.

Tsukiji is crowded and noisy, housed under dark, low ceilings, and lit by naked bulbs dangling overhead. The stalls are crammed together. Every morning between 5:00 and 9:00, the narrow alleys teem with sushi chefs and retail fishmongers hunting for fresh supplies, along with sweating workers dragging dilapidated wagons piled with seafood and men racing go-karts laden with fish. It's estimated that some 50,000 people do business at Tsukiji each day. Enough seafood passes through the market in one day to serve more than 5 million meals.

Zoran had spent three days in Tsukiji. It seemed that everything that lived in the sea was for sale, including whale, and it came from all over the world. Japan had long since depleted many of its local supplies and had turned to the rest of the world in its insatiable demand for seafood. Zoran had watched workers drag 500-pound tuna across the auction floor. He'd seen men cutting big frozen fish apart with industrial table saws.

In L.A. this morning, Zoran tossed a boiled octopus from Japan and several other items in his shopping basket, dodged a dolly loaded with pallets, and strode over to a stack of Jacuzzi-size tanks. A worker fished in the tanks with a dip net. He dumped dozens of large, live shrimp into a bin. Zoran bent over the pile of snapping tails and culled through them. He snatched a dozen of the animals and dropped them in a Styrofoam box with a few inches of chilled seawater.

Zoran hauled his purchases to a hectic checkout counter and met up with Tetsu, who was lugging his own selections. The counter was staffed by Japanese men bundled in thick coats. Piles of Styrofoam boxes and plastic bags full of fish and shaved ice sat waiting to be delivered to restaurants around the city. Zoran handed over a check signed by Toshi.

Back in the van with their purchases, Zoran and Tetsu pulled out of the parking lot and drove past a prostitute on the sidewalk. Tetsu stared at her. It was 6:30 a.m.

"She looks sixty years old," Tetsu said.

Zoran laughed sharply. "I'd need another cup of coffee for that."

They raced east toward the railroad tracks. At the Play Pen Totally Nude strip club Zoran turned left and pulled into another warehouse lot. This was the competitor of International Marine Products, a newer operation called Ocean Fresh.

Zoran and Tetsu pushed through a curtain of clear plastic strips into another frigid industrial showroom. Tetsu pulled a crumpled shopping list from his pocket and bent over bins of sea cucumbers, abalone, and slipper lobsters to examine a slippery octopus leg. He straightened up, lifting the leg until it dangled free. It was three feet long. He peered at the suction cups, then returned it to the tub.

Zoran surveyed rows of fish on palettes. He passed over jumbo flounder and red perch, but he crouched by a selection of bonito. They looked like a row of heavy artillery shells, waiting to be shot from a canon. Each had one large eye staring at the ceiling. Zoran picked the one with the clearest eye. It was nearly the length of his arm.

Besides the bonito, Zoran and Tetsu collected squid, giant clam, gizzard shad, conger eel, dried baby sardines, nori, and shoots of Japanese ginger. Tetsu had also located some fatty bluefin tuna belly, flown in from a fish farm in Croatia. It wasn't cheap, and he asked for nearly 6 pounds of the stuff. The pale slab of fat came to $230.

The two chefs strode across the wet showroom floor to settle their tab. Passing a set of double doors, Zoran saw flashes of silver, orange, and red through the small windows. Scraping sounds came from the room, and blasts of hissing.

A worker shoved through the doors, propped them open, and carted in a huge tuna fish. Frigid air burst through the opening. The chamber inside looked like a city morgue, with cold stainless-steel walls, long stainless-steel tables, cavernous steel sinks, and flexible steel wash-down hoses dangling from steel pipes. Hispanic men in floor-length yellow rubber suits bent over piles of yard-long salmon, swiping descaling brushes across the fat silver bodies with a sound like machine-gun fire. Scales flew in all directions.

They hosed the bodies off with blasts of high-pressure spray and heaved them onto a steel table, where another man wielded a long blade like a samurai sword. He pulled a fish toward him across the metal and slashed a series of precise incisions into the shining body. Seconds later he peeled a single huge slab of fat-striped orange flesh from each side. He shoved the carcass into a bin and grabbed the next fish.

In the far corner of the room stood a taller Hispanic man, older than his colleagues, and wearing a floor-length rubber apron. The market value of the single fish he was cutting was equivalent to that of twenty or thirty salmon, so he moved with less speed and more care. In front of him lay a tuna weighing probably 150 pounds. The animal's tail had been sawed off, leaving only a bloody stump, and its gills and guts had been gouged out.

With fluid strokes, the man drew his blade through the fish, then slid a massive cut of meat off the beast and onto the table. The flesh hit the steel with a slap. The swordsman wiped his blade clean on a cloth.

It was 7:00 a.m. when Zoran pulled out of the parking lot. The morning was already hot. He rolled down his window for some fresh air and gestured to the Play Pen Totally Nude sign across the street.

"Tetsu, you have an account there, right?"

Tetsu managed a weak chuckle. The only flesh on his mind at the moment was belly fat.

"Price of *toro* going up," Tetsu said.

Zoran nodded. "Somebody is making a lot of money."

A few minutes later Zoran hit congestion on the freeway. The van slowed to a crawl. The morning sun streamed into the rear window of the van, turning the back into an oven—an oven filled with hundreds of dollars of seafood on ice.

17

BLOOD AND GUTS

Zoran arrived back in Hermosa Beach with only minutes to spare. He checked the boxes of seafood. They were still cool inside. He stowed his purchases in the walk-in and rushed to the head of the classroom table.

"Today we grill *saba*!" he announced.

Kate didn't know what *saba* was.

Zoran asked the students to read aloud from their textbook again, from the section on grilling. Japanese-style grilling was another cooking technique that a sushi chef needed in his *omakase* arsenal. Even a sushi chef had to admit that sometimes fish tasted good cooked.

Zoran pulled out a plastic tub and ripped off the top. Packed inside were shiny foot-long mackerel, like giant sardines. Each fish had a bullet-shaped head, a thick body, and a tail that tapered to a set of fins like an arrowhead. Wavy black stripes ran across their backs like ripples on the sea. Their bellies were silver. Until now, the students had encountered their fish in disembodied rectangles. These were whole fish.

Kate stared at the fish. Suddenly she felt like she was back at the first day of class, staring down into her knife case. Somehow it hadn't occurred to her that making sushi would actually involve whole fish.

Zoran slapped a mackerel onto his cutting board and made a quick incision just behind the head on both sides. Kate grimaced.

"You don't want to cut all the way through," Zoran said. He would explain why in a moment.

Next, Zoran aimed the point of his knife at the mackerel's anus.

"Here's the poop hole," Zoran said. "From his bum to his neck you cut a slit—" Zoran sliced along the silver belly. Red goo oozed out the edges. "—and take out the guts."

Zoran stuck his hand inside the fish and ran his fingers through the visceral cavity. His hand came out covered in slime. He grasped the fish around the eyes and twisted the head off like a screw top. Bones cracked. He pulled off the head, and a cluster of organs and intestines popped out through the neck after it, hanging from the fish's head.

"You see," Zoran said calmly, "you don't cut all the way through the head because you want the guts to stay attached."

He tossed the head and viscera in the trash. Kate heard them land at the bottom of the can with a thump.

Zoran carried the body of the fish to the sink. He ran cold water into the belly cavity and scrubbed vigorously with his fingers. Next he produced a thin bundle of bamboo shish-kebab skewers held together with a rubber band and used it to scrape the fish's spine inside the cavity. Globs of coagulated purple blood slid down the drain.

Kate took a deep breath.

Along with humans and all other vertebrates, fish evolved from worms. Worms were the first creatures to have a circulatory system with blood, a heart, and gills. They probably lived in the sea about 540 million years ago. Early fishlike creatures appeared around 500 million years ago, though at first they were more or less just giant worms. Some of these early fish are still around today. They're called slime eels. Some people eat them.

Fish as we know them today began to branch off from the big worms around 400 million years ago and developed a more sophisticated circulatory system. Fish have a simple, two-chambered heart that pumps blood in a loop. From the heart, blood rushes first to the gills, then on to the rest of the body along a central artery that runs down the spine.

Zoran had just scraped out that central artery. Chefs call this the bloodline, and if not removed, it can ruin a dinner of fish by contaminating it with the overpowering taste and smell of blood.

Zoran gave the mackerel a final rinse and stuffed it with paper towels. "This, we'll grill," he said. "Okay, get yourselves a fish."

Kate let the others go first. When it was her turn, she lifted a fish from the box and held it aloft at arm's length. At her cutting board, she sized up the fish. It looked plump and felt slippery. She was afraid it would slide around when she tried to cut it. Slicing sushi rolls frightened her enough, and they stayed in one place.

In the comic book *Sushi Chef Kirara's Job,* the young female chef Kirara borrows a worker's knife at the fish market and guts and cleans a fish with such speed and skill that a crowd gathers. As a woman, she can't be squeamish or hesitant around blood and guts, or the male sushi chefs won't take her seriously.

Kate faced a similar challenge. She grasped the handle of her willow-leaf knife lightly between her thumb and fingers, at the very back end of the handle, as if holding the bow of a violin. Touching her knives as little as possible made her feel safer. She pressed the knife against the fish and sawed. The blade sank straight through the fish and cut its head clean off. She stared at the decapitated animal. Blood leaked out onto her cutting board.

She looked around the room and saw that her classmates were forging ahead. She stared back at the decapitated fish in front of her. She slit a gash down its belly. She leaned to the side and peered in. Parts of organs protruded through the crack. She poked the tip of her blade at the guts, as if her knife were a magic wand that could make them disappear.

She dropped the head into the nearest trash can. She picked up her fish and held it over the can. She stuck her knife inside the belly and wiggled it. Organs tumbled out into the trash bag with wet slaps. After a while things stopped falling out. Kate couldn't take it anymore. She laid the fish back on her cutting board. She didn't wash it or scrape out the bloodline. Zoran didn't notice.

"Okay, bring your *saba,* please!" Zoran yelled, heading for the kitchen.

It was time to grill. But Zoran and his Japanese colleagues at Hama Hermosa did not use a grill. It was better just to poke a few skewers into a fish and hold it over flames, or better yet, over glowing charcoal. Japanese chefs didn't use ovens, either. Baking isn't part of Japanese cuisine. Even modern homes in Japan, outfitted with all manner of appliances, seldom have ovens unless the house is completely Westernized.

Zoran stabbed three steel skewers into his mackerel to form the shape of an oriental fan and grasped the base of the skewers with one hand.

"You want a lot of salt on the tail and fins," he said, sprinkling white crystals on the fish, "so they don't burn." He cranked up the biggest burner in the kitchen. Blue and orange flames leapt into the air.

Zoran held the mackerel over the flames and yellow sparks popped around it as the oil in the fish combusted. The aroma of sizzling flesh filled the kitchen. It smelled fantastic.

When humans started burning animal flesh on sticks, one benefit of the practice was safety—heat kills bad bacteria. But there were two other reasons. One has to do with gravity. The other has to do with our noses.

Four hundred million years ago, when worms evolved toward fish, some of them added oil to their bodies while others developed simple gas-filled sacks, and thus became buoyant as swimmers.

On land it was a different story. As land animals evolved, they had to construct superstructures of tough connective tissue, fiber, and sinew to keep their muscles up and running against the constant drag of gravity. Birds had to work even harder to get airborne.

As a result, the meat of mammals and birds is much tougher than the meat of fish. The connective tissue that holds all muscles together is a protein called collagen, a name that comes from the Greek word for "glue producing." The collagen-filled sinews of horses is boiled to make glue. Human skin wrinkles with age because it loses collagen; pumping collagen back into tissues is part of cosmetic surgery. A third or more of all the protein in the body of a land animal is collagen.

The process of cooking meat—slow roasting, especially—transforms collagen into gelatin, making the meat tender and easier to eat. By breaking apart the collagen walls and the membranes of the muscle, cooking also releases the juices inside, bringing out flavor.

In addition, cooking "browns" the meat, creating chemical reactions on the surface that produce hundreds of aromatic smells. When we think of "flavor," much of what we sense is actually smell. Try cooking your favorite dinner and eating it with your nose pinched the entire time. Much of the experience vanishes.

Fish don't need to fight gravity, so their flesh consists of flakes of muscle held together with only a delicate matrix of collagen. Their muscles are naturally firm but also moist and quick to break apart. As a result, fish are easy and enjoyable to eat raw.

It is easy to ruin fish by cooking because their muscles are so delicate. The weak collagen collapses and the flesh dries out at lower temperatures than the flesh of terrestrial creatures. What's more, although cooking creates appealing aromas in fish, just as it does in meat, these smells come at the sacrifice of taste. The reason has to do with where the taste of fish comes from in the first place.

Sea creatures survive in their salty environment by loading their cells with free amine oxides and amino acids, which counter the osmotic pressure of the ocean. Without them, the water in its cells would rush out of the fish's body in a futile effort to dilute the salt in the sea, and the fish would collapse in on itself. These free amino acids are what give seafood much of its taste. They include glutamate, the key flavor component of *umami*, and a particularly sweet-tasting amino acid called glycine. Saltwater fish contain anywhere from three to ten times more of these delicious free amino acids than beef. Another important element in the taste of fish is glutamate's counterpart, IMP, the savory substance that Japanese scientists discovered in such abundance in aged bonito. IMP is created when the high-energy power pellets called ATP break down after the fish's death. Like free amino acids, tasty IMP is more abundant in fish than in animals.

When exposed to thorough cooking, however, the free amino acids and the IMP quickly combine with other molecules, dampening taste. As a result, most fish are more interesting to eat raw, or only briefly cooked—at least when it comes to texture and taste.

When it comes to aroma, uncooked fish fall flat. In the human brain, smell is linked to memory. A platter of raw fish cannot trigger the feelings of comfort and happiness that people associate with the smell of their favorite cooked foods. Perhaps that is one reason sushi chefs pay close attention to visual presentation.

Mackerel, however, is a good candidate for cooking. Mackerel are little cousins of bonito and tuna. Like tuna, mackerel swim fast most of the time, so their muscles are loaded with ATP. Mackerel also contain more glutamate and glycine than other fish. Cooked briefly over high heat, the surface of a mackerel undergoes browning, emitting a mouthwatering range of aromatic smells, while inside the flesh, sufficient IMP and amino acids remain to generate mouth-filling taste.

"Cooking time should be about five minutes," Zoran said, flipping his mackerel to sear the other side.

Marcos stabbed three skewers into his fish and leaned against the kitchen table, waiting for his chance at a burner.

"I'm going to kill you guys," he said. He drummed his hands against the edge of the table. "I was the best marshmallow griller in my Boy Scout troop."

Several students stood at the burners and cooked their fish.

"I could do this back at the hostel," Marcos said, still waiting. "I bet it would impress the ladies."

Marcos had met a few girls since arriving in Hermosa Beach. But when he'd told them that he was studying to be a sushi chef, so far the response had been lukewarm. 'A sushi chef? That's pretty random.'

'Not many men can cook, you know,' Marcos would say.

Now he imagined himself in the kitchen of the hostel where he was living, surrounded by admiring young women, all waiting for him to grill them a fish. He hopped about, testing different stances with his skewered fish. He decided that the coolest posture for fish grilling would be to hold the skewers behind his back, like a pool player executing a behind-the-back shot. In his head, the girls went wild. He laid his fish back on the table and raised his hands, palms down, like a rock star trying to suppress applause.

"One at a time, ladies, one at a time."

Kate paid him no attention.

"Cutting that fish was *disgusting*," she was telling one of the other women in the class. The other woman hadn't been bothered by it, but she offered Kate a sympathetic smile. Kate went on. "I mean, he just gave us a *fish*."

In a few minutes, Marcos and Kate advanced to the row of burners. Zoran strode into the kitchen and sniffed the air.

"Kate, you didn't clean your fish properly!"

From the flames, Kate's mackerel stank of burnt blood, intestines, and bacteria.

Marcos was still preoccupied. "To really impress the ladies with sushi, I think I need to become a *freestyle* sushi chef," he said. He pretended to toss his mackerel up and slice it in midair, with sound effects. He sighed and stared at his fish. "It's looking all juicy." He pulled it from the flames and held it up to his face. The skin was a crisp golden brown. "*That's* some marshmallow skill, right there."

Afterwards, the students ate their fish, but Kate had no desire to eat her stinky mackerel. She knew she'd failed to prepare it to specification. But as she packed up her gear after class, she felt a peculiar sense of accomplishment. She had done something that she could never have imagined herself doing before. She had cut the head off a fish.

1 8

EAT THE PIE

That evening at Hama Hermosa, a few people trickled in for dinner, including some friends of Toshi's at the back bar. Fie helped Toshi serve his friends *omakase*.

Fie had rolled a traditional Japanese worker's bandana into a cord, then pulled back her shiny flaxen hair and wrapped the cord around her head and tied it. On a Japanese sushi chef, this lent a degree of machismo. On Fie, it was an unprecedented fashion statement. Standing behind the sushi bar, in her tight black T-shirt and Japanese headband, Fie radiated a whole new category of authority: she was a Westerner, she was a woman, she was beautiful, and she was a sushi chef. Toshi, a head shorter than Fie, reached up and adjusted her headband, then stood back and nodded.

Before long a pair of big Caucasian men in their fifties strode in. One was wearing a yellow baseball cap. At first they didn't notice Fie, who stood working at the far end of the bar. They bellowed out boisterous greetings to Toshi.

"You look great, Toshi!"

"It's good to see you!"

They ate whatever Toshi served them. Partway through their dinner, working awkwardly with chopsticks, one of them asked, "Hey, Toshi, what's this sauce?"

Toshi glared at the men. His eyes narrowed. Finally he grunted, his voice low and threatening. "Secret . . . sauce."

Then his face relaxed and opened into a huge, crinkly-eyed smile. He laughed uproariously. So did the men. But Toshi didn't answer their question. Instead, he called Fie over and introduced her.

The men gazed at Fie, goggle-eyed. They forgot all about the sauce. They immediately purchased a giant bottle of premium sake to share with the chefs.

Everyone raised a glass. *"Kanpai!"*

The men knocked back their sake and poured more.

"So," the man with the yellow baseball cap said, leaning toward Fie, "how did *you* end up behind a sushi bar?"

Toshi sagged against the back wall of the bar and surveyed the restaurant. For twenty years, his old restaurant in Venice Beach had filled up every night with admirers. He'd been a superstar. Now his restaurant was empty. He'd been hoping business would pick up again this summer, but so far it hadn't. Worse, the after-effects of his stroke were still sapping his charisma. He felt exhausted after serving just a few courses of sushi.

The men raised their glasses again. *"Kanpai!"* Then they added, "To Fie!"

The man in the yellow cap rested his elbows on the bar and beamed at her, as she served them *nigiri*. He chewed slowly. "That's good," he said, his eyes glazing over. "It's not Toshi. That's Fie. I can *taste* the difference."

They downed more sake and heaped more praise on Fie. Toshi watched from the sidelines.

"I might as well retire," he muttered.

Fie flushed red. She pulled back from the bar. The two men apologized.

"Hey," the man in the yellow cap said to Toshi, raising his voice, "you know how guys are with beautiful women."

But Fie wasn't just a pretty face. She put care into the food. Her sushi was good. Toshi nudged her back into position. She topped four *nigiri* with something red and marbled. She armed herself with Toshi's blowtorch and seared the surface of each slice with a burst of blue flame. Toshi sagged lower against the wall and watched.

Fie applied a dab of creamy sesame dressing with wasabi to the top of each *nigiri*, then plated all four on a dark brown ceramic platter. She was about to hand it across the fish case when Toshi hissed at her. "Fie!"

Startled, Fie turned. Toshi was scowling. He pulled her *nigiri* off the brown platter and replated them on a pair of bright white plates. Now the browned flesh stood out against the white background, and each pair of *nigiri* looked special. Fie nodded. She added pinches of chopped green onion and served the plates. The man in the yellow cap chewed, a smile spreading ear to ear. "Fie! That's *incredible!*"

Fie allowed herself a shy smile. "It's Kobe-style beef."

"Beef? I thought it was tuna! Oh, that's good."

"You're getting all my favorite things," Fie said.

For their last dish, Fie served them *toro nigiri*. When they had finished, both men leaned back in their chairs. The man with the yellow cap rubbed his belly.

"That was incredible. Very, very, *very* nice." Slowly, he nodded. "That was worthy of Toshi."

Toshi pushed himself off the shelf. "I'm not feeling so great," he said. "I need to head home and rest."

The men became subdued for a moment.

"Toshi," the yellow cap guy said, smiling again and raising his voice, "soon you'll be back to normal!"

Toshi nodded. He hoped he was right. He slipped out through the swinging door into the kitchen. Before the door had even closed the men had turned back to Fie.

"Okay, so what nights are *you* here?"

Fie told them her schedule. The men sat for a few minutes, downing the rest of their sake. The man in the yellow cap gazed at Fie.

"God love the human race for people like you," he said. "You're spanning the globe." He thought hard for a moment, then issued his final declaration of the evening.

"Life is a great big—" he paused "—pie. And you should eat it."

19

BIG TEST

On Monday morning, Zoran set up a sign on the sidewalk in front of Hama Hermosa: "Student Sushi Bar, 2 Nigiri $1, Rolls $3–$5."

Hama Hermosa wasn't normally open for lunch, but every Monday from now on, Zoran would open the restaurant's doors at lunchtime, and the students would serve sit-down customers off the street, using the real sushi bar in the back room. Toshi insisted that students at the academy get as much experience serving customers as possible. He believed it was the best way for them to learn. Kate was excited. She hoped that serving customers again would help lift her spirits. She'd invited her mother to come.

In preparation, the students spent the morning cooking rice and loading the fish cases at the back bar with *neta*. Around noon, customers started trickling in.

Kate was nervous at first, but as soon as she started chatting with her customers she felt the same rush of enjoyment she'd felt at Paramount Pictures. She served a man who'd brought along his two sons, both about Kate's age. Then Kate's mother arrived. The man and his sons ordered a few items from the menu and asked Kate about the school. She explained a few things about sushi. Kate's mother listened, intrigued. The men asked Kate to make them something special—something that wasn't on the menu.

She made them an inside-out roll with grilled eel, avocado, cucumber, and tempura-fried shrimp. She tucked the roll in tight, the way Zoran had showed her, and squeezed it closed. She tossed the roll in tempura crunchies. She sliced and plated it, and squeezed stripes of sweet eel sauce back and forth across the plate. She chuckled to herself. With those stripes, she should call it a zebra roll. The slices of roll held together long enough for the men to gobble them up. Kate chatted with the men some more.

Afterwards, Kate's mother was beaming. 'You know,' she said, 'I think you'll be good at sushi. You're good at visual design.'

Kate smiled and nodded. It was like Toshi had said: "You gotta eat with your eyes."

Unlike the catering job at Paramount, today Kate had a chance to get to know her customers. When they got up to leave, she was sad to see them go.

Kate was feeling great until Zoran made an announcement. In a few days, Toshi would be giving the students their first big test of the semester. It would be on rolls.

The day before the roll test, Zoran had a surprise for the students. He taught them how to cook fried eggs—special fried eggs for sushi. In Japanese, the dish was called *tamago yaki,* and it was a standard sushi topping. Kate was thrilled. After her popping-open rolls, her crooked *nigiri,* and her bloody fish, she was glad for something that felt familiar.

Tamago yaki is both sweet and savory; in English, it's usually called "sweet egg omelet." Each student mixed ten eggs with some dashi—the kelp and bonito broth—plus some of the sweet rice liquor called mirin, along with a little sugar, soy sauce, and salt. Zoran demonstrated the tricky cooking technique. The special square pan had to be hot, but not so hot that it would brown the egg. He poured a thin layer of the egg mixture into the pan and folded the layer into a rectangular omelet. Then he poured in another thin layer of egg and lifted the first layer so the new egg would flow under it. He flipped that several times, wrapping the egg around the rectangle and building on it. He repeated the procedure over and over. As the rectangle of egg grew in size, the flips Zoran executed became more difficult and dramatic.

The skills required to fry *tamago yaki* call for long practice, so they were traditionally considered a barometer of the chef's general mastery. When trying out a new sushi shop, a customer would order a *nigiri* topped with sweet egg omelet. If he didn't find it up to par, it was considered acceptable for him to leave without ordering anything else. Today, most sushi restaurants buy pre-made *tamago yaki*.

When Zoran finished, he had created a solid block of thin compressed layers of egg. He sliced a small rectangle off the end. It was four fingers long and two fingers wide, perfect for the top of a *nigiri*.

Kate spent the rest of the class in the kitchen. Frying eggs was fun, and she was pretty good at it. None of her efforts produced a perfect block of egg, but she came close.

As the day of the test approached, one of the other two women in the class dropped out—the Japanese-American girl. Her sushi had been better than Kate's, but she'd become discouraged and quit.

Kate had come a long way since the first two weeks of school, when every day she'd contemplated quitting. She had stuck with it. She'd been eating better, too. She'd gained 10 pounds.

But she couldn't shake the feeling that her classmates still saw her as a flake, and judging by some of the sushi she'd been making, she was worried they might be right. She didn't feel ready for the test.

On the morning of the test, Zoran scribbled on the whiteboard, jotting down a list of rolls. The students would make two American-style inside-out rolls: one California roll, one spicy tuna roll. In addition, they would make two Japanese-style thin rolls: one cucumber, one tuna.

"*Ohaiyō!*" Toshi strode into the classroom wearing his chef jacket, shorts, and a pair of oversized basketball sneakers. There was a bounce in his step. Seeing his students gave him energy.

The students rushed to their stations. Toshi read off the list of rolls on the whiteboard, then turned to the students.

"Before we start, the most important thing—let's make a nice square." It wasn't clear what he meant. He glared down the table.

"This is very important!" He paused. "Six minutes, all rolls! If under six minutes, plus three points. If over seven minutes, minus five points. Six to seven minutes, no change. And after you finish I want to see whether your station is dirty or clean. So make sure it's all under control now."

The students scrambled to pick up stray bits of food from the floor. They washed their hands again. Toshi issued final instructions.

"When you finish, place everything on your cutting board. Clean. Then move back." He paused again and shouted. *"Clean!"*

Zoran stood at Toshi's side, gripping a digital track-and-field stopwatch. Toshi's eyes narrowed. "Ready?"

In unison, the students bellowed their response. *"Hai!"*

"Go!"

Zoran clicked on the stopwatch. The students threw open the lids of the metal nori boxes. Their fingers flew into the dishes of water. They clapped the excess water off their hands and reached into their canisters for rice. After thirty seconds of silence, Toshi turned to Zoran and chuckled.

"Ooh, everyone's so serious now."

The numbers on the stopwatch flew by. The students were still on their first roll. Zoran looked at the time.

"Two minutes thirty!" he yelled.

Kate squeezed closed her first roll. By three minutes she had started on her second. She had wanted to impress Toshi, but she was way behind. But so was everyone else.

"Four minutes!"

No one had completed the second roll. Toshi scowled. He turned to the whiteboard and erased the "6" from "6 minutes" and scrawled in an "8."

"Six minutes!" Zoran called. No one had even begun a third roll.

"I changed it to eight minutes," Toshi announced. "C'mon, let's *go!*"

The students were frantic now. Kate was one of the first to complete the third roll. One more to go.

"Eight minutes!"

The students kept working. Kate and Takumi started slicing. Then Marcos began to slice. One of the other students straggled far behind. At nine minutes, he was still pressing rice onto nori for his third roll.

"*Ten* minutes!"

Kate started plating her slices. As did Takumi.

Finally, at twelve minutes—double the original time limit—Kate finished. She was in first place!

She arranged her tray of sushi on her cutting board and stepped back from the table. One by one the others pulled in behind her. The last student to finish clocked in at 15:50. Zoran clicked off the stopwatch.

Toshi sighed. He strode around the table carrying a clipboard with scoring sheets. He examined each student's sushi, checked the floor, then scribbled on the clipboard. Kate's inside-out rolls looked good. But her slices of cucumber roll were popping open. Toshi returned to the head of the table, his expression severe.

"Every single roll should be two minutes, *max*," he growled. "That's your target. Even two minutes is too long. It's *easy*—thirty seconds."

The students stared at their cutting boards.

"We've got to be more serious," Toshi said. He glanced around at the trays. His eyes passed over Kate's tray. "Some of your rolls are exploding!"

Toshi demonstrated a cucumber roll. With two quick squeezes he created a boxy shaft, long and narrow with right angles. It wasn't a roll at all, it was a block. It seemed as if his hands had hardly moved.

"Square!" he yelled. He sliced the roll and turned the slices on end. The nori framed a perfect white square of rice, and the block of green cucumber sat smack in the middle. "Centered!" he yelled. Toshi looked up at the students, then he raised his voice to a shout. "Just *make* it!"

He paused to let his words sink in, then changed the subject.

"Next Friday," he said, "test on special roll. Everyone come up with a nice signature roll. Something special. Think about it."

After class Kate ran into Jay. He knew she was struggling.

"How'd you do today?" he asked.

"Good!" Kate said. Then her face fell. "My *kappa* broke."

Jay smiled. "Keep practicing."

Week 6

20

SUSHI NATION

$\mathcal{T}$he following Monday the students set up for their second student lunch counter. Marcos wiped down the back sushi bar and dumped tubs full of ice into the *neta* cases. A stream of ice cubes flew across the top of the fish case and clattered onto the bar. Zoran closed his eyes.

"That was me!" Marcos yelled. "And I am sorry."

The spilled ice began to melt. Water soaked into seat cushions. Pools formed on the tile floor. Marcos jammed perforated steel plates into the cases on top of the ice. He finally fit them in but they sat at odd angles. One of his classmates walked through the seating area and slipped in a puddle.

Just then Jay's friend Jeff, the restaurant consultant, strode into the room. As part of his consulting work, Jeff matched up sushi chefs with restaurants, all over the United States. From time to time, he would stop by the academy and check out the latest batch of students. He'd ask Jay and Zoran for their assessments. Jeff might recommend the promising students for jobs when they graduated.

Jeff stood in the doorway and watched the students work. He'd just missed Marcos's antics with the ice. Zoran walked over and stood next to Jeff.

"My phone has been ringing off the hook," Jeff told Zoran, shaking his head. "It's unbelievable."

Every week this summer, Jeff had been getting more calls asking for sushi chefs. He'd never seen it like this before. What surprised him in particular was where the calls were coming from: Kansas City, Milwaukee, Des Moines, and Boise. Even Stillwater, Oklahoma.

"It's exploding!" Jeff said. It reminded him of L.A. in the 1970s and early 1980s. But now a lot of the calls were coming from *white* restaurant owners, opening sushi bars in the American heartland. It looked like a whole new wave, the second front in the sushi invasion. A few days ago, Jeff had talked about it with Jay. "I give these people so much credit, to have the guts to do it," Jeff had said. "True pioneers. To open sushi in Stillwater, Oklahoma?! Wow." Jay had been getting calls, too, asking about the academy. 'Do you have a school in Chicago?' 'Do you have a school in Texas?'

The numbers were astonishing. The restaurant owners who'd already opened one sushi bar in the Midwest now wanted to open three more, and the profit figures they cited to Jeff were way above what restaurants made in L.A.

When Howard Dean was running for president in 2004, a conservative political group attacked him in the Iowa primary by referring to his campaign as a "latte-drinking, sushi-eating, Hollywood-loving . . . freak show." The funny thing was, Starbucks Coffee and Blockbuster Video were opening locations one after another in Iowa, and sushi bars were popping up, too. At least four restaurants now serve sushi in Des Moines and another seven sell sushi in Iowa City and the town of Waterloo, where teenagers order so many rolls that the chefs can't keep up. When a columnist for the *Des Moines Register* recently defended Sioux City from the disparagements of a snobby New Yorker, she cited the existence of good sushi as one of Sioux City's selling points.

Across the Midwest, restaurants serving sushi have been opening in every major city. By mid-2006, there were twenty-five of them in St. Louis, twenty-three in the Twin Cities of Minneapolis and St. Paul, twenty-two in Indianapolis, twenty-two in Cincinnati, twenty in Cleveland, sixteen in Columbus, thirteen in Kansas City, eleven in Oklahoma City, eleven in Milwaukee, ten in Wichita, and six in Omaha, Nebraska—and that was just the restaurants that had formally incorporated in each state. Most had opened since the year 2000. Even Peoria, Illinois, now has at least three restaurants serving sushi.

In Indianapolis, home of the Indianapolis Motor Speedway and a mecca on the NASCAR circuit, people aren't shy about their sushi. "I firmly believe," one writer declared in the *Indianapolis Star,* "that inside every red-blooded, beef-devouring American beats the heart of a sushi lover."

Chicago, America's meat-packing capital, has become a city of raw fish. Even a cursory search of Chicago and its suburbs turns up 150 restaurants serving sushi, sixty-nine of them having opened since 2000. Chicago shopping malls have sushi in the food courts. Fans of the Chicago Bears can buy sushi while watching football at Soldier Field Stadium. Wealthy residents of Chicago can pay $500 to eat sushi off naked women.

Vying for dominance with Chicago is Texas. The Dallas/Forth Worth area boasts at least 100 restaurants with sushi on the menu. "It's not a trend anymore," a food critic recently said of Dallas sushi, "it's a near onslaught."

In the Dallas suburb of Plano, the local Wal-Mart has installed a sushi counter. The Wal-Mart sushi comes courtesy of a company called Advanced Fresh Concepts (AFC), which plans to franchise 200 more sushi counters in Wal-Mart stores around the country.

AFC started out in 1986 with a takeout sushi counter in a Vons supermarket in L.A. The company expanded rapidly into other grocery stores under the brand name Southern Tsunami. In 1991, it opened its first supermarket sushi counter outside California— in San Antonio, Texas. By 1996, AFC had 300 takeout sushi counters in American supermarkets. Now it has at least 1,900, including locations in Arkansas, Indiana, Iowa, and Kansas. In addition to Wal-Mart, AFC sushi counters can be found in Vons, Safeway, and Harris Teeter, as well as in university dining facilities, hotels, and casinos. AFC even supplies sushi to the U.S. military.

Smaller takeout sushi franchisers have sprung up in AFC's footsteps, such as Philadelphia-based Genji Express, which supplies Whole Foods Market grocery stores, and a new operation called Sushi Avenue, based in Minnesota.

A publication called *Japanese Restaurant News* estimates that the total number of Japanese restaurants in the United States has roughly doubled in the past decade, to more than 9,000. Some of those restaurants don't serve sushi, but many non-Japanese restaurants do, at recently installed sushi bars. The chefs come from all over. Sometimes they're Japanese, but just as often they're Korean, Chinese, Taiwanese, Vietnamese, Burmese, Thai, Mexican, and Caucasian. A 2001 survey in Chicago found that nearly a third of the sushi chefs working in the restaurants surveyed were Latino.

In addition to the more than 9,000 restaurants, *Japanese Restaurant News* estimates that some 3,000 retail outlets serve takeout sushi in the United States, including sushi counters in grocery stores. These outlets have become so ubiquitous that many Americans, particularly in the Midwest, now get their first introduction to sushi in their local supermarket rather than in a restaurant.

To Jeff, the vast new sushi market opening in the Midwest held promise, but also great danger. Americans in the heartland had the potential to become more sophisticated sushi eaters than their predecessors. Right now, compared with the coasts, the Midwest was a blank slate. But it wouldn't be for long. Jeff wondered if there was a way to stop the history of American sushi from repeating itself.

Jeff watched the students. It would take a new kind of chef to educate customers and spread the Japanese approach to sushi in America—a chef who had mastered Japanese tradition but who could act and think like an American. A chef like Toshi could yell and scream in the anything-goes atmosphere of Hollywood, but now, with middle America in the mix, things were different.

The stakes were high because Jeff saw another trend, too. Back in Japan, the younger generations were becoming Westernized. Japanese traditions were in danger of dying out. Eating habits had changed dramatically. A Westernized version of curry rice, imported via Britain and usually made with beef and potatoes, had become one of the most popular meals in Japan, along with McDonald's hamburgers, pizza, and spaghetti.

It was possible that if the authentic sushi experience were to survive anywhere, it would be in the United States. If Americans learned to appreciate the sushi tradition, they might be saving it not just for themselves but for Japan as well.

21

MANHOOD OF SHRIMP

*W*hile Jeff was talking with Zoran, back in the kitchen Marcos was inserting bamboo skewers through curled-up shrimp to straighten them. The shrimp were to lie flat on top of the *nigiri*. He stuck the skewer into the tail, just under the swimmerets, and worked it through to the head. It wasn't as bad as the task Zoran had given them a few days ago. Zoran had set a box of large live shrimp on the table and made the students rip their tails off while the animals were still wriggling.

The muscles of shrimp, prawns, and lobsters are full of enzymes, and are prone to digesting themselves into mush as soon as the animal dies. That's why retailers keep lobsters alive in their stores, and why sushi chefs keep high-quality shrimp alive until the last minute.

Shrimp didn't join the elite ranks of sushi toppings until after World War II. Raw shrimp had long been a popular dish in western Japan. When Tokyo-style sushi spread to the rest of the country after the war, chefs in western Japan began topping *nigiri* with the raw tails of freshly killed shrimp. Some chefs also cooked "mantis shrimp," which are not actually shrimp but a different crustacean with a strange, elongated tail.

Today, most sushi bars serve two types of shrimp: raw, fresh tails, which are glistening, transparent, and sticky; and smaller, cooked tails with meat that is firm and white with pink highlights.

Sushi bars in America usually list the former as *ama-ebi*, or "sweet shrimp." In Japan people call them *ama-ebi* or *botan-ebi*. They are relatively expensive. The smaller cooked shrimp usually go by the name *kuruma-ebi*, or just *ebi*, and are cheaper.

The smaller, cooked shrimp are generally of the black tiger or Mexican white varieties. Environmentalists decry the methods that produce these animals. Fishermen catch them with trawl nets that also snag nontargeted sea life, including baby fish and endangered sea turtles, although U.S. fishermen have taken steps to minimize such by-catch. Overseas farming operations have destroyed millions of acres of mangrove habitat to grow these shrimp.

The larger sushi shrimp, served raw, are generally of the spot prawn or pink shrimp varieties that belong to the genus *Pandalus*. Fishermen harvest them from the wild, mostly with traps or trawls that are far less damaging.

Every *Pandalus* shrimp starts out male. He spends his first two or three years as a bachelor, during which time he generally loses his virginity. Once he's had his fun, his testes transform into ovaries and he matures into a female. At which point, she turns around and hits up the new generation of strapping young males for more sex. There is some evidence that if females are especially numerous, the males can delay their sex change and remain playboys for an extra season or two. Likewise, if there aren't enough females, the males may give up their bachelorhood and switch early.

The shrimp Marcos was working on were tiger shrimp tails, recently defrosted. Three other students joined him and helped insert skewers. When they had finished, the result looked like a bowl of seafood Popsicles. Zoran strode into the kitchen and glared into the bowl.

"What the hell is this?" He picked up one of the shrimp. It was still curved.

"Probably one of mine." Marcos said.

"Come on, man," Zoran spat. "What's the point if it's not straight? I *showed* you how to do it." Zoran folded his arms across his chest and stepped back.

"Marination is up to you guys," Zoran said. "I'm not going to say anything." He strode away.

One of the students remembered Zoran's saying that the sweet vinegar from a bucket of pickled ginger was favored by many chefs. They agreed that would work. First, the shrimp would need to be briefly blanched. Marcos dumped the skewered shrimp into a pot of boiling water.

Crustacean flesh develops delicious aromas and flavors simply by spending a few minutes in boiling water. Most meats can't achieve such high levels of smell and taste without the application of flame or intense heat, and there are a couple of reasons for this. Crustaceans counteract the osmotic pressure of saltwater with an especially tasty and concentrated array of amino acids, particularly the same sweet-tasting glycine found in mackerel. Crustacean flesh also contains a high concentration of sugars. With the application of a little heat, these amino acids and sugars react with each other, creating the same sort of delicious and aromatic molecules produced in the meat of mammals and most fish, only at much higher temperatures.

When the students' shrimp had floated to the surface, the flesh had turned from transparent to opaque. Marcos hefted the pot off the burner and hustled it toward the sink, shouting as he moved, "Hot pan!"

He'd underestimated the weight of the water. When he hit the edge of the sink his skinny arms couldn't lift the pot over it. He pushed it against the side of the sink, trying to force the top over so the water would spill out. Steam billowed in his face. Zoran was screaming at him.

"Quick! Quick! So they don't keep cooking!"

Marcos spread his legs, grimaced, and shifted sideways to get a better grip. Finally, the water streamed out with more clouds of steam. Then he dumped the shrimp into an ice bath. He wiped his brow and carried the bowl out to the classroom.

"Well," he announced, "we've got some semi-straight shrimp."

That was only the beginning. Several students gathered around the bowl to remove the skewers and peel the shells off the shrimp. Then, they sliced off any irregular flesh at the head end to create a neat, straight line. They trimmed the tail flippers at a prescribed angle. They carefully sliced at the belly tendons until they could spread the shrimp flat in a butterflied position; if they sliced too deep, they'd cut the shrimp in half. Zoran hovered over them, offering pointers.

"You don't *need* to marinate shrimp for sushi," he said. "Often chefs in Japan don't. But Americans like everything sweet."

But you do have to wash the shrimp because they are full of shit. Takumi rubbed each of his shrimp in a bowl of saltwater, scraping his thumb along the shrimp's tiny digestive tract to remove it. Most of the other students forgot, leaving their shrimp laced with poop.

Zoran stood at the head of the table, overseeing the assembly line. "When you guys start working in a sushi bar, this is what they're going to have you do first thing. Lots of sushi *ebi*."

Finally, they dumped the shrimp into a couple of bowls of pickled ginger vinegar to marinate.

Takumi switched on the lights over the back sushi bar, and the motley crew took their stations for the Monday lunch counter. They were open for business.

Marcos remembered the rush he'd felt at the Paramount Pictures party, when hot girls had flirted with him at the sushi bar. But since then, he hadn't been able to use his status as a sushi chef to meet any hot girls. He was 17. If he were a *Pandalus* shrimp, pretty soon he'd be losing his testicles.

Sushi was the bait, and now he had some skills. He squeezed together a California roll and a spicy tuna roll and put them on a plate with a dish of soy sauce. He stood out on the sidewalk in his chef uniform and tried to look handsome.

Two women walked toward him.

"Heyyyyy," Marcos drawled, "you ladies want some sushi?"

"Thanks, we've already eaten." They eyed the plate. "Did you make this?"

"Yeah!" Marcos plugged the restaurant, but they walked on.

A pair of very pretty girls approached, purses and cellphones dangling. "Heyyyyy, you ladies want some sushi?"

The girls smiled. "No, thanks!"

Marcos gazed after them, forlorn. "Maybe I'm just not cute enough."

After five minutes Marcos gave up and retreated inside. "Wow," he said, "marketing is a *lot* harder than it looks. I thought everyone out there would want to eat free sushi." He thought for a moment. "Maybe we need to get a commercial on Fox."

Bored and hungry, Takumi sliced a few thin pieces of tuna and disappeared into the kitchen. Alone, he spread fresh tomato paste on the tuna, drizzled it with olive oil, and sprinkled on chopped chives and garlic chips—Italian carpaccio. The Japanese weren't the only ones who ate raw tuna. He scarfed it down.

At the sushi bar the students were discussing what it was, exactly, that they were supposed to yell when a customer came in. The workers at the Subway sandwich shop across the street had it easy. All they had to do was yell, "Welcome to Subway!"

"It's *ee-RA-shee mase*," Marcos said.

"I don't know," Kate said. "I just wait till everyone else is yelling it, and then I go, '*Ra-ra-ra-ra.*'"

Just then a pair of attractive women walked in. Nearly in unison, the students belted out an approximation of "*Irasshaimase!*" The women sat right in front of Marcos. Now he just needed to impress them with his sushi skills.

Marcos cleared his throat and greeted them, a quaver in his voice. The women ordered albacore *nigiri*. Marcos pulled the albacore from the *neta* case, his fingers trembling.

"So," the brunette asked Marcos, "how long have you been doing this?"

"About six weeks, I guess," Marcos said.

"We used to come here all the time," the brunette said.

Marcos turned up the charm. "Well, we're glad you're here."

Marcos squeezed together four *nigiri*. He crammed them onto a plate that was much too small. He forgot to sauce them. He handed the plate across the bar. The brunette handed it back. "Could we get some sauce on these?"

Marcos blushed. He dabbed a blob of sauce on each piece of fish. The brunette popped one in her mouth. She grimaced and squeaked out a noise that suggested revulsion.

Marcos looked terrified. "Too much wasabi?"

"No," the brunette said. She fished around in her mouth with her fingers. "There was a *bone* in there."

"Oh." Marcos hung his head. "Sorry." Regardless of who prepared the fish, it was the responsibility of the chef who served it to ensure it was suitable to eat.

Kate's mother came, this time with Kate's brother. Kate served them a fancy roll.

"This is very pretty, baby," her mother said. Kate smiled.

Later, her mother snuck up to where Kate was working and snapped a photo. Kate rolled her eyes. *"Mom!"*

Afterwards, Kate grabbed some cucumbers, rice, and nori, and headed home to practice her rolls.

2 2

GETTING FISHY

"Everybody ready to get fishy today?!" Zoran yelled the next morning. "From here on out, fishy, fishy, fishy!" He had an evil grin on his face. "You're going to need to know the Japanese names for every single part of the fish," he said. He peered down the table. "And Takumi, you'll have to know the English names." Zoran went on. "If the sushi chef says to you, '*Sōji sakana*,' he means clean up the fish. Not fillet. Just clean up. Take out the gills, the guts."

More guts? Kate steeled herself. This time she didn't want Zoran telling her that she "hadn't prepared her fish properly." She was sick of being the class flake.

Zoran drew the outline of a fish on the whiteboard. He labeled all the fish parts on the diagram with their Japanese names. The students scribbled furiously in their notebooks. Zoran set out a cardboard box on the table with a thud. Mackerel again.

"*Saba!* Today, we are going to make *saba* sushi—and sashimi."

In the old capital of Kyoto, mackerel was one of the most common fish used in early Japanese sushi, back when chefs pressed entire fillets of fish onto sushi rice in boxes with heavy stones. But mackerel was never used raw for sushi. Nor was it used cooked.

"We usually marinate it with salt and vinegar," Zoran said. "The thing you should know about *saba* is that it's susceptible to parasites."

Mackerel is perilous to serve raw. Mackerel is so difficult to keep fresh that Japanese chefs sometimes call it the fish that "spoils even while still alive." Humans can also pick up more than fifty different parasites from eating raw or undercooked fish; removal of parasites can require surgery. A worm called anisakis is one of the most prevalent parasites, and its larvae love living inside mackerel.

The clever larvae of anisakis swim around looking delicious. They *want* to be eaten, and usually a small crustacean will oblige. The larvae live happily in the stomach of the shrimp or krill until a mackerel comes along and eats the crustacean. Then the larvae burrow into the lining of the fish's gut or, less often, into its flesh.

Mackerel serve the larvae's purpose only because sooner or later a mammal will eat the mackerel, preferably a dolphin, porpoise, or whale. Once in the stomach of a mammal, the larvae molt and become adult worms. The worms use a mouth like a boring tool to drill into the mammal's stomach wall. They mate and lay eggs, which emerge in the mammal's feces, starting the cycle again.

The larvae can end up in a human stomach just as easily as in a dolphin stomach. When a human eats an infested fish without cooking it, he feels a tingling in the throat, and within a few hours may suffer violent abdominal pain and nausea. If he's lucky, he'll vomit up the larvae.

If not, he'll suffer for a week or so until the worm, realizing that it's not inside a dolphin, gives up and dies. By then, the person's doctor may have misdiagnosed the situation as stomach cancer. Even without swallowing a live larva, people sometimes react simply to the chemicals in the fish that the larvae produced.

But heat kills the larvae easily. Some people would argue that grilled mackerel smells and tastes so delicious that there's no point in risking anisakis illness by eating it uncooked.

Nevertheless, sushi chefs continue to prepare and serve mackerel uncooked. In theory, salting the fish and then soaking it in vinegar may well kill the larvae, for the same reasons that salty and acidic environments kill bacteria. Salt sucks the water from cells, causing them to shrivel. Acids bombard cells with hydrogen ions, warping their enzymes.

Unfortunately, experiments have shown that parasitic larvae can survive for nearly a month in a 20 percent salt solution. Japan has one of the highest incidences of anisakis illness in the world—about 2,000 cases a year.

"*Saba* is also very oily," Zoran added. "About sixteen to twenty percent fat. The marination helps cut down on the oil. *Saba* also has a very fishy taste."

Fish that are alive, and fish that are freshly killed, don't taste or smell fishy at all. A perfectly fresh saltwater fish emits two primary smells. One of these smells is the scent of the ocean—or rather, of the bromophenols produced by algae that fish eat. Surprisingly, the other smell is the odor of geranium leaves. The fats in fish are the unsaturated kind, as they are in plants. Fish skin and plant leaves both contain an enzyme that breaks unsaturated fats down into fragments that smell "greenish" and a bit metallic, like a newly crushed geranium leaf.

Soon after death, however, fish start to smell fishy. Fishiness comes from the same phenomenon that gives fish much of their flavor. In their fight against the osmotic pressure of saltwater, sea creatures fill their cells with tasty amino acids. But fish in particular also fill their cells with a related amine called trimethylamine oxide, or TMAO.

Unlike the amino acids, TMAO has no taste. Nor does it have any smell. But after the fish dies, bacteria on the fish, and enzymes in the fish itself, steal the oxygen away from TMAO, leaving behind TMA.

TMA by itself stinks. It's what gives old fish their foul smell. It's also present in human bad breath and in bacterial infections of the human vagina. A rare genetic disorder called trimethylaminuria can prevent people from metabolizing routine amounts of TMA in their food. The devastating result is that their sweat smells like rotting fish. For obvious reasons, it's a disorder that can cause severe depression.

In addition, bacteria on the surface of the fish quickly digest proteins in the fish after death, creating noxious fumes, including ammonia, putrescine, and cadaverine.

Salting and marinating fish with vinegar doesn't just help control parasites. It also reduces fishiness.

Covering fish with a heavy layer of salt draws moisture out of the flesh by osmotic pressure. As the water inside the flesh rushes to the surface to dilute the salt, compounds like TMA and stale-smelling fatty acids emerge along with it.

Meanwhile, the acetic acid in vinegar fires hydrogen ions at TMA, just as it does at bacteria. When a hydrogen ion hits a molecule of TMA, the fishy-smelling compound gains a positive electrical charge, which allows it to dissolve easily in water, removing it from the air and terminating the smell.

Mackerel were not the only fish that early sushi chefs salted and marinated. In fact, the sushi vendors on the streets of nineteenth-century Tokyo rarely served anything raw. They had no access to refrigeration. They salted and marinated—or blanched, or seared—all their seafood so it would keep long enough to serve. Sushi chefs in old Tokyo used so much salt and vinegar that people called sushi shops *tsuke-ba*—"pickling places."

The need for preservation generally had a fortuitous effect; salting and marination often improve the taste and texture of raw fish. One of the reasons for this is that muscle, like mold, contains a lot of enzymes. In muscle, enzymes convert fuel—sugar—into energy. Fish muscle, however, generally contains many more enzymes than the flesh of land animals.

This is partly because fish of many species lead lives of extraordinary self-sacrifice. They consume as much food as they can, building up their muscles and fat reserves, and then they embark on long, grueling migrations. Toward the end of these migrations they manufacture huge masses of sperm or eggs. When they run out of fat during these mating marathons, they literally start to eat themselves for the sake of the next generation. The many enzymes in their flesh deconstruct their own muscle proteins into amino acids. The fish can then use them for energy and the raw material for building sperm or eggs. The closer the fish get to spawning, the more wasted and frail they become.

Like the enzymes in mold, the enzymes in fish muscle continue functioning even after the fish dies. As a result, cooking can actually ruin the taste and texture of fish. If you heat a piece of fish at too low a temperature for too long, the warmth speeds up the work of these cannibalistic enzymes, and the fish eats itself right there in the pan. As with crustacean meat, the result is mush.

Salting raw fish at room temperature, however, lets the enzymes work slowly, deconstructing a little of the protein into the tasty components of *umami*. The salt fends off bacteria long enough for the enzymes to accomplish their task, and the salt itself amplifies the effect of *umami* on the human tongue.

Mackerel flesh digests itself to the peak of *umami* in about twenty-four hours after salting. Any longer and the *umami* degrades. Before the advent of modern transportation, runners from the coast of the Japan Sea carried 100-pound boxes of freshly salted mackerel to the inland city of Kyoto on foot. They hiked all night along thirty miles of mountain paths so that the fish would arrive just in time to reach their peak level of *umami*.

Vinegar, meanwhile, unfolds complex fish proteins, firming up fish flesh and turning it opaque. Early sushi chefs also marinated some of their fish in soy sauce to help it keep longer.

To this day, hard-core sushi aficionados argue that to truly qualify as sushi, the fish must *never* be completely raw. Instead, the chef should always somehow alter the fish, whether through salting, marination, or cooking, or some clever combination of preparation techniques.

Zoran ripped the top off the box of mackerel. Kate peered inside. These mackerel were bigger than the previous ones—about 18 inches long. Zoran laid one on his cutting board. He removed the head and guts and cleaned the fish. Now was time to teach the students to fillet.

"Gather round," Zoran said. He showed them how to cut from the anus back to the tail fin. "Just break the skin first. Once you break the skin you can go in for another try." He sliced deeper now, his knife blade horizontal, separating the tail muscle from the ribs. As the knife glided through the animal, Kate heard a series of faint staccato thuds, like a pencil rubbing across a washboard.

"Hear that?" Zoran said. "Brrrrrr." It was the blade hitting the ribs along the spine. "That's good," Zoran said. It meant he was getting all the flesh off the bone.

He spun the fish around and cut from the head along its back in the same fashion, separating the flesh along the backbone. The knife came out at the tail. Zoran lifted off the whole side of the fish. All that was left on the frame was bone.

When it comes to muscle, fish are much more efficient body-builders than land animals. Fish don't waste energy or materials fighting gravity. Butchering a cow by removing its head, hide, feet, organs, and bones leaves only about a quarter of its body weight as muscle. On average, filleting a fish harvests 40 percent of its body weight as muscle—and often more, depending on the season and species. In addition, fish are generally cold-blooded, so they don't expend energy keeping themselves warm. They are more efficient at converting their food into meat.

Zoran turned the fish over and repeated the process on the other side. Now he had two perfect fillets, plus the carcass.

"*San-mai oroshi,*" Zoran said. The term meant "three-piece breakdown," the most common fillet technique. Zoran chucked the carcass in the trash and straightened up. "Your turn."

The students pulled fish from the box and filed back to their stations.

"Once you cut," Zoran yelled, "it's very hard to put back together. Think before you cut. We're in no hurry, guys."

Kate grasped her knife at the very back of the handle again, to put as much distance between her hand and the blade as possible. She turned away and sawed without looking. The head came clean off. This time, after she gutted the fish she washed it. She even scraped out the bloodline.

Kate stared at her fish. The whole room reeked of the pungent, oily odor of mackerel. Zoran looked at Kate.

"You okay, darling?" Zoran said.

Kate stuck her knife in the fish's asshole and started cutting.

While everyone's mackerel fillets lay salting in the refrigerator on woven bamboo colanders, Zoran pulled from the fridge what looked like elongated beige footballs, each one encased in shrink-wrap.

"Albacore," Zoran said. He laughed. "To the Japanese, albacore is the lowest of the tuna—the worst!" He shook his head. "But Americans like the flavor." Albacore is most often canned as "white meat tuna."

Zoran explained that most albacore are filleted and frozen at sea. "We buy them pre-filleted, and when you work in a sushi restaurant, you will, too. You can eat it raw, but because the flesh is so soft, we usually sear it."

Raw albacore tends to disintegrate under the knife. Searing tightens up the edges. It's a bland fish, so searing also adds taste.

Zoran extracted one of the long football-shaped pieces of meat from its plastic package.

"The first thing we need to do is feel for bones. If you find them, remove them before cooking." Marcos nodded. "Now," Zoran went on, "cut off the belly edge so you can tell your customers, 'This is albacore belly.'" He smiled. "It makes them feel special, like tuna belly. Honestly, it tastes a *little* different, not much. But it will make them feel like a million dollars."

The students practiced searing albacore on skewers over the kitchen burners. Zoran glanced at the clock and pulled the salted mackerel from the refrigerator.

The fillets were beautiful. Everyone gathered around and admired them. They glistened silver and blue with dark wavy stripes against the old-fashioned bamboo colanders. The room suddenly belonged to a nineteenth-century Japanese fish monger instead of a twenty-first-century American sushi school.

The students laid their mackerel fillets into a stainless-steel pan. They poured in rice vinegar to begin the process of marination.

"Take a ten-minute break," Zoran said. "Then, sashimi."

23

RAW DEAL

The Japanese tradition of eating fresh raw fish has nothing to do with sushi. Sushi began as a way of preserving old fish, and street vendors turned it into a crude snack food.

Centuries earlier, the Japanese nobility were already feasting on elegant meals that included slices of fresh raw meat called sashimi. Sashimi didn't have to be fish. It could be anything, even the meat of deer, wild boar, or birds.

In ancient China, people ate thin slices of raw meat or fish drizzled with a misolike dressing. The practice continued into the twentieth century in southern China, until the Communist government outlawed it to prevent illness from parasitic worms. In Korea, beef and fish sashimi are still popular, often served with spicy red pepper paste and vinegar.

The Japanese probably learned to eat raw meat from their Chinese and Korean neighbors. The Japanese called the dish *namasu*, a term that appears in Japanese texts from 1,200 years ago. *Namasu* was a sort of raw-meat salad. The chef sliced the meat into long strips, then tossed it with a dressing that might contain ginger paste or the crushed leaves of a pungent herb called water pepper, as well as miso and dashi.

Probably beginning around 800 years ago, people began to use the word *sashimi* as well as *namasu*. *Sashi* means "to stick or pierce," and *mi* means "meat." There are two theories about the origin of the word *sashimi.*

One is that the chef would "stick" a fin from the fish among the slices as a decoration that indicated the type of fish. The other is that *sashi* was a euphemism for *kiri,* "to cut." In the culture of the samurai, calling the meal *kirimi*—sliced meat—would have raised unpleasant connotations of sword fighting and human bloodshed. In medieval Japan, human bloodshed was the last thing anyone wanted to think about when they sat down for a nice meal.

The habit of eating sashimi with a side dish of soy sauce instead of dressing probably originated after 1600, when the new shogun moved the capital to Edo. Today, chefs serve sashimi not just with soy sauce but also with a dab of wasabi. They also serve it with a garnish, which usually consists of a mound of shredded white radish.

Zoran handed out chunks of giant Japanese radish and bellowed, "*Katsura-muki!*" It was time to practice the dreaded "column peel."

Kate gritted her teeth and held the chunk of radish and her vegetable knife up to her face. Then, breaking her grandmother's cardinal rule, she sliced toward herself. She carved off a nice, thin sheet of radish.

If customers who ate sashimi had any idea of the work that went into preparing the garnish alone, they would never leave the shreds of radish on their plate. In fact, chefs serve radish with sashimi for a good reason, and it is meant to be eaten. The same chemicals that give radish its spicy taste also help inhibit the growth of harmful bacteria.

Zoran spun his radish chunk and shaved it into long, paper-thin pieces, like ribbons of silk. He folded each sheet twice lengthwise, curled the fingers of his left hand, and pressed his hand down on the folds. His right hand chopped in a blur, the cleaver thudding fast. Fine slivers of radish piled up in the wake of the blade.

The room fell silent as the students tried to imitate Zoran. The sharp smell of radish rose from the table. The students' strips were chunky and their cutting action slow and deliberate. Zoran's body jiggled rhythmically back and forth, his cleaver thudding away at high speed. Suddenly, into the silence burst Zoran's voice, with a song.

"When you're happy and you know it, *katsura-muki!*"

Silence fell again, but for the staccato thuds of cleavers hitting wood. When Zoran had finished he watched the students.

"Stop!" he shouted. "Everyone has been watching too much *Iron Chef* French! Your conception of *thin* is completely different from mine. Are any of you aware of how thick your slices are? Are any of you doing anything to correct it? Are we going to have to stop and go back and do thin vegetable slicing every day instead of fish?" Zoran looked menacing. "Because I will!"

The students bent back over their work. It took them each half an hour to slice and chop one 4-inch chunk of radish into garnish.

Zoran set up his cutting board with a slab of albacore tuna, a variety of decorative plates, his radish shreds, and a stack of bright green perilla leaves. Called *shiso* in Japanese, perilla is a lemony, Chinese member of the mint family. Like radish, perilla leaf is thought to have medicinal properties, including an inhibitory effect on bacteria. It is healthful and meant to be eaten, too.

"Okay," Zoran said, "first, you need to make sure you have a clean plate, and you need to make sure it's not hot out of the dishwasher. You don't want your plate to cook the fish!"

Zoran chose a round china plate with a wide blue pattern around the rim. He squeezed a handful of shredded radish onto the plate, like a pyramid of cotton candy. After all the work that had gone into it, now he covered it with a sloping leaf of perilla.

Zoran leaned over his cutting board and traced six fluid arcs through the albacore with his knife. Using his steel chef's chopsticks and the fingers of his left hand, Zoran lifted four pieces and laid them on an angle against the leaf. He set the other two directly on the plate, at a contrasting angle, slightly staggered. He slipped a lemon wedge behind them to one side, spooned a dollop of bright orange onion and carrot sauce in the crook between the two sets of slices, topped the left side of the sauce with a tiny pyramid of chopped green onion, and pressed a wad of wasabi in the lower right corner of the plate.

Nothing was symmetrical. Everything was off center. Yet Zoran's platter was a masterpiece of balance and captured motion. In less than sixty seconds he'd created a landscape of blooming shrubs, climbing forests, ranging mountains, and a beaming sun, surrounded by a deep blue lake, all within the confines of a 10-inch plate.

In a sense, making sushi and sashimi has much in common with creating a Zen garden. On the grounds of a Buddhist temple, a monk snips away at the trees and shrubs until they have been reduced to abstract symbols evoking nature's beauty in miniature. A sushi chef snips away at fish, reducing them to abstract morsels of the sea. Zoran, the gruff Australian air force veteran, was a Zen gardener in disguise. The students stared in awe at the plate.

Unlike sushi, sashimi should always be eaten with chopsticks. Takumi and one of the other students whispered to one another. They were both left-handed. Zoran had placed his slices in the direction that a right-handed customer would approach with chopsticks. That was the easiest way for him to arrange them, and the easiest way for a right-handed customer to pick them up. To achieve that, a left-handed chef had to think backwards. Unless, of course, the customer was also left-handed. The best sushi chefs consider this, and reverse their arrangements if the customer appears to be left-handed.

At the end of class, only one sashimi arrangement had captured the elusive Japanese aesthetic. Takumi, like Zoran, had succeeded in building a miniature Zen garden out of garnishes and fish.

2 4

MACKEREL GAL

The following morning Kate armed herself with a new weapon. After handling mackerel the day before, she'd gone home with itching hands. Today she'd arrived with a pair of latex gloves.

Mackerel belong to the genus of fish called *Scomber,* and they are responsible for an ailment called scombroid poisoning, which is one of the reasons they have a reputation for spoiling quickly. If mackerel aren't properly chilled, bacteria that are otherwise harmless can grow and release toxins. One of those toxins is histamine, which generates the symptoms of an allergic reaction. Contact with histamine had probably caused Kate's itching hands. Scombroid poisoning can occur with mackerel's bigger cousins, the tuna, and is thought to be one of the most common forms of seafood-based food poisoning in the United States.

"Okay, now get your *saba* out," Zoran said. "*Saba* for breakfast! Oh, boy."

More mackerel. Kate pulled on her latex gloves like a surgeon. The fillets from yesterday, salted and marinated, were ready to use.

First, Zoran demonstrated how to remove the stomach lining and ribs from the lower corner of each fillet. He felt with the pads of his fingers along the center line and plucked out bones with special tweezers. Then he flipped the fillet over so that the mackerel's skin was showing.

"This is a *hikari mono*," Zoran said. "That means 'shiny-skinned fish.'"

Sushi chefs divide all fish into three basic categories: red, white, and blue.

Red is a narrow category, and tuna is the primary member. Swordfish also qualifies. Unlike most fish, these fish have blood-red meat.

White includes fish with pale flesh, including sea bream, snapper, flounder, and sea bass. Most fish in the ocean have pale, colorless flesh.

Blue refers to fish that have silvery-blue skin, such as mackerel. Blue includes fish that sushi chefs in Japan serve frequently but that Westerners encounter less often, such as gizzard shad, horse mackerel, and halfbeak. Because the skin of these fish is silvery, sushi chefs also call them *hikari mono,* or "shiny things."

Sushi chefs began categorizing fish by color and shine in the early 1900s. Historians think that geishas in Tokyo's entertainment district may have been the first to popularize these categories by using them when dining with their clients. In Tokyo today, young people use a variation of the term "shiny fish" as a form of slang. They refer to girls who wear glitter and shiny clothes as "mackerel gals" because they look like shiny-skinned fish. In fact, mackerel have a reputation the world over for their ostentatious shine. In England, calling a man a "mackerel" meant he was a dandy; in France, it meant he was a pimp. It is from the latter usage that we get the term "mack daddy."

"Now," Zoran told the students, "you want to keep the shine on."

What really distinguishes blue, or shiny, fish at the sushi bar from other categories of fish is that the chef serves them with the attractive surface of the fish still attached to the meat, as part of the presentation. Mackerel can have reddish flesh, but they don't qualify as red because chefs serve them with their shiny scales still attached. Conversely, many large fish—tuna, yellowtail—also have shiny blueish skin, but they don't qualify as *hikari mono* because their skin and scales are too tough to eat.

Fish with small scales can swim faster because they create less drag in the water. In relation to body size, tuna have relatively small scales. In relation to body size, so do mackerel. Mackerel are much smaller fish, though, so their scales are tiny. They feel velvety to the touch and people ingest them without realizing it.

However, on mackerel, the scales lie underneath a layer of transparent protective skin that *is* too tough to eat. The sushi chef must remove the outer skin without removing the scales. It is one of the trickiest tasks in all of sushi making. It's like trying to remove a sticker from a wall without damaging the paint.

While the students watched, Zoran tugged horizontally on a corner of the outer skin at the head end of his fillet. A layer of transparent film rolled slowly off the fillet, leaving behind the luminescent blue and silver colors on the surface.

Zoran flipped the fillet over, tilted his knife, and cut a slice off the tail end. When he turned the slice right side up, it retained an attractive, silvery-blue slanted edge, the hallmark of carefully prepared shiny-skinned fish.

That slice was for *nigiri*. Next, he cut nine slices straight down through the fillet for sashimi. He constructed a sashimi platter, another Zen landscape on a plate.

The students hunched over their fillets and extracted bones along the flesh side. Certain fish, including mackerel, salmon, trout, and herring, are especially problematic to prepare because their muscles contain floating pin bones that are unattached to the main skeleton. Bone pulling itself is a challenge. Soon the students' fillets were pocked with craters.

When Kate finished pulling bones, she tried to grasp the edge of the skin on her fillet. But with her latex gloves she couldn't get a grip. And she'd started from the tail. Zoran was watching. "Try from the other end," he said.

She flipped it around. She got a grip and tugged. She pulled a little too steeply and too fast. The shine and color all came off with the skin.

She sighed in frustration. She peered at the other students.

None of them were doing much better. Even the ones whose sushi usually looked perfect had created fillets that were ragged and colorless. Mackerel was hard.

Kate admired the clean, asymmetric lines of Zoran's sashimi arrangement. *That's* what she wanted to make. She cut her fillet and pushed the slices around on a plate, but couldn't replicate it. Kate had a good artistic sense, but the Zen-like beauty eluded her.

Zoran appeared at Kate's side and arranged her sashimi for her.

Zoran slipped back to his station. He had another trick up his sleeve—a small wooden box. He lined the bottom of the box with translucent strips of simmered white kelp. He pressed in a fillet of mackerel, then stopped himself.

"I've got to think in reverse," he said. He rearranged the mackerel, so the shiny skin faced down. Then he packed rice on top.

Zoran looked up at the class. "This is how sushi originated in Japan," he announced. The students stopped working and gathered around. "Before they pressed sushi by hand," Zoran said, "they pressed it in a box. It's called *hako-zushi*"—box sushi. This was a small-scale variation on the method of pressing fish and rice in a box with heavy stones.

Zoran inserted the top of the box—or rather, the bottom— and pressed down hard. He flipped the box and lifted it off. The kelp had created a transparent glaze over the patterned colors of the mackerel. He sliced it into bite-size pieces. In parts of western Japan, around the old capital of Kyoto, this style of pressed box sushi is still considered "normal" sushi, as opposed to the Tokyo-style sushi that has colonized the rest of Japan and the world.

The students dispersed back to their stations. The other woman in the class took a bite of her mackerel, chewed it thoughtfully, then spit it into the trash. The student next to her yelped.

"Ugh!" he said. "That's the sixth time you've done that!"

She shrugged. "I can't eat anything raw. I'm pregnant."

She offered her mackerel sashimi to Kate. "Do you want to take this home?"

"Not a good idea," Kate said. "Mackerel is making me nauseous and itchy."

At the end of class, Zoran reminded them, "You will have another test in two days."

Kate looked up.

"The test will include a special roll for each individual," Zoran said. "Each of you will have to come up with your own. Something creative."

Soon a vision popped into Kate's head. Love hearts.

2 5

RUSSIAN ROULETTE

Zoran strode grimly to the whiteboard. He hated teaching creative rolls. He grabbed the Magic Marker.

"Types of American special rolls?" Zoran asked.

The students called out names—dragon roll, rainbow roll, caterpillar roll (covered with thin slices of avocado), Philadelphia roll (smoked salmon and cream cheese), and others. Zoran jotted them on the board.

"Companies mass-produce picture menus of all these kinds of rolls," he sneered, "and then different restaurants give them different names."

Most American special rolls are based on a basic inside-out roll, usually with a topping. They rely on gooey, fatty ingredients and sauces, and the shock value of unlikely ingredients.

Zoran tossed the marker back into its tray and slapped a long list of American rolls on the table. He'd printed it from the Internet. There was a candy roll, a dynamite roll, a pesto roll, a ragin' Cajun roll (tempura alligator), and a holiday roll (cranberry salsa and turkey). A restaurant near San Francisco served a Prozac roll, though it didn't actually contain Prozac. Marcos had heard of a roll called "the screaming orgasm." He wasn't sure what went in it.

Zoran demonstrated a quick caterpillar roll. The students tried their hand at it. Takumi made one and arranged it across the plate in an S-curve as if it were crawling. He poked two slivers of cucumber in its head for antennae. He stood back and stared at it. He muttered to himself in Japanese. "If you look at it too long, it gives you the heebie-jeebies."

"Okay," Zoran announced, "you have the rest of class to work on a creative roll."

The students started testing their own ideas in preparation for the upcoming test. Zoran set about making the only special roll he considered worth eating—a Japanese-style *futo-maki,* or "big roll."

The Japanese-style big roll has the nori on the outside, of course, like the thin rolls, but takes a full, 7-by-8-inch sheet of nori instead of half a sheet, and several ingredients are included as filling rather than just one. Zoran filled his big roll with crab meat, boiled whitefish, sweet egg omelet, cooked spinach marinated in soy sauce, simmered shiitake mushrooms, and simmered gourd shavings. He squeezed it closed. He looked up and surveyed the students' progress.

"Come on, guys! It's taken you thirty minutes to make three rolls!" Zoran yelled. "Gotta work on your speed. The customers are going to go home."

Zoran pointed proudly to his Japanese-style big roll.

"This is the best roll." He gestured at the American rolls the students had been making. "All that other stuff is *crap!*"

Most of the students were experimenting with a version of a standard inside-out roll. Most of the rolls involved large quantities of cream cheese and messy sauces. Kate's involved fruit.

Takumi, meanwhile, had devised an entirely new roll structure. He built two small rolls and packed them side-by-side inside a larger, rectangular one with more rice, with the nori on the outside, Japanese style. He squeezed it closed with his bamboo mat, then cut off a slice. He examined the cross section. It was a geometrically perfect rectangle, containing two perfectly centered squares. He nodded to himself, and said, "domino roll."

Takumi started on a second creative roll. He built a standard thin cucumber roll and sliced it. He stood the pieces on a plate, in a circle, cross sections facing up. It looked ordinary, but inside one piece Takumi had replaced the cucumber almost entirely with wasabi paste—enough horseradish to make a grown man weep.

Takumi spun the plate. The pieces of roll circled like bullets in the chamber of a revolver. The plate came to a stop. Takumi giggled. "Russian roulette roll."

A writer was visiting the classroom to learn about the academy. Takumi held out the plate to him. The visitor selected a piece and bit down.

Most commercial wasabi served in sushi bars isn't wasabi at all. It's a mix of horseradish powder, mustard powder, mustard extract, citric acid, yellow dye no. 5, and blue dye no. 1. Real wasabi is a rare and finicky plant. It's hard to grow, nearly impossible to keep fresh, tricky to prepare, and absurdly expensive. It's also much more delicious than its contrived counterpart.

Wasabi and horseradish are cousins. Along with mustard and regular radishes, they belong to the cabbage family. Being a cabbage has its drawbacks. Members of the cabbage family do not possess legs and can't run away from predators. Instead, cabbages have evolved a high-tech defense system that would turn heads at the Organization for the Prohibition of Chemical Weapons. Inside their cells they store an innocent-looking, sugar-laced compound called glucosinolate. In separate compartments nearby, the plants store an enzyme called myrosinase.

When an insect or slug, for instance, bites into a member of the cabbage family, it's in for a rude shock. By breaking into the plant's cells, the predator cracks open the compartments, and the compound and the enzyme mix. The enzymes rip the sugars off the glucosinolate, converting it to an intense irritant called iso-thiocyanate, known to most people as mustard oil. Mustard oil is a highly volatile substance that converts rapidly to a gas and irritates mucous membranes in mammals. It's often used in cat and dog repellent. Mustard oil is so toxic that it damages the plant as much as it hurts the predator, which is why cabbages must store it with the sugars attached.

True wasabi is native only to Japan and Sakhalin Island, a Russian outpost off Japan's northern coast. It creates a derivative form of mustard oil called methylsulfinyl isothiocyanate. In humans, sulfinyl in small amounts can trigger a beneficial immune response, activating enzymes that detoxify noxious chemicals in our bodies. The Japanese collected wild wasabi as a medicinal plant as early as the tenth century. Wealthy nobles probably began eating small amounts of wasabi with raw fish as a flavorful spice and a hedge against food poisoning. Real wasabi tastes sweeter, more subtle, and less spicy than the horseradish that passes for wasabi today.

To activate true wasabi, the chef grinds the tuberlike rhizome of the plant on a piece of shark skin. The fine, toothlike scales of shark skin are the most effective tool for breaking the compartments that separate the compound and the enzyme. Grinding the plant about ten minutes prior to serving it allows the enzymes to produce the isothiocyanate. Any longer and the heat and flavor rapidly dissipate. Mixing wasabi (or horseradish) into soy sauce, as most Americans do, dampens the flavor and aroma even more quickly.

Contrary to what many sushi chefs and customers believe, wasabi can't kill bacteria on raw fish. But it does create conditions in the stomach that inhibit populations of bacteria from growing, and thus it may have some utility against food poisoning.

Wasabi plants grow only in shaded gravel streambeds with constant cold running water, making them difficult to cultivate. But in the city of Edo after 1600, sashimi became popular and demand for wasabi increased, so farmers began to grow it. Yet average citizens seldom ate wasabi. The leaves of the wasabi plant resembled a leaf depicted in the shogun's family crest. For average citizens to eat wasabi was thus considered an insult to the aristocracy. Most people ate regular mustard with their sashimi, not unlike the fake wasabi sushi chefs serve now.

Today, a modern Japanese wasabi farm could be mistaken for a black-topped country road curving through a gully. The farms consist of streams that farmers have widened to accommodate rows of plants. The farmers cover the streams with black curtains to provide shade so that from above, the streams resemble strips of asphalt. The highest-quality wasabi comes from a mountainous region southwest of Tokyo called Amagi. Wasabi experts refer to all other wasabi simply as *bachi*—"from someplace else."

For many years people assumed that wasabi wouldn't grow outside Japan. In the 1990s, a California real-estate developer named

Roy Carver learned that true wasabi could fetch $100 a pound. He'd tried growing exotic mushrooms, Jerusalem artichokes, and black truffles, and now he decided to apply modern greenhouse technology to cultivating wasabi. He chose coastal Oregon, where the climate was similar to Amagi. He visited growers in Japan, but when he started asking technical questions they clammed up. He convinced a Japanese friend to conduct espionage. Carver managed to smuggle several cultivars of wasabi back to the United States, along with Japanese wasabi-growing manuals.

No one had ever succeeded in growing wasabi in greenhouses. Carver hired a Vietnam vet and former pastor as farm manager. He hired a botanist with a PhD as science advisor. They trucked in 9,000 cubic yards of river rock to a sandy plot on the Oregon coast. At enormous cost, they installed twenty-three greenhouses with a state-of-the-art irrigation system. A computer controlled the temperature and nutrient flow to mimic a Japanese mountain stream.

The farm had its first commercial harvest in 1997. Word spread, and Carver's acts of espionage returned to haunt him. One day a black Lincoln sped into the farm. Asian men poked cameras from the windows, photographed everything not under cover, and raced away in a spray of gravel. Carver hired a security guard. On several occasions low-flying planes circled the farm. One Sunday morning at 6:00, a man jumped the 8-foot perimeter fence, snapped photos, and took notes until the guard chased him out.

Whenever Carver gave real wasabi to Americans to taste, the reaction was astonishment and delight. They had no idea that most wasabi was fake, and when they discovered how delicious the real thing tasted, they wouldn't go back.

The problem was that most Japanese sushi chefs in the United States weren't receptive. They told Carver and his sales team that Americans wouldn't be able to tell the difference between real wasabi and horseradish powder. Americans didn't appreciate subtlety, the chefs said, they just liked their sushi spicy hot.

Along with high electrical bills for the irrigation system and high labor costs, lack of demand from chefs destroyed Carver's dream. In 2001, he ripped out the greenhouses and started importing cheaper, frozen wasabi from China. It's still true wasabi, but the quality isn't quite as high. He sells it in tubes as Pacific Farms 100% Real Wasabi Paste. Many of his customers are American chefs.

The farm manager has continued to run the import and packaging operation. One day a couple of years ago, the manager received a phone call. A man was calling on his cellphone from a toilet stall. His friends had bet him $200 that he couldn't eat a fist-size ball of Pacific Farms Wasabi Paste. Now he was refusing their offers to rush him to the emergency room. The manager tried not to laugh, and told him to wait it out.

As luck would have it, the visiting writer at the California Sushi Academy had selected the piece of Takumi's Russian roulette roll that was full of fake wasabi. It was a much smaller amount than a fist-size ball, but the effect of the isothiocyanate in the horseradish was immediate and overwhelming. His eyes squinched closed and he gasped, while Takumi stood by and smiled.

Marcos had loaded his first attempt at a creative roll with far too many ingredients and couldn't get it closed. He'd slimmed it down. The result was nothing special, but it was simple and well-formed.

Zoran sauntered by and examined it. He nodded. "Looks good. Very good. Something's sinking in."

Marcos was stunned. Suddenly his head swarmed with grandiose images. What he really needed to do was come up with a creative roll that was far more ambitious—something wild, something that would blow everyone away.

The other students finished their creative rolls. Kate had quietly tested several ideas. She'd decided on a plan.

2 6

TASTES LIKE CHICKEN

On the drive to school the next morning, Kate was in a good mood. She liked her plan for her creative roll. She was looking forward to the test.

She was also proud to have actually filleted and skinned a whole fish this week. She hadn't done a superb job, but the mackerel had been difficult for everyone. For the first time all semester, Kate felt like one of the guys. She pulled her Mustang into a Krispy Kreme shop and bought a box of donuts. When she got to school she set them on the back sushi bar, a present for her classmates.

Zoran had a present for the class, too—a pop quiz. The students sat at the bar, hunched over their papers. Zoran patrolled the room, his arms folded across his chest. Suddenly his voice broke the silence.

"Who's trying to get brownie points by bringing in donuts?"

Kate raised her hand. "Me!"

"Well," Zoran snorted, as though donuts were the most disgusting thing in the world, "*I* won't eat them."

Kate frowned.

After the quiz, Zoran explained about the next day's test. "Toshi will give you the roll test. Then you will have ten minutes to create your special roll and plate it." He glared around the room. "*Ten* minutes."

He let them practice their creative rolls. Takumi rebuilt his domino roll, and he refined it by adding curry powder to the rice. Marcos swigged black coffee and put his idea into action. His new creative roll was sure to impress everyone. It was composed of chicken wrapped in sheets of potato, then deep-fried. He ran around the kitchen, bursting with creativity.

Jay's friend Jeff, the restaurant consultant, stopped by to make an announcement.

"I've got a sushi restaurant that's looking for a student to work part-time in L.A.," he told them. "It's a win-win situation. You'll learn and you'll get paid. Fifteen dollars an hour. I also got a call from a nightclub."

At the word *nightclub* Zoran laughed. "*Nyōtai-mori!*" he shouted. It was the Japanese word for sushi served on a naked woman.

Jeff continued. "I'm coming to you guys first. Anyone interested?"

Kate was seized with excitement. She could imagine herself having a lot of fun making sushi at a nightclub. Several of the students raised their hands, but Kate didn't. On the roll test the previous week, in spite of her speed, her score had been the lowest in the class. If she spoke with Jeff directly, maybe he wouldn't find out about her test score.

"Okay," Jeff said, and turned to go. The students were to contact him through Zoran or Jay, so he could get the school's assessment at the same time. Nevertheless, Kate took a deep breath and sidled up to Jeff as he was leaving.

"Anything in San Diego?" she asked, eyebrows raised.

"California is tough," Jeff sighed. "There are opportunities in Des Moines, Kansas City, Utah. The opportunities are out there, especially in the Midwest. It's harder if you want to stay around here."

Kate pursed her lips. Then she screwed up her courage and asked him to keep her in mind for the nightclub job. He said he would.

The students finished their creative-roll practice. Marcos was way behind. His elaborate new roll had taken forty-five minutes. He took a bite and chewed. "Tastes like chicken," he muttered.

27

MANGO LOVE

Kate's alarm went off at 4:20 on the morning of the test. She drove to the Laundromat and downed a Coke and Snickers bar for breakfast while her chef's jacket spun in the washer. She was determined to get good marks on her uniform.

Zoran was also awake. He was downtown, buying a thousand dollars' worth of fish, including 22 pounds of eels. It was just as well that Kate didn't know about the eels.

When class began, Zoran checked everyone's uniforms. Kate's was clean, but Zoran was busy praising another student who had pressed his with an iron. Zoran checked knives, tapping blades on his thumbnail and scribbling on his clipboard.

While they waited for Toshi, Kate cracked open a Red Bull caffeine drink and rummaged in her bag. She pulled out a heart-shaped cookie cutter and started punching heart shapes out of a mango.

Toshi bounded into the room.

"*Ohaiyō gozaimasu!*" he boomed, so fast that the syllables blurred together. The students snapped to attention.

"Today I'm going to do three tests," Toshi announced. "First, spicy tuna and California roll, four minutes. Next, *kappa-maki* and *tekka-maki*." Cucumber and tuna thin rolls. "Then, special roll."

Toshi paused before beginning the test on the first two rolls. "Please, under four minutes. Anyone can do it slow. Okay?"

"*Hai!*" the students shouted.

Zoran reached for the digital stopwatch.

"Ready?" Toshi asked.

One or two of the students responded. "*Hai.*"

Toshi scowled. "*Ready?!*" he bellowed.

"*Hai!*" they chorused.

Kate noticed that some of the other students' hands were shaking. She looked at her own hands. They were steady.

"*Go!*"

Marcos raced ahead and finished first. The others took close to five minutes, but their speed had improved. Toshi moved on to the next test—two thin rolls. Again, Marcos finished first. But on both tests, he'd clocked in without cleaning his cutting board. Takumi had wiped his cutting board clean both times before declaring himself finished.

Kate had tucked her rolls firmly together the way Zoran had showed her, and they stayed together. The practice had paid off. Toshi glanced at her rolls and nodded his approval.

"Okay!" he yelled. "Specialty roll, ten minutes! The clock is ticking!"

The students scrambled. Takumi quietly built his domino roll. Marcos rushed around in a frenzy, constructing and frying his potato-chicken roll. With seconds remaining, he plated it and squirted on a fancy pattern of sauce. Toshi examined each roll, taking notes on his clipboard.

Kate was glowing. She'd made an inside-out roll with salmon, cream cheese, and tempura-fried mango, presented on a bed of tempura crunchies. Two mango love hearts perched at the back of the plate. It was sweet and yummy. It was pretty. It held together. Most important, it was Kate.

Toshi examined Kate's roll. He nodded again and scribbled on the clipboard. When he arrived at Marcos's roll, he gave Marcos a long, cold stare. He gestured at the roll.

"This isn't sushi," he said, his voice quiet. "There's no rice."

Marcos flushed. "It has to have rice?"

"It looks good," Toshi said, "but it's not sushi."

Marcos blinked.

Toshi turned to the whole group. "Great job, everybody." He looked around. "Any questions?"

Marcos stammered, still red in the face. "Are all special rolls supposed to have rice?"

"We're supposed to be doing *sushi*," Toshi answered.

On his way out, Toshi leaned down and peered at Takumi's domino roll again. The geometry was exact, and the cross sections were colorful. Toshi smiled at Takumi. He spoke in Japanese. "That's cool."

That night Takumi helped out behind the sushi bar, assisting the senior chefs with *omakase* for a group of American customers. As usual, he started off shy and reserved. But the customers were boisterous and kept buying beers for the chefs, and Takumi drank a little too much. He began to chat and then joke with the Americans in broken English. He made them a plate of Italian-style raw tuna carpaccio. They loved it. Then Takumi got a glint in his eye.

Moments later, he reached across the fish case and placed a small plate in front of them. On it were six slices of cucumber roll, in a circle. He told them what it was. Then he spun the plate.

2 8

COMEDY CLUB

Saturday night, Zoran and Fie worked behind the front sushi bar. Business was slow. When the couple Fie had been serving had left the restaurant, she surreptitiously poured the beer they'd bought her into the sink. She was watching her figure. So was one of the men at the bar. A few minutes later, he asked her to marry him. He added that she could still have a boyfriend on the side, if she wanted. He laughed. "I don't want to do *all* the work!"

Fie plastered a smile on her face while she made him sushi. "Sounds like a good deal," she said.

"No one's offering to marry me!" Zoran bellowed. He glanced around, eyebrows raised.

The man seemed not to have heard. He was staring at Fie. "It's a wonderful offer," he said.

Fie kept her eyes on the roll she was slicing. "It's a wonderful offer," she repeated.

He nodded. "Think about it."

Zoran turned sideways and pretended to watch the television above the bar but he was keeping his eye on the man. Fie plated the roll and squirted on sauce. She slipped past Zoran to deliver it. Zoran whispered in her ear. "Let me know if you want me to say something."

She nodded. "Okay."

The ticket printer chattered out a new order. Zoran ripped out the ticket and pulled ingredients from the fish case. The man ate a few slices of the roll and watched Zoran work.

"So," the man asked, "what are the skills required to be a sushi chef?"

"You have to be polite," Zoran replied.

In the comic book *Sushi Chef Kirara's Job,* the young Kirara has a conversation with a disillusioned older woman chef.

"Since you are a pretty girl," the older woman tells Kirara, "you must have been through a lot."

"What?" Kirara asks.

"Like being given a hard time by customers who've been drinking, or sexually harassed by co-workers, or seduced by the owner."

Kirara protests. "I haven't experienced anything like that."

"You don't need to play ignorant with me. Female chefs are discriminated against. There's no way you haven't experienced anything like that."

At 7:00 p.m. on Sunday, a low-slung silver sports car growled past the restaurant. Visible in the cockpit was the silhouette of a head with a jutting chin. A few doors down, the car stopped in front of the Comedy & Magic Club. The car's door hissed open vertically and out stepped Jay Leno.

Leno was here for his weekly Sunday-night gig at the club, where he tested new jokes before using them on the *The Tonight Show.*

At the sushi academy, Toshi taught every class that a sushi chef had to be an entertainer as well as a cook. Some years Toshi hired actors and comedians to help the students learn to perform behind the sushi bar. He'd taught Zoran to perform. Now, Zoran was up against Jay Leno, appearing in the same block. Tonight Zoran had the better act.

Zoran was dangling a raw octopus leg in front of three women at the bar. They gazed at it, vacillating between amusement and horror.

"Would *you* eat it?" one of the women asked.

"It's *delicious!*" Zoran said. He snatched up his knife and cut a disk of flesh from the leg. He squeezed a lemon wedge over it, sprinkled it with salt, and held it out for their inspection. "Raw octopus leg!"

The women stared, wide-eyed, as Zoran popped it in his mouth with a flourish. They squealed.

"Ew!"

"It's really quite nice," Zoran said, chewing. "So next time, ask for the shiny octopus."

Suddenly Zoran keeled over sideways, his face contorted. The women gasped.

Zoran shot back up, chuckling. The women laughed.

A few seconds later Zoran coughed and started choking. Again they stared. He broke into a smile. They laughed some more.

Then Zoran's knees buckled out from under him. He grabbed his throat and yelled, "Water!" The women broke into uproarious laughter.

Kate had returned to San Diego for the weekend, elated. On the creative-roll test, Toshi had given her high marks in each category: preparation, presentation, and originality. And she was excited about the prospect of the sushi job in the nightclub.

Kate hadn't sharpened her knives before leaving for the weekend. She hated sharpening her knives, and she wasn't much good at it. She still worried about slicing off the tips of her fingers. She knew a sushi chef was supposed to care for her own knives, but she was feeling so good about her mango heart roll that she decided to treat herself to an indulgence.

On Sunday afternoon she walked into a professional cutlery store in San Diego. They were startled to see a white girl with a pierced nose pass them a case full of Japanese hand-forged blades. She said she wanted them sharpened.

Zoran would be furious if he found out.

Week 7

29

LONG GOOD-BYE

On Monday morning, Zoran stared at the table, then lifted his chin. He had an announcement to make.

"I'm leaving," Zoran said, his face tight. "I fly out on the twenty-eighth." He would be returning to Australia. It wasn't his choice to go, he said.

The students looked stunned, especially Kate. That was just two weeks from now—only two-thirds of the way through the semester.

The hum of refrigerators and freezers filled the room.

"Who is going to be our teacher?" Kate asked.

"Maybe Tetsu. Maybe Toshi. Maybe both." Zoran paused. "Okay, just to let you guys know." He glanced at the clock, then told the class to begin preparing for today's student lunch counter.

The students swung into action. Kate switched on the radio. Hip-hop thumped into the room. They loaded ice into the fish cases and set out chopsticks, soy-sauce dishes, and napkins. In the kitchen, Marcos skewered fillets of albacore and seared them over the big burner. He wondered if the two women he'd served last week would return. He'd served them a bone in their fish. It didn't seem likely they'd come back.

Around noon, five people walked in and sat at the bar. They looked like businesspeople. The man in front of Kate ordered a cucumber roll. She wet her hands and clapped her fist into her palm with authority. She gathered a handful of rice from the canister and squeezed together a cucumber roll.

After a few minutes Kate's mother and brother walked in. Kate greeted them with a big smile. She made them a couple of rolls and sliced them, using her long, willow-leaf blade. The cutlery store had made her knife very, very sharp. She was relieved to have found a way to avoid sharpening it herself. But now she had to be extra careful when slicing.

Two more people walked in. Marcos looked up. It was the women from last week—the ones to whom he'd served bones. They glanced around the room, surprised. "Wow, it's full!"

Marcos flashed them a smile. "I was wondering where you ladies were." He finished squeezing together a rainbow roll—colorful strips of fish pressed atop a California roll. "So, how you ladies doin'?" Marcos's father was in town, and just then he arrived with his girlfriend. Suddenly Marcos had four customers, all special. And there was nowhere for his dad to sit. Zoran intervened, directing them to a table.

A young couple arrived and Zoran seated them at a second table. Then a heavyset man with long hair strode in. Seventeen customers now waited for food. The students hustled, sliding past each other to the lowboy and the fish cases, grabbing ingredients.

Marcos squeezed together a few tuna *nigiri* for his father and his father's girlfriend. He crowded them onto a tiny plate with wasabi and pickled ginger, and he delivered it to their table. On the way back, Marcos tried to flirt with the two women. They seemed more interested in the sushi than in him. At least they hadn't found any bones.

Marcos's dad's girlfriend spread wasabi across the top of the *nigiri* like frosting and then bit the *nigiri* in two. The other half fell from her hands. She was quick, and caught it before it landed in the soy sauce. The heavyset man with long hair stirred a glob of wasabi into his soy sauce, forming a paste. Then he dipped his pickled ginger in the paste and ate it as an appetizer.

Another couple walked in, then even more customers arrived. They had to wait to be seated. The students kept hustling.

The heavyset man finished his wasabi-laden lunch.

"This was really excellent," the man said. "Thank you." He

handed the students some cash. "Keep the change. Next time I'll bring thirty friends. We'll *fill* the place!"

As the other customers left they, too, complimented the students on the food. The students beamed.

After class, the students sharpened their knives. Except Kate. Her knives were nice and sharp. She left a note for Jeff, the restaurant consultant, reminding him that she wanted the nightclub job, and left.

3 0

FROM FRESHWATER

*T*he next morning, Kate was on rice duty. She arrived at school early. After half an hour, on her eighth rinse, the rinse water was still cloudy. She worked her hands through the frigid water, mixing and rubbing the rice. She lifted the heavy bowl and poured the water out again. Her hands were turning numb.

This is going to give me arthritis, Kate thought. Sushi apprentices in Japan did this every day for two years before they were even allowed to touch fish? Maybe the California Sushi Academy wasn't so bad. Kate put the rice on to cook just as Zoran took roll. She rushed to the classroom.

"Today, salmon," Zoran was saying. "In Japanese it's called *sake,* or *shake* to distinguish it from sake." In Japanese the two words are written with different characters—one for salmon, another for rice liquor—but they are pronounced the same. Sushi chefs had fiddled a little with the language to avoid confusing themselves behind the sushi bar.

"Now," he went on, "I have some news for you. The Japanese don't usually use salmon for sushi. When I was in Tokyo with Toshi, some tourists asked a sushi chef for salmon, and he stood looking at them as if they were crazy. You know why?"

No one did.

"Parasites. Salmon are susceptible to parasites."

In fact, they're worse than mackerel. A study in the 1980s found anisakis larvae in every one of the fifty wild salmon the researchers took from Puget Sound. And because salmon swim in freshwater as well as the ocean, they can carry the larvae of tapeworms, too. In 1981, the Centers for Disease Control issued a warning after a tapeworm outbreak in California was traced to salmon sushi. Tapeworms are a primary reason why traditional sushi chefs seldom serve freshwater fish raw. Once a tapeworm takes up residence in a human, it can grow to a length of several feet. A museum in Tokyo dedicated to parasites houses a tapeworm that was extracted from a man who'd eaten a raw trout, a freshwater relative of salmon. The worm in the museum is nearly 30 feet long.

Unlike bacteria, parasites are complex, multi-celled organisms. Cooking will kill them, but so will cold enough temperatures. The solution for raw salmon, Zoran explained, was to freeze the fish in the restaurant's industrial freezer. Some people consider unfrozen fish a requirement for high-quality sushi, but unfrozen salmon are a very bad idea. The chefs at Hama Hermosa froze their salmon for a minimum of seventy-two hours before thawing and serving it. Most sushi chefs are less strict about freezing mackerel because they salt and vinegar it.

The lower the temperature, the more quickly the parasites die. In the United States, the FDA recommends that distributors or restaurants freeze *all* fish that will be served raw for eighteen hours at −31°F, a temperature that only a high-powered blast freezer can achieve. At the more conventional temperature of −4°F, the FDA points out that the fish has to be kept frozen for an entire week to destroy parasites. Most home freezers don't go much below 0°F.

The FDA simply issues recommendations. Individual states must implement their own regulations, and many have. As of the summer of 2006, California still had no statewide codes to enforce fish freezing. Fish suppliers are supposed to track any health risks, and local health inspectors do visit sushi restaurants regularly and hand out scorecards that must be posted at the entrance. People do not generally get sick from eating salmon sushi. Nevertheless the "Kids Page" on the California Food and Drug Web site puts it this way: Eating sushi "may not be very safe for you."

Salmon belong to one of the oldest families of fish in existence. Along with freshwater trout, salmon go back 100 million years.

There is evidence that the group of creatures we generally think of as fish did not first evolve in the ocean. Like salmon and trout, all fish may have their origins in freshwater. Between about 350 and 400 million years ago the earth exploded with new life forms. In the ocean, the wormlike fishes evolved into new species. Some of these moved into freshwater. There they developed skeletons made of hard bone. Subsequently, many of them returned to the ocean with their new equipment and recolonized the sea. These may well have been the ancestors of the ocean fish we know today. Many others stayed behind. Forty percent of all species of bony fish still live in freshwater.

Salmon live in both worlds. Salmon are born in freshwater, spend from one to five years in the sea, and return to freshwater and fight their way up raging rivers to spawn in the streams of their birth. Why go to such trouble?

In the relatively cold climates at higher latitudes, where salmon live, the ocean provides a richer buffet of nourishing food than freshwater. But freshwater streams are safer places for babies to grow up. By taking advantage of both environments, salmon eat well, and their eggs and young have high survival rates.

Salmon smell their way back to their birthplace. As they begin their trek upstream from the ocean, they eat the last meal of their lives. From then on they will survive by burning their own fat and digesting the proteins in their own muscles.

As they head upriver they also undergo astonishing anatomical changes, not unlike Dr. David Banner's transforming into the Incredible Hulk. At sea, salmon are handsome and respectable-looking silver fish. By the time they return to their home streams, depending on the species, they have developed green heads, bright-red skin, bizarre color patterns, beaked jaws with nasty teeth, and hunched backs.

These monstrous fish flail around in streams that are much too small for them, the males ramming and biting each other and the females attacking everything that moves. The females turn on their sides and whack their tails into the gravel, digging depressions to lay their eggs. The toughest males duke it out for the right to spray sperm on the eggs. The violent orgy ends in death for all the salmon.

Meanwhile, bears swipe salmon from the water by the fistful. Bears are finicky sashimi eaters. They eat only a few bites of each salmon before tossing it aside and ambling back into the water to catch another. They leave lacerated salmon strewn across the forest floor.

At a sushi bar this behavior would merit eviction, but in a forest it's welcome. Plants living near salmon streams contain large amounts of nourishing nitrogen, and tests have shown that up to 70 percent of it came from the ocean, via salmon. Tree growth near salmon streams is three times greater than near comparable streams without salmon.

"Now, to farming," Zoran said. He explained that most salmon served in sushi is farmed salmon.

Industrial pollution began killing off wild salmon in major rivers around the world as early as the nineteenth century. In England, the last salmon in the Thames were caught in 1833. The construction of dams destroyed many salmon runs as well.

Norway pioneered the farming of salmon in the 1970s, followed by Scotland. The Europeans expanded salmon farming into Canada, the United States, and Chile. Today, a handful of multinational corporations control much of the industry, and farmed salmon account for half of all salmon sold. Fishermen who catch high-quality wild salmon have trouble staying in business because cheap farmed salmon glut the markets.

Salmon farming has made salmon more plentiful, but in a sense it has also created a new kind of fish. And for sushi, most Americans prefer this new kind of fish. The reason is simple. As Zoran liked to put it to his customers at the sushi bar, "Farmed salmon don't work for a living."

Wild salmon work hard. In the wilds of the Pacific Northwest and Alaska, free-swimming salmon continue to throw themselves year after year into the grueling marathons that return them to the streams of their birth. To fortify themselves for the trip, they hunt a variety of wild prey, including miniature shrimp called krill.

Krill eat algae. As a result, they are full of a photosynthetic pigment called astaxathin, similar to the carotenoid that makes carrots orange. Many kinds of fish absorb this pigment, giving their skin a red tint, but only salmon absorb it into their flesh, which is why salmon meat has a unique, orangey pink color. Flamingos eat small crustaceans similar to krill and are pink for the same reason.

To a sushi chef, salmon doesn't qualify as a red fish. It's a white fish because the color doesn't belong to the fish. Salmon farming operations must add pigment to the feed or their farmed salmon will turn out white and disappoint the consumer.

In the wild, salmon gain flavor as well as color from their prey. As they hunt, they swim hundreds of miles to return to the mouths of their native rivers. By the time the fish are caught, they're well-exercised.

By contrast, farmed salmon are couch potatoes. They mill around in pens, gorging themselves on rich, oily fish meal. Companies manufacture the meal by grinding up fatty fish such as mackerel, herring, sardines, and anchovies in giant industrial blenders.

Sometimes Zoran would serve his customers two different *nigiri,* one topped with wild salmon, one topped with farmed salmon. The flesh of the wild fish was usually dark, pungent, and—depending on when and where it had been caught—relatively lean. It didn't melt in your mouth; you had to chew it. The taste was strong and the flesh had texture.

The farmed fish was soft, pale, and striped with thick streaks of fat. And, by comparison, it tasted bland.

The recent popularity of fatty tuna in sushi has led people to value a rich, fatty, melt-in-your-mouth sensation over flavor and texture. The aquaculture companies have been happy to oblige. Fat, lazy salmon are what they do best.

Unfortunately, lack of flavor and texture isn't the only downside. All that fat in farmed salmon is loaded with around seven times the PCBs—polychlorinated biphenyls, likely a cause of cancer—that wild salmon contain. Since 3 pounds of smaller fish are necessary to produce 1 pound of salmon, the salmon "bio-accumulate" more of the toxic PCBs from eating the smaller fish than they would from eating krill directly.

Many farming operations also pump their salmon full of antibiotics, as disease can run rampant in the crowded pens. On the other hand, farmed salmon are less likely to transmit parasites to humans.

Traditionally, the favorite sushi toppings in Japan were lean, firm fish like snapper and flounder. In the past, Japanese fishmongers sliced off the fatty portions of their fish and tossed them on the floor for their cats. When an entire fish had a high fat content—mackerel, for example—they salted it and marinated it with vinegar to cut through the oil, just as Kate and her classmates had learned to do. But after Western food became popular in Japan, the Japanese started to include the fatty cuts of fish in sushi, too. That said, Japanese chefs tend to consider farmed fish inferior.

In the United States, the preference of diners for bland fatty salmon has been a bonanza not just for aquaculture but for sushi chefs as well.

"If you want to open a restaurant," Zoran said, "salmon is your moneymaker. Very cheap to buy." He meant farmed salmon, of course. "You can make a lot of sushi from a big salmon fillet."

"Now," Zoran said, "I have a problem. I ordered salmon with the head on, but I got salmon fillets. Sorry."

No fish heads? Kate was not upset by this news. Zoran unwrapped a green cellophane package.

Most fish are either fairly thin or fairly plump. For example, a snapper is a tall, narrow fish, while a tuna is a wide, tubular fish. Both extremes cause complications when breaking fish down into *neta* blocks that can be sliced easily for sushi. But a salmon is just right—a relatively big fish, thick enough in cross section, but not round. So cutting salmon is simple—another reason sushi chefs like it.

Zoran laid his palm on the featureless orange slab of salmon flesh and sliced off a rectangle the width of his hand. The resulting block was ready to be wrapped in plastic wrap and stored in the fish case at the sushi bar.

Zoran laid his palm on the fillet and cut off another large rectangle. "See, four finger wide." He looked around at the students. "Got it?"

They nodded. Zoran distributed several fillets around the table and the students paired up. First, they felt the flesh for pin bones to extract with their tweezers. Bent over the stainless-steel table in their white coats, with their steel blades and instruments, they looked like surgeons.

Kate had crossed over to work with one of her classmates. He took his Western-style chef's knife from his case and cut the fins off the fillet, then handed the knife to Kate.

Kate laid her palm on the fillet. It was slimy. She sawed through the flesh to create a hand-sized block. When the knife hit the skin on the underside of the fillet, it stopped cutting. She gave up and handed the knife back to her classmate.

He couldn't get his knife to cut through the skin, either. Zoran noticed. He grabbed the knife and tested it on his thumbnail.

"Whose knife is this?" Zoran asked, looking at Kate.

"Mine," the other student said.

Zoran stifled a laugh. "It's not sharp!" He tapped the blade theatrically on the flesh of his palm. Kate winced, but the knife drew no blood. Zoran glared at the man and shook his head. "You *can't cut fish* if your knife *isn't sharp*." He strode away.

Kate jogged back to her station and fetched one of the knives she hadn't used since they'd been sharpened. It cut through the skin with one quick slice. They broke the rest of the fillet down into blocks and wrapped them in plastic wrap.

"Think about what flavors go well with salmon," Zoran instructed them. "Because now I want you to come up with salmon sushi of your own. Your own style. Fusion is okay. Whatever you want."

The students frowned.

"Come on!" Zoran yelled. "Let's go. Salmon sushi, your style!"

Zoran burst into action. He squeezed out six quick salmon *nigiri*. He topped one with sesame seeds and an ultra-thin wedge of lemon. On another he sprinkled bonito flakes over a sliver of rinsed white onion. Another he topped with a dash of teriyaki sauce, and another with creamy sesame dressing. The fifth he painted with sweet miso and egg yolk, then he seared it with a blowtorch. He peeled up the last slice of salmon and slipped half a perilla leaf between the fish and the rice.

"There!" Zoran barked. "Six different salmon *nigiri* in a few seconds. You have to think quick because your customer is going to come in and want something different each time."

That evening Kate returned to the classroom. Jay was teaching a night class for a group of civilians, and Kate was his intern. She gave the students pointers and chatted with them while they worked. After the class a woman came up to Kate. The lady said she liked Kate's style, and handed her a twenty-dollar tip.

It had been a good day. Kate's knife had been sharp in class. And so far the new fish lessons weren't that bad—no fish heads, no fish guts, no fish blood. No problem.

31

CONGRATULATIONS FISH

Kate strode into the classroom the next morning and placed another box of Krispy Kreme donuts on the sushi bar. She set something else out, too—an apple. It was for Zoran. She was surprised at how sad she was that he was leaving.

Zoran strode into the classroom and took roll.

"So, is this next fish called a snapper or a sea bream?" He chuckled. "It's *so* confusing. There are hundreds of varieties of sea bream and snapper in the world. What's it called in Japanese?"

"*Tai*," someone said.

"Right! Where does the name come from? In Japanese, there is a word—" Zoran solicited help from Takumi on the spelling "—*omedetai*." It means "congratulations." "If you're having a celebration in Japan, they serve you *tai*. A sumo wrestler, when he wins a championship, what does he get? A huge *tai*! That's part of the winning—a giant *tai* sashimi."

In old Tokyo, people considered sea bream a high-class fish, while tuna was a despicable, low-class fish. *Tai* were so high-class, in fact, that they were too expensive for most street vendors to use in sushi. Only the fanciest sushi shops sold *tai*.

In the twentieth century, as sushi escaped its low-class roots, sea bream occupied a place of honor in sushi bars. Only in the past few decades has tuna risen through the ranks to challenge the supremacy of *tai*. Many Japanese still consider *tai* one of the best sushi toppings. A Japanese saying, "*uo no tai,*" states simply, "the *tai* of fish." People utter it when they want to indicate that something is the best of its kind. There's also a proverb, "*kusattemo tai.*" It means, "even rotten, it's still *tai.*"

Sushi menus in America often simply list the fish as "snapper," a catch-all category that can include a variety of sea breams, snappers, sea bass, and ocean perch. True *tai* is a single species of sea bream called *Pagrus major.* It lives in the waters around Japan, Korea, and Russia.

Excavations of ancient shell and bone heaps indicate that Stone Age diners loved this fish. The oldest collection of poetry in Japan, the *Manyōshū,* dates from about 1,300 years ago and includes poems that celebrate the sea bream, putting the fish on a par with the beloved bonito, the source of flavor for dashi.

Sea bream are more closely related to tunas, bonito, and mackerels than salmon are; yet, sea bream are very different fish. Tuna, bonito, and mackerels look like streamlined silver bullets. Sea bream aren't built for speed. They are tall, narrow fish with high foreheads and colorful skin and fins—rather like the absent-minded character Dory in *Finding Nemo,* but red instead of blue. Instead of swimming quickly across expanses of open ocean, they putter around reefs and rocks along the bottom. Like salmon, they get their red color from the astaxathin pigment in the crustaceans they eat, but the color accumulates in their skin instead of their muscles.

The Japanese love *tai* so much that they have added *tai* as a suffix to the names of many fish that aren't sea bream at all. Something similar has happened in the United States, with the local equivalent of *tai.* In 2004, researchers analyzed the DNA of "red snapper" at retailers in eight states. They discovered that three-quarters of the fish weren't red snapper at all, but other fish entirely.

"When we do *tai,*" Zoran said, "one thing we have to be careful of is the top fin. The pointy little prongs. They contain poison."

Kate's mouth fell open. *Poison?*

"If you're unlucky enough to get one that breaks off in your finger," Zoran said, "you're going to have to get it surgically removed." It wasn't clear if he meant the spine or the finger.

"Ready?" Zoran yelled. "It's going to get messy!" He wrestled a Styrofoam box out of the fridge.

Kate peered inside. The box was full of foot-long pink fish wrapped in plastic. They were stubby and funny-looking. They still had everything—heads, mouths, big eyeballs, and tails. And poisonous spines.

"These are New Zealand farm-raised. These are red snapper. How can you tell?"

"They're red?" someone said.

"Very good!" Zoran laughed.

Actually, the fact that a farm-raised snapper was red at all was a neat trick.

Sea bream and snappers are slow-growing fish and can live to ripe old ages, anywhere from twenty to sixty years. When sea bream are babies, eels eat them—one of many examples of one sushi topping eating another. When sea bream get older, they mostly eat shrimp and crabs.

When it comes to sex, snappers are the opposite of shrimp. They all start out as females. After a year or two, some of them perform a sex-change operation on themselves and become male. Because these fish take so long to mature, populations of sea bream and snapper grow slowly. A population of mackerel that is left alone can double in size in just three or four years. For sea bream, it can take fourteen years. Furthermore, the fish are predictable. Every year big groups of them return to the same spots to spawn.

All this means that fishermen can easily catch too many of these fish and wipe them out. In parts of the United States, populations of red snapper are in trouble, which is one of the reasons retailers substitute other species.

Long before the Norwegians started farming salmon, the Japanese started farming *tai* to supplement wild stocks. They bred Frankenfish *tai* that grew 40 percent faster. They even used human pregnancy hormones to induce the fish to spawn. By the mid-1990s,

Japanese aquaculture companies were farming six times as many *tai* in floating cages as fishermen caught in the wild.

The only trouble was, the farmed *tai* didn't look like *tai*. In their floating cages at the surface, the fish got suntans and turned black.

So the farmers erected tents over the cages to keep off the sun. Then the fish became too white. The farmers learned to feed them krill a few months before harvest, so the fish would become red by the time they went to market. Feeding them paprika can achieve similar results. Sushi aficionados say farmed *tai* don't taste as good as the wild ones, but no one seems to have complained of paprika-flavored fish.

In the kitchen, Zoran set a snapper on a cutting board in the sink under cold running water. He pointed to the poisonous fins along the back.

"Don't rub your fingers the wrong way."

He held a knobby steel instrument in his hand—a scaler. He leaned over the sink and scraped the scaler down the fish with quick, vigorous thrusts from tail to head. Scales popped into the air and flew in all directions. The students dodged the flying disks.

"Make sure you get the scales off its ass, too!" Zoran yelled. "You think this is bad, you should see a big *tai*." He paused and formed a circle with his thumb and finger, the size of a silver dollar. "The scales are this big. If one of those hits you on the head, watch out!"

Because sea bream and snapper are slow-moving fish, they don't need tiny scales to reduce drag. They'd rather have the extra protection of bigger scales.

Now Zoran scaled the head. "If you're preparing a whole-fish presentation, don't forget to scrape his chinny-chin-chin, too." He scraped the scaler under the jaw, as though giving the fish a shave. Zoran peered into the fish's wide-open eye. "Hallo!"

Zoran set down the scaler. "Now, you want me to take the head off here?" He smirked. "There's going to be blood and guts. Yes? Okay."

First, he snipped off the spines with scissors. "I once knew a sushi chef who got one of these spines in his finger, and it blew up to a huge size, from the poison."

Zoran tapped the blade of his fillet knife on the fish, just behind the front fin. "You can't cut right here; it's hard as a rock." He shifted the blade a quarter-inch toward the tail. "If I was preparing a whole fish presentation, I would have cut out the gills first. We'll do gills next week." He paused. "You want to see it now?"

Someone said yes. Zoran jabbed his knife into the gills and cut through cartilage. There were loud snapping sounds. He pulled out the veiny, blood-red fans of tissue and held them up.

Zoran's face suddenly brightened. "Takumi-san, do you have a good recipe for *atama*?"

Takumi nodded. "Ah, yes!"

"Okay," Zoran said, "everybody has to take their gills out."

"What?!" Kate blurted.

"Takumi is going to make us something," Zoran said. *Atama* was the Japanese word for head. Normally, a chef wouldn't have to remove the gills because they'd be thrown out with the head, but now Takumi was going to use the heads.

Zoran reset his knife behind the fish's front fin. He raised himself over the cutting board and thrust downward with a cut that crunched through bone. He pulled off the fish's head, smearing globs of blood across the cutting board.

"Next step," Zoran said, "cut from the ass down the belly. Clean out the guts. And the bloodline—very important."

Zoran inserted the point of his knife into the fish's anus and sliced an incision forward toward the chin just as he'd done with the mackerel. He stuck his fingers into the visceral cavity and yanked out a cluster of organs and guts, then held the fish over the trash can and used a bundle of skewers to scrape out more globs of purple blood. He stuffed a paper towel in the body cavity and wiped it clean.

"All right, your turn. Get your fish."

Kate and Marcos went first, standing side by side at the kitchen sinks.

Kate picked up her scaler. She stood up very tall and tilted her head back, so her face was as far from the fish as possible. She peered down her nose to see what she was doing. She scraped the scaler down the side of the fish. Scales popped off. She kept going. When she'd finished most of the body, she turned to her classmates.

"Do I have to scrape his head, too?" Kate asked.

"Yeah," someone said.

She turned back to the sink. This time she leaned into the work. She thrust out her chin, wrinkled her nose, and kept scaling. She rinsed the fish off with water. Then she realized she had only done one side. She sighed and flipped the fish over.

When she'd finished, Kate transfered her fish to the table and grasped her triangular fillet knife between thumb and fingers, again holding it like the bow of a violin. She poked the tip of the knife into the gill and winced, as if she'd poked herself.

Zoran strode over. "You okay?"

"No," Kate said.

"Hold your knife properly," Zoran said. "You're going to hurt yourself."

With Zoran's help Kate removed the gills. Today was the first time she'd used her fillet knife this week. It was very sharp.

She gritted her teeth, chopped off the head, and scraped purple gunk from inside the head. Her bowl filled with goo. She cut open the belly and organs popped out—yellow, green, and white tubes like slimy sausages. She grasped some of them with her bare hands and tugged them loose. She scraped out the purple bloodline, then looked to Zoran.

"What do I do with the head?"

"Cut it!" he said, his voice much too chipper.

"In half?!"

"Yup."

Kate tried but the head wobbled, and nearly slid out from under her.

"Don't hurt yourself!" Zoran said. "Knife down, more power."

She tried to adjust, but Zoran stopped her. He took the knife, held it vertical, and put his entire body weight on it, shoving it down through the mouth. The blade jerked toward the cutting board, splitting the fish's skull. Finally, the two halves of the head lay flat, still connected by a section of bone. Zoran swung the knife down with a heavy whack. Blood splattered. Kate shut her eyes.

In the kitchen, Takumi collected the fish heads. He believed that everything in the world had a spirit, and he wanted no usable part of an animal to go to waste. In the comic book *Sushi Chef Kirara's Job*, the young female chef Kirara shares this philosophy. She treats the fish in her kitchen as small deities that possess emotions. At the end of a night working behind the sushi bar, Kirara sees leftover sushi, and sheds tears as she throws it away.

Takumi blanched the snapper heads, then sautéed them with salt, pepper, and a sprinkling of flour. He simmered them in a stockpot with leeks and dashi, and a splash of soy sauce and sake, while he scaled and cleaned his fish.

"Bring your fillets," Zoran told the class, "I need you all in the kitchen."

Snapper is best served with the skin on because it adds flavor and color. But the skin is too tough to serve raw. Herein lies a conundrum. A sushi chef needs a way to cook the skin but not the meat.

Zoran laid his fillet on a bamboo colander skin side up, and poured boiling water over it. Instantly the skin tightened and curled at the edges. He grabbed the fillet with bare fingers and dunked it into a bath of ice water.

"If you don't heat the skin enough," Zoran said, "it's going to be too chewy. If you heat it too much, it'll cook the fish."

Kate stepped up. She laid her fillet on the bamboo. She did exactly what Zoran had done, but when she touched the steaming fillet, she yelped.

"Agh! I can't lift it up. It's *hot!*"

The fillet sat there, cooking. One of her classmates leapt in and grabbed it. He winced from the pain and tossed it in the ice bath for her. Each student took a turn. All of them flinched as they burned their fingers. Zoran called a fifteen-minute break.

Kate's fingers were smarting. It had been a long morning. She wandered over to the stove, where Takumi hovered over his pot of soup. He smiled and served her a bowl. A fish head stared up at her.

Kate had been raised on chicken casseroles. She hesitated, then sipped the broth. She took another sip. She picked the fish head out and nibbled at it.

"Pretty good!" Kate said.

Takumi nodded. He thought the head contained the best-tasting meat because the jaw and fin muscles got constant use. He showed Kate how to pick the best morsels from the head with chopsticks. Then he fished in his bowl. He extracted an eyeball.

"This is good," he said, and swallowed it.

Zoran called the class back into session—it was time to make sashimi and sushi with the snapper fillets. After scalding the crap out of one's fingers, the key to presenting snapper was to put that colorful cooked skin on display.

"When Western customers see the skin," Zoran had told them earlier, "they say, 'Ew.' So you have to educate the customer."

Kate peered closely at her glistening slices of snapper. Under the textured skin, the flesh was a matrix of transparent gelatinous capsules of muscle.

The muscles of most creatures are divided into two types: fast-twitch fibers and slow-twitch fibers. Fast-twitch fibers are the sprinters—the muscles move quickly, but they also tire out quickly. Slow-twitch fibers are the marathoners—the muscles move slowly, but they keep going for a long time.

Fast muscles are light-colored or translucent. At Thanksgiving dinner, the turkey's white meat is fast muscle—turkeys only beat their wings in short bursts. Turkeys spend most of their time walking around, which is why their legs are slow muscle. That's the dark meat. The muscles of many mammals, including humans, are dual-use and contain both types of fibers.

Fish muscle ought to consist mostly of slow-twitch fibers because fish are constantly swimming around. But water is a weird place.

Swimming through it slowly is easy, especially if you're shaped like a fish. But if you try to go fast, the density of the water suddenly hits you like a wall. Resistance increases exponentially with speed.

This means that for most fish, the muscles they use constantly are barely noticeable—just a thin pair of dark fibers running down each side of the body, usually right under the skin. The cross section of a salmon steak, for example, has small triangles of dark meat nestled against the skin on either side. These are the slow-twitch fibers that the salmon uses for most of its regular swimming. If fish never needed to swim fast, they'd all be narrow shafts.

The rest of a fish's muscle—from 60 to 90 percent of it, depending on the species—is an emergency power pack of pale, fast-twitch fibers that kicks in when the fish needs to sprint. Fast-twitch fibers function well in quick, short bursts because they contain their own fuel supply of preloaded carbs. Enzymes inside the fibers convert this fuel into quick energy. The conversion occurs so fast that the fibers soon exhaust their supply of oxygen. They can keep functioning for a while without oxygen, but not for long. They soon shut down for refueling, and the sprint is over.

By contrast, slow-twitch fibers burn fat for fuel, which requires lots of oxygen. These fat-burning factories hire fleets of delivery trucks to fetch oxygen and bring it to the factory, so they don't have to shut down. The trucks are proteins called myoglobin. Meanwhile, inside the factory, part of the machinery that uses oxygen to burn fat are proteins called cytochromes. Myoglobin and cytochromes both possess a kind of hook for holding on to oxygen. The hook is made of iron. These iron-containing proteins are red, though they turn brown when cooked. That's why dark meat is dark.

The pale muscle Kate was looking at in her snapper consisted almost entirely of fast-twitch fiber. The category of white fish in sushi—sea bream, snapper, flounder—contain an especially high percentage of fast muscle. These fish also tend not to embark on long-distance seasonal migrations, so they don't store up reserves of fat in their bodies as do mackerel, salmon, or tuna. For these reasons, many Japanese sushi eaters have traditionally preferred them. The gelatinous capsules of muscle in Kate's fillet represented a lean, light-tasting meat that had an almost crunchy texture in the mouth.

The Japanese like *tai* in particular for its clean, sweet taste. *Tai* falls short on *umami*—it contains only three-quarters of the IMP of bonito. But *tai* is rich in the sweet-tasting amino acid glycine, with three times more of it than tuna.

"This is a very nice-tasting fish," Zoran said, as he sliced pieces for sushi off his fillet. He squeezed together some snapper *nigiri*. He lined them up on a tray and placed a pinch of mysterious green paste atop each one.

"Try this," he said.

Kate ate one. It was like nothing she'd ever tasted. There was none of the fatty richness of salmon or yellowtail. Mingled with the subtle sweetness of the fish and its skin was an unusual bouquet of flavors from the mysterious paste—notes of lime, clove, and oregano, along with a spicy zing. Her face filled with wonder. It was the most delicious thing she'd eaten all semester.

Zoran looked pleased. He revealed his secret. The green paste was a mush of the rare and flavorful Asian citrus fruit yuzu, laced with green chili pepper. It augmented the sweet snapper perfectly.

The students practiced making *nigiri* with their fillets. Kate sliced her fish with her willow-leaf knife. It was the third time she'd used it this week, but it still had a decent edge.

Zoran patrolled the room, watching the students make *nigiri*. He shook his head. They stood hunched over, turning and squeezing close to their faces like nearsighted old ladies darning socks.

"You all look like this." Zoran slouched over and moved his arms through a series of big, plodding motions. "Stand up, hold your hands up, keep your movements small and efficient. Hold your fish up high—" he dangled a slice in the air "—then form your rice. If you need to give your *nigiri* extra squeezes because it still hasn't formed properly, do it like this." He stood up straight, arms cocked out in front of him, and spun the *nigiri* on his palm. "That way the customer thinks you're busy making good sushi, not trying to fix your bad *nigiri*!"

Zoran strode to and fro, yelling like an army recruiter. "Be confident! Be proud! *I want to be the best that I can be!*"

After class, Kate congratulated herself. She'd done things today that she had no idea she was capable of doing. While the others sharpened their knives, she slipped out of her uniform and gathered up her gear and knife case. She left the apple sitting on the sushi bar and headed for the door. Zoran watched her. He'd noticed that Kate hadn't been staying after class to sharpen her knives.

He called after her. "Sharpen your knife!"

Kate turned, but didn't stop. "Huh?"

"Sharpen your knife tonight!"

Kate nodded. "Okay."

3 2

UNLEASH THE BEAST

*K*ate didn't sharpen her knives. She figured they were still sharp enough. When she walked into the classroom the next morning, she noticed that the apple was gone. She bumped into Zoran a few minutes later. 'I ate your apple,' he said.

As Zoran took roll, Kate took a swig from a tall black can. The shorter cans of Red Bull weren't cutting it anymore. This morning she'd switched to a caffeine drink twice the size—Monster Energy. On the side of the can it said "Unleash the Beast," which was appropriate considering what sat waiting for them today in the walk-in.

"You're going to have fun today!" Zoran said. "What do you call yellowtail in Japanese?"

Yellowtail is one of the most popular fish in sushi. Yet even aficionados can't agree on what it is called. For starters, it's not to be confused with certain types of flounder and snapper that are also called yellowtail.

Zoran laughed. "This is going to get really confusing." He wrote on the whiteboard:

- *mojako*—1 to 2 inch fry
- *wakashi*—2 to 6 inch size
- *inada*—6 to 16 inch
- *warasa*—16 inch to 2 feet
- *buri*—mature

Yellowtail is what the Japanese call an "ascending fish." As the fish grows through different life stages, the name of the fish changes because it tastes different at each stage. Eating an *inada* (a young fish on its way north to feed for a few years) is different from eating a *buri* (an adult fish on its way south to spawn), even though they are the same species. The term "ascending fish" comes from an old Buddhist term referring to a young man who becomes a monk.

To make matters more complicated, people in different parts of Japan use a totally different set of names for the various stages of yellowtail. The names Zoran had listed were the ones people in Tokyo use. Around Kyoto, people divide the maturation of yellowtail not into five levels, but into seven, and use seven separate terms unrelated to the Tokyo terminology. People in other parts of the country have different names still. It's a wonder anyone can walk into a restaurant in Japan and order the fish at all.

There is an additional complication. In western Japan, people once used the word *hamachi* to refer to the adolescent fish's fourth stage. Zoran explained that now *hamachi* refers simply to any farmed yellowtail because farmers harvest the fish on the cusp of maturity.

"Don't say 'farmed,'" Zoran told them. "It sounds unprofessional. Say 'cultivated.'"

The Japanese have long prized wild yellowtail in winter, particularly *buri* caught in the Japan Sea as they head south after several years of feeding in rich northern waters. They are firm, flavorful, and rich—nearly 20 percent fat. But they, too, can carry the parasitic larvae of the anisakis worm, and the fatty flesh spoils quickly. *Buri* weren't especially popular for sushi.

In the 1970s, yellowtail farms began to supply large quantities of fatty fish all year long, and the Japanese began to eat a fattier diet. Now, as in America, customers at sushi bars in Japan often prefer the soft, buttery flesh of farmed yellowtail, even though they have less flavor than their wild counterparts. The farmed fish are nearly 30 percent fat. Sushi traditionalists consider this to be too much fat. Zoran, for one, wouldn't eat farmed yellowtail. He said it was too oily.

Zoran gave the students an overview of yellowtail farming. In the wild, the fish spawn in the sea off southwestern Japan. Their fry—the little *mojako*—mass inside mats of floating seaweed. Some seventy other species of tiny fish also live in the seaweed, but the *mojako* dominate. Fishermen easily capture them alive while each fish still weighs only a third of an ounce.

In the wild, these fry would have grown bigger and spent years swimming long distances and chasing prey as they matured into *wakashi, inada,* and *warasa.* Finally they would have come of age as *buri* and been caught as a winter treat. Instead, they will lead a life more akin to the lives that produce veal and foie gras, although with less discomfort. Like farmed salmon, farmed yellowtail are pampered and lazy—for the most part.

Fish farmers feed the fry three or four times a day. The tiny fish quickly grow to a hundred times their initial weight. The farmers vaccinate the fish because disease is a constant danger under crowded conditions, just as on salmon farms. Then the fish are transfered into floating pens.

Disease isn't the only problem. Humans like to eat yellowtail, but yellowtail also like to eat yellowtail, which makes them a tricky species to manage. At night, when the fish stop swimming and drift at the surface, the farmers cull through them and segregate them into different pens by size, so the big fish don't gobble up the smaller ones.

Every day the farmers fire feed pellets out of a canon into the pens. The feed pellets are similar to the ones salmon farmers use, packed with ground-up fatty fish such as mackerel, herring, sardines, and anchovies, often along with extra doses of oils and vitamins.

The yellowtail eat so much of this feed, and get so little exercise, that the excessive amounts of fat they accumulate actually weaken the matrix of connective collagen fibers that holds their muscles together. That's why farmed yellowtail is so soft.

Independent researchers have conducted thorough investigations into farmed salmon, revealing that the fish accumulate much higher levels of PCBs from their feed than do wild salmon. So far, yellowtail have not been the subject of similar studies, even though lots of people eat high-fat farmed yellowtail in sushi. It would not be surprising if farmed yellowtail have the same problem.

Most yellowtail served in sushi—regardless of the region, type of restaurant, or price the customer pays—come from the same cluster of yellowtail farms, located off the coast of western Japan. Farmed yellowtail now account for 70 percent of all finfish aquaculture in Japan. Only a quarter of the yellowtail on the market in Japan are still caught from the wild.

"*Kanpachi* is lean, wild yellowtail," Zoran went on. *Kanpachi* is a closely related species to *hamachi*. "If someone wants yellowtail, but not as fishy and not as fatty, you can serve them *kanpachi*."

But aquaculture companies have begun producing fatty farmed versions of *kanpachi,* too. Before long, the words *lean* and *wild* may not apply to fish at all.

"Today we have three fish," Zoran said, smiling. "Three *big* fish. One of the fish is from Japan and we can eat it raw. The other two we can just practice hacking up." The farmed fish that had arrived by plane from Japan was fresher than the fish from southern California.

Zoran pulled the fresher, Japanese *hamachi* from the walk-in. It had lost its head and organs. Its tail remained intact, though it wasn't especially yellow. Zoran told the students that most yellowtail was shipped headless to save weight. The body was two feet long.

He laid the fish gently on a towel on his cutting board and wiped it with another towel. Kate admired its lustrous surface. It was amazing to her that it could look so fresh and have come all the way from Japan.

"A lot of American customers eat *hamachi*," Zoran said, "but say they don't want mackerel. It doesn't make sense to me. I think this is more fishy-tasting than a mackerel." He ran his hand across the surface of the fish. "First thing, take off the scales, right?"

He rubbed his scaler across the fish. Kate braced herself for the horrible scraping sound. It didn't come. The scaler just slid smoothly back and forth. Zoran looked up at the students and smirked. "The scales are so small that this won't work. We have to *cut* them off."

Yellowtail scales aren't as tiny as mackerel scales, and for a chef, that means they are inconvenient—too big to eat, too small to scrape off. Zoran used his willow-leaf knife to saw lightly across the surface of the fish, as if he were skinning a big mango. The outer skin and scales came off in strips.

"Okay, let me show you the other fish." He led the students into the kitchen. He set a pair of oversized polyethylene cutting boards on the kitchen table, then disappeared into the walk-in.

When Zoran reemerged, he had a whole fish in his arms. The thing was three feet long. It still had everything, including its head. Zoran dumped it on one of the cutting boards with a thud and returned for a second one just like it. The tail fins on these fish were distinctly yellow.

"These are cheap," Zoran said. "Two dollars a pound—and you get what you pay for." He waved his hand in front of his nose. "Wow, they stink!"

Takumi laughed, and nodded.

"You can't do anything," Zoran said, "until the scales are off. Good luck!"

Good luck? That was it? Kate stared at the enormous fish, and made the mistake of breathing through her nose. One of Kate's classmates started sawing sideways, cutting off scales. The surface of the fish was curved so steeply that he could slice only one narrow section off at a time.

He stepped aside to let Kate try. She used her willow-leaf blade, but she had trouble getting it to go where she wanted it. The knife had dulled since yesterday. She pushed too hard and cut into flesh. She recoiled and stepped away, leaving a gash. Skinning such a big creature seemed more like skinning a person than a fish. Her classmate kept sawing. It took fifteen minutes just to complete one side. Kate watched.

"What are scales for?" she asked.

It was a good question.

Hundreds of millions of years ago, ocean worms burrowed in the mud for safety, but when they evolved toward fishdom they began to swim out in the open. They developed body armor for protection. The earliest fishes were called placoderms, from the Greek for "plate skin," and they had big bony plates on their heads and necks.

The problem with armor plating is that it's cumbersome. Scales evolved as a less protective but more liberating compromise. What the fish lost in safety they gained several times over in speed and agility. Scales are so useful that they appear all over in nature. The bodies of snakes are covered in scales. Sharks evolved their own version of scales separately from fish. So did insects, for use on their wings.

Some fish have unusual scales, or none at all, or they lose or gain scales depending on their life stage. These fish are generally off-limits to kosher eaters. According to the Torah, for example, eels are not kosher. Some rabbis consider swordfish not to be kosher because they lose their scales at a young age, in order to swim as fast as possible.

Zoran watched the students slicing scales off the yellowtail with their hand-forged blades. It was laborious work.

"Can you believe it's 2005," Zoran said, "and we're still using this technology?"

He walked to the sink and came back with a steel scouring pad.

"This isn't the Japanese way," Zoran said, "but you can actually use this. Most restaurants that sell a lot of *hamachi*, they don't have time, so they use this." He looked at the pad in his hands. "It works." Then he put it away. Zoran's students did things the Japanese way.

Zoran surveyed the room and put his hands on his hips. "Oooh, I am *not* looking forward to taking the guts out. It's going to smell." He turned to Kate. "Come on, Kate, I haven't seen you doing any."

Kate moved tentatively toward the big yellowtail. She sawed across the surface again. She progressed 2 inches with her dull knife, then cut too deeply again and exposed flesh. She glanced up but Zoran had left the room. One of her classmates stepped in to bring the scaling line back to the surface. She tried again. This time she progressed 4 inches and stopped. She turned to the student next to her.

"Your turn," she said.

Other students weren't faring much better on the other fish. It looked like a burn victim.

Zoran reappeared with a Magic Marker.

"Look out, fish. Tattoo time!" He drew a dotted line behind the head, indicating the best path for decapitating the beast. He stepped out of the way. Kate's classmate sawed down into the neck along the line, opening a deep gash. He turned to Kate. "Want to take a peek? Put your hand inside?"

In spite of herself, Kate peered into the gash. Her hand flew to her mouth. She pulled away. Her classmate kept sawing, making crunching sounds. Kate shook her head.

"It's the cracking into the bones that gets me," she said.

He couldn't get the knife all the way through the thick spine. He gave up and cut along the belly. Bloated organs popped out like salamis. A sack of eggs slid into view, encased in a net of purple veins. The stench was overpowering.

Kate grabbed her nose. "Dis-*gust*-ing!"

Zoran laughed.

Kate's classmate ran his fingers delicately along the guts, trying to determine the best way to remove them. Zoran butted in and simply ripped the organs out in handfuls and dumped them in the trash, spattering blood and globs of tissue all over the cutting board.

Now it was time to fillet. A large tubular fish like a yellowtail requires a more complex fillet plan than the "three-piece breakdown."

With a fillet knife, Zoran traced long incisions around the edges of the fish, then deepened the cuts. He removed an entire side of the fish. Then, he divided it lengthwise with two new incisions on either side of the pin bones.

Zoran had produced two long blocks of flesh, roughly triangular in cross section and tapered at the tail end. Each long block contained about a quarter of the fish's muscle mass. A busy sushi bar might go through one or two of these blocks a day.

This fillet plan was called *go-mai oroshi,* or the "five-piece breakdown." It produced four quarters of meat, plus the carcass. The students tried their hand at filleting the other side, and then the other fish. When they had finished, Zoran grabbed one of the carcasses and dangled it over the trash can by its tail.

"Look at all the meat you're throwing away," he said. If the students had been working for a restaurant, these fillet cuts would probably have gotten them fired. Zoran released his grip, and the carcass dropped into the garbage.

Everything the students had just been through happens every few days in any sushi restaurant that cuts its own fish—except at about quadruple the speed and with a lot more fish. In the kitchen behind any sushi bar, the carnage is fast and furious.

In the old days, sushi chefs wrapped their fillets of fish in kelp. Now sushi chefs enclose blocks of *neta* tightly in plastic wrap so they don't dry out in the refrigerator. At Hama Hermosa, the chefs went through a mile and a half of plastic wrap every month.

Kate laid paper towels in a *neta* tray. Zoran loaded the tray with the slabs of meat. He pointed to different shadings of flesh in each piece. Most of the meat was pale, fast-twitch muscle. But the edges of some pieces were dark purple—a sure sign of the presence of iron, and the machinery for employing oxygen for endurance swimming. Together, these sections of dark flesh had composed the narrow strip of slow-twitch muscle that had stretched down each side of the fish, under the skin.

"Americans don't like this meat," Zoran said. "If it's fresh, Japanese customers will eat it, no problem."

The paler, fast-twitch flesh, meanwhile, contained curving, slanted sections of muscle.

While slow-twitch fibers run parallel to the fish's body, fast-twitch fibers of fish nest against each other in geometrically complex sheets that angle off the fish's midline by as much as 45 degrees, forming a series of spiral tracks down the body. The geometry is perfectly calibrated so that all the fibers at a particular point along the length of the fish contract together, regardless of their distance from the backbone. This allows for the maximum exertion of force.

Zoran straightened up. "Isn't this fun?" he asked, smiling.

After a morning of bloody violence, the students descended into meditative silence and practiced sashimi with the butchered yellowtail. They remembered not to eat it because it wasn't fresh. One customer had no such compunction. A housefly buzzed around the table and landed on the sashimi, sampling it with apparent relish.

Kate was trying without success to slice a piece of fiber from her yellowtail using her willow-leaf blade. Zoran materialized next to her. He held out a cheap, mass-produced knife.

"Try this," Zoran said.

Zoran leaned on the table and glared while Kate tried the cheap knife. It cut right through the fiber.

"Your knife isn't sharp," Zoran said. After three days of heavy use, Kate's high-carbon blade had lost its edge.

"Today, I want you to stay after class," Zoran said. "Don't go home. I want to see how you're sharpening your knife."

"You saw it before," Kate said.

"Well," Zoran said, "you're obviously not doing something right."

Suddenly Kate winced and dropped the knife. She squeezed her left hand into a fist, pressing her thumb against her index finger. She'd finally cut her finger. Bright red blood oozed out. She rushed to fetch a Band-Aid. Zoran stopped her.

"Don't leave your fish lying out, Katie."

She hesitated.

"You're not dying," Zoran said. "I can see that. You haven't cut a major artery, have you?"

She shook her head.

"Okay, so put your fish away first. Never leave fish lying out."

When Kate returned, nursing her cut finger, Zoran addressed the class.

"Honestly, you guys, today your knives are the sharpest I've ever seen in any class, ever. Very good job."

He paused.

"Except Katie. Everybody has to help Katie sharpen her knives today. Don't let her go home until she's sharpened her knives. We have to help her along."

And with that, Kate was no longer one of the guys. Once more, she'd become the flaky girl who couldn't do anything right. Moments later, when no one was paying attention, she shut her knife case and slipped out of the building.

33

FLATFISH

With a few simple words, Zoran had dragged Kate all the way back to the first week of school. It was as if she had not gotten past day two, when Zoran yelled in front of the whole class, 'Kate, your knives are *terrible!*' The worst part of it was, it was her own fault.

She arrived at school early the next morning and helped wash and cook rice. She moved briskly around the cypress tub, mixing vinegar into the rice, while Zoran introduced the day's lesson.

"Today we're doing *hirame* and *karei*," Zoran said. "What's the difference?"

One of the students hazarded a guess. "Ugliness?"

"Well, maybe!" Zoran unwrapped two fish. They looked as if they'd been run over by steamrollers.

Hirame and *karei* are Japanese names for the fish that Americans call flounder, halibut, turbot, sole, or plaice, depending on the region and species. Regardless of the names, the main thing about them is that they are all *flat*—flat as pancakes. And really weird-looking. Both of their eyes are on the same side of their head, and their mouths open sideways, like in a Picasso painting.

Zoran pointed at the two fish. One was large and one was small.

"You might say size. But there's another difference."

The students were stumped.

"See this?" he said. "The small one faces right. The big one faces left."

Because flatfish are so flat and strange, most people don't notice the obvious characteristic that separates the 550 or so species of flatfish into two distinct camps. They point in opposite directions. And just to confuse things, there is at least one species of flatfish, called the starry flounder, that goes both ways. Off the coast of California, half of all starry flounders face right. Off the coast of Japan, all starry flounders face left.

The Japanese refer to most left-sided flatfish as *hirame* and most right-sided ones as *karei*. The best way to tell them apart is by the price tag. At sushi bars in Japan, *hirame* have a reputation for being more delicious. Most *karei* are cheaper, and the Japanese eat them cooked more often than raw.

Flatfish as a group haven't left behind much of a fossil record. But in a sense, they didn't need to. Flatfish are themselves striking evidence of the process of evolution. They reveal evolution at its best—and at its worst.

For fish that want to eat an unsuspecting sea bug or worm for lunch, lying sideways on the sand makes sense. That way, the fish look less like predators and more like rocks. Over time, as the fish lay on their sides imitating rocks, the flatter fish were more successful. Soon they became so flat they simply disappeared into the sand.

Flatfish also evolved in such a way that both eyes ended up on one side of the fish's body. Picasso may have considered this beautiful, but generally it's not the sort of development that counts as an improvement. Imagine a child trying to get through grade school with both eyes on the same side of his nose.

Yet without such seemingly bizarre mutations, the myriad creatures of the planet—including us—would never have evolved at all. While mutations often cause problems, some are fortuitous, and over time the useful ones add up. Having both eyes on one side of the head could be considered an aesthetic disaster for some, but for a fish that hunts by lying on its side and ambushing passing prey, it's a vast improvement. It's much easier to catch things when you have depth perception.

In a sense, every flatfish today still passes through the entire multi-million-year process of evolution, but compressed into about a week. Flatfish are born perfectly normal. For their first month, a baby flatfish swims around looking like a regular fish. It must come as a rude shock when, over the course of just a few days, its cranium, brain, jaw, nose, and eye sockets all suddenly rotate over to one side.

Scientists aren't certain what genes cause the change, but they do know what triggers it. The young fish's thyroid gland releases a sudden surge of hormones. One side of the fish seems to respond more slowly to the hormones than the other. When researchers suppressed the hormones, the fish never went flat. It remained upright and grew into a more or less regular fish.

In the case of the starry flounder, where some individuals lean left and some right, the left-sided ones are the oddballs. In all vertebrates, optic nerves carry information from the right eye to the left side of the brain, and from the left eye to the right side of the brain. In left-sided starry flounders, these optic nerves wrap around each other twice.

While the starry flounder may lean left or right, a species of southern flounder can lean male or female. Which way they swing depends partly on the temperature of the water. Heat generates males. Where cooler waters prevail, the embryos tend to swing female.

For the Japanese, *hirame* are such high-class fish that sushi vendors on the streets of old Tokyo rarely sold them. Throughout much of the twentieth century, *hirame* have, like *tai,* enjoyed pride of place at fine sushi bars in Japan.

This may seem surprising because flatfish have less flavor than most other fish. They don't get much exercise. They spend most of their time lying around impersonating sand. But sushi connoisseurs appreciate flatfish for several reasons. One is the subtlety of their taste. While most flatfish muscle lacks a high concentration of flavor elements, it does contain a variety of interesting amino acids.

Another attraction is texture. Flatfish muscle contains a high proportion of a connective protein called elastin. The result is what Japanese diners call *kori-kori.* The term suggests a combination of crunchiness, elasticity, and firmness. Another example of food that is *kori-kori* is lightly cooked broccoli or asparagus.

Many Japanese enjoy the sensation of *kori-kori* and the gradual release of delicate tastes that come from raw flatfish. Flatfish sushi or sashimi rewards slow, thorough chewing. Some experts recommend that people eat flatfish sushi with their eyes closed, in order to fully appreciate the texture and the subtle interplay of flavors.

Flatfish have an additional attraction, and the Japanese consider it one of the best features in all of sushi.

Americans who think fatty tuna belly is the pinnacle of Japanese sushi are mistaken. Zoran pointed to the outermost edge of the larger flatfish's body.

"*Engawa*," he said. "The adductor muscle is a delicacy. Japanese customers will eat this before they eat *toro*."

Many kinds of flatfish swim without using their main body muscles. In fact, they hardly bend their spines at all. Instead, they have evolved continuous fins running down each edge of their flattened bodies, plus a row of special muscles along the base of each fin. These fin adductor muscles undulate, propelling the fish forward. The fish floats across the sand like a hovercraft.

The word *engawa* is an architectural term. It refers to the veranda-like walkways that run around the outside of a traditional Japanese home. Early Japanese fishermen apparently saw a resemblance in the edge fins that run around the outside of flatfish. The *engawa* muscles contain more elastin, so they're even chewier, but they also have more flavor, since they get more exercise. In addition, they're rich with fat. The main body of a flatfish is 1 to 2 percent fat. The *engawa* is 15 to 20 percent fat.

In the United States, most people have never heard of *engawa*. Some fish purveyors know enough to set it aside. It's sometimes referred to in English as "dorsal fin muscle." Actually, since a flatfish is a regular fish lying on its side, half of all *engawa* is technically "anal fin muscle." But that's not something sushi chefs emphasize.

"The *karei* is local," Zoran said, "so we're not going to eat it. We'll eat the *hirame* raw." Again, the local fish wasn't as fresh as the one that had ridden several thousand miles in a jet.

Zoran produced eight more right-eyed flatfish, each about 10 inches long. He produced three *hirame* as well—left-eyed flatfish, nearly twice as big. The students each took a small fish.

Like yellowtail, flatfish have small scales. Once more, the students had to slice the scales off before filleting the fish. Their knives kept slipping and cutting into the flesh. One of the students quit and rubbed his knife on a whetstone.

Marcos stopped, stood up straight, and let his arms flop down to his sides. He sighed. "This is so hard!"

"Anybody getting super-frustrated?" Zoran asked.

Marcos raised his hand. Kate looked up glumly. She raised hers, too. Zoran brought over the steel scouring pad he'd shown them the day before. He smiled sweetly at Kate and whispered, "Don't tell." She took a turn with the scouring pad first, and scrubbed her fish in the sink.

Next Zoran showed them how to clean a flatfish.

"Lots of guts and blood in this fish," Zoran said as he cut open the belly. Blood and organs gushed into Zoran's metal tray. Kate glanced away, but then she turned back and watched. Zoran explained how to fillet a flatfish while preserving the precious *engawa*—the adductor muscle along the fins.

"See this line? That's its spine. Cut a line along the spine." He made an incision down the midline, deepened the cut, then brought the knife around to the edge of the fish and cut repeatedly in the direction of the ribs. He pulled the flesh away from the bone a little farther with each cut. Working carefully so as not to damage the *engawa,* he produced four fillets—one on each side of the top, one on each side of the bottom. Flatfish, like big tubular fish, qualified for the "five-piece breakdown."

Zoran peeled away the skin along the edge and exposed the *engawa.* The adductor muscle was composed of a glistening string of pale pointy capsules of transparent flesh.

The students went to work. Kate had trouble making her first incisions. She looked around. She cleared her throat.

"Zoran, could you help me?"

He strode over and picked up her triangular fillet knife. He cut one fillet for her, partway through, and handed her the knife. He smiled. "Easy, see!"

Zoran circled the room. "What do you enjoy better," he asked, sounding cheerful, "cutting fish, making sushi, or cooking?"

"Cutting fish," Kate said, her voice dripping with sarcasm.

Zoran chuckled. He took a few more turns around the room, examining the students' work. He returned to Kate's station.

"Takumi's and Kate's fillets are the best," Zoran said, examining Kate's fillets over her shoulder. "Very good."

Kate stared at Zoran's back as he walked away.

Takumi finished filleting his *karei* and tried his hand at the larger *hirame*. He saved the heads, of course. He also rummaged through the guts of the larger fish until he located a grayish-pink organ shaped like an ear. Later, he would marinate it in sake, grind it to a paste with soy sauce, and use it as a sauce. In Japan, *hirame* sashimi served with the fish's own pulverized liver is a delicacy.

Suddenly Zoran bellowed out instructions.

"In three minutes I want you ready to make *kappa-maki*!" he yelled. Cucumber rolls. "Come on, come on!"

Kate gritted her teeth and rushed to set up for sushi. A couple of the students ran to the refrigerator and yanked out cucumbers. Zoran snatched one and started cutting it himself. Marcos was still fidgeting with his flatfish.

"Come on, Marcos!" Zoran yelled. "The customer has just ordered *kappa-maki*." No response. Zoran glared. "Earth to Marcos!" Zoran counted down. "Ten, nine, eight, seven . . . Go! I want two *kappa-maki* on your plate in three minutes!"

The students jabbed their fingers in water, clapped, and assembled rolls. Pieces of cucumber tumbled around their cutting boards. The smell of nori and vinegared rice filled the room. When they were mostly finished, Zoran interrupted them.

"Okay, stop what you're doing," he said. "Is your station clean? You're going to make a California roll—one *futo-maki* and one *ura-maki*." A big roll and an inside-out roll.

Zoran counted down again. "Ten, nine, eight, seven . . . Go!"

Claps punctuated the silence. Zoran circled the room, hands behind his back.

"Kate," Zoran yelled, "needs work on cutting!"

She frowned, lowered her head, and kept working. One by one the students completed their rolls and stepped back from the table.

"How was that for a wake-up?" Zoran shouted. He surveyed the table. Suddenly he hung his head and spoke in a soft voice. "I just wanted to see you make sushi before I leave."

During cleanup, Zoran disappeared upstairs. When he returned, he made an announcement, "There is a catering internship tomorrow. Who wants it?"

"I do!" Marcos said. He needed internship hours badly.

"Go upstairs and talk to Toshi."

Meanwhile, Kate forced herself to sharpen her knife. Zoran hovered nearby.

When she'd finished, she changed into tight jeans and a tank top and strode out to the parking lot. She pulled a soccer ball from her Mustang and kicked it hard against the wall of the restaurant. She was frustrated with herself, and with Zoran. It seemed as if he deliberately gave her encouragement and then followed it with criticism—building her up just to knock her back down. At the same time, she knew he was trying to help her succeed. Her own shortcomings hadn't helped things, especially when it came to her knives. On top of all that, she hadn't heard back from Jeff about the nightclub job. She worried that Jeff didn't think she was good enough.

Marcos came outside in his chef's pants, a T-shirt, and bare feet. He smoked a cigarette and watched Kate bust out a repertoire of fancy soccer moves. She bounced, sprinted, and juggled the ball with her feet and knees. The top of her pink thong underwear showed above the waistline of her pants.

"Kate," Marcos blurted out, "you should move in with me!"

Kate laughed. She suggested instead they eat lunch at her favorite Jewish deli. "We'd have to go downtown. You want to go?"

"Hell, yeah!" Marcos said.

Ten minutes later they were speeding down the freeway in the Mustang with the windows down. Kate switched on the stereo.

"I know Zoran wants me to cry," she said over the music. "And I'm *not* going to." She pursed her lips and shook her head. After a few minutes, she added, "My parents thought I was a chronic underachiever."

"They couldn't just call you lazy?" Marcos said. "They had to come up with some kind of medical condition?"

"Yeah!" Kate laughed. She drummed her fingers on the steering wheel. "So what's this catering thing tomorrow?"

"I don't know," Marcos said. "Toshi just said there'd be famous people there." He imagined himself on a movie set. "You want some sushi? You're going to have to give me your number, *Miss Jennifer Garner.*"

Kate laughed. "She's already knocked up!"

"Oh, yeah." He frowned, then bobbed his head to the music. He stared out the windshield. Somewhere out there in the haze were the hills of Hollywood. "I've never met a movie star before."

34

OLD GLORY

That evening, for the first time in weeks, Hama Hermosa was busy. The wait staff didn't walk, they ran. Customers lined up in the foyer. Behind the front sushi bar, Zoran, Fie, and Tetsu—the head chef—fired sushi out into the dining room like machine gunners in a pillbox. Tetsu still resembled a bear, but not a sleepy one. He grabbed fish from the *neta* case like a grizzly hunting salmon in a river. Zoran worked head down, cranking out orders as fast as he could. Fie tried to keep up.

In the back room, Toshi looked happy and relaxed. He was holding court before an audience of ten customers at the back sushi bar. It was just like old times. The frenetic activity of the restaurant swirled around him. In the center of it all, Toshi was an island of cheerful calm. He took everything in, keeping watch over his customers, his waitresses, and his chefs. He constructed elaborate *omakase* courses and refilled sake glasses. His movements were full of flourish and he radiated stage presence. Every few minutes he laughed and toasted with his customers and bellowed out commands to his staff. Frank Sinatra crooned on the sound system.

A woman sauntered into the back room with her date.

"Toshi, how are you?" she squealed.

"Beautiful!" Toshi yelled. They sat down. Toshi screamed over his shoulder. "Filipé! Towel! Towel!"

The busboy materialized with hot hand wipes.

As Toshi prepared another *omakase* dish, a man sitting at the bar said, "Toshi, can we have something more upbeat?"

Toshi gyrated his hips behind the bar and screamed, "Sheila! Music!"

The hostess appeared, wearing a tight red tank top with gothic script across her breasts that said, "Fuck Off." She strutted over to the stereo. The Sinatra was replaced by pounding hip-hop. The man at the bar nodded his head to the beat. Toshi refilled the man's glass with sake. The man wagged a finger at Toshi and shouted, "Toshi, you're bad, bad, bad!"

Toshi grinned and raised his own glass. "*Kanpai!*"

The customers shouted, laughed, hugged each other, and joked with Toshi. Toshi raised his arms high over the sushi bar and rolled together sushi hand rolls in the air. His customers gazed up, mesmerized. Toshi lifted a squeeze bottle aloft and squirted sauce onto the rolls, deepening the spell.

Two women sat down at the bar with a boy about 7 or 8 years old. Toshi leaned over the fish case. He raised his eyebrows and smiled. "You like sushi?"

The boy nodded.

"Okay!" Toshi said, and squeezed him out a *nigiri*. He painted it with *nikiri* sauce and handed it across the fish case. "This is tuna!"

Toshi turned back to his other customers and thrust the sake bottle toward them. The man held up his hands. "No more!"

"One more!" Toshi yelled, his face a theatrical scowl. The man accepted. They raised their glasses. "*Kanpai!*"

Toshi knocked back his glass, but the man dumped his cup of sake out onto his plate. He laughed so hard his face turned red. Toshi glared at him, pointed an accusing finger, then relaxed and laughed, too.

35

SPY KIDS

Kate still needed intern hours to graduate. Zoran was teaching a half-day course for civilians on Saturday morning. She signed up to be his assistant.

The class went well. Zoran didn't yell at her. The only downside was that after the class, Kate discovered she'd locked her keys in the car. While she was sitting on the back stairs, waiting for the AAA truck, Zoran rushed past and then stopped. He reminded her that Toshi would be away catering a movie set that night. There would be a station free at the back sushi bar. Did she want it?

Kate felt a shiver of excitement. Takumi was usually the only student allowed to serve customers behind the sushi bar during dinner, like one of the chefs. She nodded and said yes.

That evening Kate stood at her own cutting board behind the back bar, hands clasped behind her back, a nervous smile on her face, waiting for customers. The hostess seated the first few groups in front of the more experienced chefs. Then a couple in their fifties sat right in front of her. They ordered a California roll.

Suddenly Kate's universe shrank to seaweed, rice, and fish. She built the inside-out roll, tucking it in tight. It held together. The couple seemed to like it, and they ordered another type of inside-out roll. She made that, too. Then they ordered salmon and yellowtail *nigiri*. She laid blocks of *neta* presentation-side down, as Zoran had instructed her. She sliced the fish, laid the slices presentation-side up, then squeezed the *nigiri* together.

Zoran was far away, working at the front bar. Next to Kate, one of the Japanese chefs kept a kindly eye on her. He threw in an order of seared *toro* for her couple, on the house.

The woman got the sense that Kate was a student and chatted with her. She told Kate that their son was dating a female sushi chef from Japan! Kate started to have fun. They fell into conversation, and she made them more sushi.

In the parking lot out back, Toshi, Takumi, and Marcos hosed dirt off the van for the trip to the movie set. Marcos wiped the van dry and turned to Toshi.

"Toshi, man, let's go pick up some ladies in Hollywood!"

Toshi scowled and strode back into the kitchen. Marcos helped Toshi and Takumi load equipment into the van. Soon they were hurtling down a six-lane boulevard toward the freeway. Toshi was driving. Takumi sat in the passenger seat and Marcos sprawled on the bench seat behind them. After ten minutes Toshi turned to Takumi.

"Did you bring the rice?"

Takumi nodded. "Yes."

Toshi sighed. "Sometimes I forget to bring the rice."

"What do you do then?"

"We say, 'Today's special: sashimi.'"

Takumi laughed, then went silent. "You're making me nervous." He craned his neck around and peered into the back for the rice.

The men were speaking in Japanese. Behind them, Marcos was lost in his own world. He was on his way to a Hollywood movie set, where he might meet a famous actress. This was too cool. Marcos yanked his cellphone from his pocket and started dialing. He uttered a long, drawn-out, surfer-dude "Heyyyyy, man" into the phone. His voice was big inside the small van. "Yeah, dude, I'm going to, like, Hollywood to make sushi!" He pronounced it "soooshi."

Toshi turned in his seat and shot Marcos a glance. He looked back at the road and imitated Marcos's surfer-dude drawl, in English.

"Heyyyyy, man," Toshi said. He switched to Japanese. "Give me a break."

Takumi chuckled.

Marcos dialed another number.

"Heyyyyy!" His drawl was even louder. "Yeah, I got this catering gig in L.A., and we're, like, going to Hollywood to make sushi!"

Toshi looked at Takumi. "He's kind of annoying."

Marcos kept talking. "Yeah, man, I could show you guys a fucking good time out here." Pause. "You lazy stoners." Pause. "I've got another call. Okay, peace."

Toshi snorted.

Marcos made yet another call. When he hung up, Toshi peered into the rear-view mirror and switched to English. "Heyyyyy, Marcos, you gotta stop making phone calls."

Marcos laughed. "I gotta talk, man!"

Toshi pondered this for a minute. "Marcos, are you still in high school?"

"Yeah."

"So you used your summer vacation for sushi school?"

"Yeah."

They were both silent, then Marcos spoke. "Heyyyyy, Toshi, it sucks that Zoran has to leave."

"He doesn't like you guys."

Marcos was surprised. "He doesn't?"

"Just kidding."

In the gloom ahead, Toshi could make out big white trucks, bright lights, and swarms of people. He slowed and steered the van toward the center of the hubbub. Men with walkie-talkies stopped the van and told Toshi where to park. A helicopter circled overhead. LAPD motorcycle cops stood guard.

Marcos gaped. The whole street was closed off. Gleaming vintage cars were parked along the curb. Inside one sat two men, with bright lights shining all around them. Movie cameras pointed into the car from different directions and grips bristling with tools and equipment stood around holding curtains and poles. Marcos didn't see anyone who looked like Jennifer Garner.

Marcos and Takumi lugged the portable sushi stand from the van into a small parking lot. They navigated around stacks of dollies, clusters of tripods and lights, battered black equipment cases, and heaps of cables.

They unpacked the 25-gallon ice chest and bottles of soy sauce. Toshi noticed that their chef's jackets were hanging open. "Do those up," he barked.

A man strode over to Toshi. "What are you doing?"

"Making sushi for you guys."

"Oh." The man relaxed. "Cool. Like, California rolls and all that?"

Toshi nodded.

Toshi surveyed the crowd of grips and technicians working in the lot, then turned to Takumi.

"Since you don't speak English, they're going to think this sushi is really authentic."

They both laughed.

Three grips converged on the sushi chefs. One set up a 6-foot collapsible table. Another rigged a high-powered spotlight to illuminate it. A third lugged over an ice chest full of bottled water and deposited it on the pavement. He peered at Toshi and Takumi. "Sushi, huh?"

When they finished setting up, Takumi laid his knife case on the table and flicked it open. Marcos froze.

"Oh, man," Marcos said. "I forgot to bring my knives."

Toshi glared. "What a stupid *idiot*! *My* student, student of California Sushi Academy! You forgot to bring your knives to make sushi?!"

"Sorry, Toshi."

Toshi growled. "*Sensei!*"

"Sorry, Sensei."

The lot went quiet. Muted conversations simmered among the technicians. A single cricket chirped somewhere in the bushes. Another grip strode over to Toshi. "You ready?"

"Yes."

"I'll be your first customer. A spicy tuna roll. Make me cry!"

"You got it," Marcos said, reaching into the fish case. He assembled a cone-shaped hand roll, his movements tentative. A man with white hair approached.

"Wow, sushi. When are you going to be ready?"

"Now," Toshi said. "What do you want?"

"Everything," the man laughed. "This is *only* the third night in a row I've had sushi!" The man peered over the fish case at Marcos. "A blond guy making sushi?"

Suddenly the sushi stand was mobbed. Men and women of all shapes, sizes, and ethnicities threw out orders for *nigiri* and hand rolls. Toshi and Marcos both worked furiously. As soon as Marcos had served one person, there was another waiting—a woman in shorts carrying a hammer, a man in slacks wearing a leather jacket, a black guy in a Hawaiian shirt and sweatpants, an Asian guy with an eye patch. They streamed in from all over the set.

Marcos was frantic. Soon he needed a break. He shot a glance at Takumi, who stood behind the table watching. "Hey, Takumi, you want to jump in here?"

Toshi intercepted the invitation. "No!" he told Marcos. "You keep going."

Toshi made room for Takumi to squeeze in next to him.

Marcos's hands trembled, but he worked as fast as he could, head down, his brow glistening with sweat under the spotlight. The movie people stared at him, hungry, waiting. They were an arm's length away, watching everything. He screwed up an order.

"Pay attention!" Toshi hissed.

A cute girl with a ponytail stepped up in front of Marcos. "I have two orders," she said.

Marcos barely looked up. "One at a time."

"Okay." She smiled. "One order of salmon." She watched Marcos while he worked. "Are they teaching you?"

He laughed. "They're trying."

She told him her second order. He delivered it. She tried to catch his eye, but Marcos was staring down at his raw fish and seaweed, gauging what he needed next. She thanked him and turned away.

A man in line had a coiled wire running into his ear, like a Secret Service agent. He spoke into a miniature microphone attached to his lapel. "Let me know when the actors get here."

Moments later a cluster of beautiful young women strode into view. The crowd cleared around them. The women were dressed in clothes from the 1960s. At the center of the group was a 16-year-old girl with a familiar face. She was gorgeous and looked friendly. She stepped up to the sushi bar. She smiled sweetly and asked Marcos for a vegetarian roll. She watched him with interest.

Marcos had his head down in the raw fish and seaweed. He nodded, but he didn't look up. He focused on the *nigiri* he was squeezing.

Next to him, Toshi's hands flew. He handed the girl the roll she'd asked for. Marcos glanced over at Toshi in frustration. "You're so much faster!"

"You're too slow!" Toshi shot back.

Marcos still hadn't looked up.

The girl was Alexa Vega, star of the *Spy Kids* movies. She gave Marcos one more look, smiled, then walked away. She popped a piece of sushi in her mouth. Marcos never even noticed.

Back at Hama Hermosa, after all the customers had left, Kate stayed and helped the chefs. She put away ingredients, wiped down the counters, and washed dishes. She hadn't done that before. When she hopped in the Mustang to drive home, she was the happiest she'd been in a long time.

Week 8

3 6

SEA SNAKES

The Japanese call freshwater eels *unagi,* and saltwater eels *anago.* Most eel served in contemporary sushi is the freshwater variety. Either way, sushi chefs never serve it raw. They cook it, and often heat it a second time in a toaster just before serving. Eel muscle contains too much collagen—the tough connective tissue—to eat raw. Cooking gelatinizes the collagen.

The Japanese ate freshwater eel long before it became a sushi topping. Shopkeepers in old Tokyo killed live eels to order. They grilled them, a meal that continues to be popular. Even after the invention of *nigiri,* sushi chefs didn't serve freshwater eel on sushi rice because they judged it to be too rich and sweet. Instead, they boiled and served saltwater eel, which has a lighter taste. Connoisseurs still consider saltwater eel a better match for sushi.

In America, it has taken the popularity of sushi to get people interested in eating eel. There is some irony in this, because eel is one of the oldest and most adored dishes in Western cuisine, going back to the ancient Greeks. Eel pies were a popular street food in Paris and London, and eel was a staple ingredient for recipes in early English cookbooks. The early European settlers in America had little experience eating, say, lobsters, but eels made them feel right at home, and they ate them in abundance. After the Civil War, though, something changed. Americans decided they were above eels. In Europe, eel is still a popular dish.

To be fair, eels can seem primitive and grotesque. They are nocturnal and serpentine, and they emit slime, though slime is actually a sign of clean living, since the mucus protects the eels against bacteria. Eels even have a history as an instrument of terror. The Romans used dried eels as belts with which to discipline young boys.

Rabbis judged eels to be not kosher, but that was a mistake. Eels have scales; they're just very small and embedded deeply in the skin, which makes it easier for eels to slither in tight spaces.

Eels also seem to stir some deep sexual impulse. The Japanese believe eel meat to be an aphrodisiac.

How eels themselves have sex has been the subject of great curiosity through the ages. No one ever saw them mating. Aristotle concluded that they spontaneously arose from mud. A Greek naturalist society in the second century AD decided that eel sex must involve a lot of rubbing, and that mucous must be the eels' sexual fluid. Sigmund Freud's first assignment in medical school was to discover where eels hid their testicles. He couldn't find them.

In the 1890s, European scientists came closer to solving the mystery of eel sex by studying "glass eels." Glass eels are miniature, oceangoing eels. They are transparent and look like little shards of glass. The scientists discovered that glass eels are actually just baby freshwater eels. Mysteriously, the glass eels all seemed to be swimming toward Europe from some distant point in the sea.

An obsessed Danish biologist named Johannes Schmidt launched expedition after expedition, sailing deeper into the Atlantic on each journey. The glass eels he caught were smaller and younger the farther he went. In 1922, after eighteen years, he finally discovered where they were all coming from: the Bermuda Triangle.

As far as scientists can tell, all American and European freshwater eels are born in or near the seaweed-filled Sargasso Sea, in the Bermuda Triangle. After hatching, the baby eels leave the Sargasso and start swimming. They don't stop until they reach their destination. That destination could be a river in Iowa or a river in Germany. The journey to Europe can take a glass eel two or three years to complete. Relative to body size, it's the equivalent of a human swimming to the moon.

Asian eels do the same thing, except in the Pacific. They're all born at one place in the Philippine Sea, and from there they journey to rivers all over Asia.

Adult eels live in their freshwater homes for eight to ten years, some much longer. They eat until their bodies contain nearly 30 percent fat, and toward the end of their lives they slither back to the sea to mate.

As they leave freshwater, their digestive systems dissolve and disappear. They will never eat again. Like salmon, they survive by digesting their own fat, and after that, their own muscle protein. Scientists assume that they return to the Sargasso and Philippine seas to mate, but to this day no one has witnessed eels spawning, and no one knows how they travel so far without food. In human terms, it's like having just one chance at sex before you die, but you have to swim from the moon to earth—without stopping to eat—to get it. No wonder the Japanese consider eels an aphrodisiac.

The *unagi* at the sushi bar have not lived out their natural life. They start out as glass eels in the Sargasso or Philippine seas. They arrive at freshwater and begin to swim upriver. But everywhere they go—whether throughout Europe, across Asia, or up and down the East Coast of the United States—people with nets have lined the riverbanks. The people catch the baby eels in droves.

Fishermen refer to the eels at this stage as elvers. Buyers from Taiwan and China show up in Maine, South Carolina, and Florida and often pay hundreds of dollars a pound. During particularly lucrative years, people have made more money selling elvers than they could have made by selling heroin. Sometimes people use guns to secure the best fishing spots.

The buyers ship the elvers alive to huge farming operations back in Taiwan and China, where they are grown to market size. Then they slaughter them, broil the fillets, and slather them with soy sauce that's generally loaded with corn syrup, caramel color, and MSG. They vacuum-pack the fillets, freeze them, and ship them to sushi bars around the world.

Dedicated sushi chefs buy their eels live, and the best chefs stick to *anago,* saltwater eels. The saltwater eel is a close relative of the freshwater eel, and scientists think it undergoes a similar life cycle with a similar migration.

Eels taste best when the chef cuts them open while the animal is still squirming, because in eels, the taste component IMP breaks down rapidly. On Monday in class, Zoran told the students that at Tsukiji Fish Market in Tokyo, he and Toshi had eaten eel at a stand where, three feet away, a man filleted the animals alive.

"They actually have to pin it down," Zoran said. "Do you know what they use?"

"Hammer and nails?" one of the students asked.

"Almost. Here, I'll show you a picture." Zoran produced a stack of gruesome photos. "Eel is a true test of a sushi chef, because it is very difficult to prepare. They put them on the cutting board and put a big spike right through the eye."

Zoran put the photos away and showed the students a package of prepared eel from China.

"*Unagi* is easy, right? We just open the package and put it in the toaster." He held up his hand. "But *never* cut *unagi* at the sushi bar. You don't want customers to see you taking it out of the package."

Zoran tossed the pack of *unagi* back in the fridge. "But *anago,* we have to fillet and then cook." He sent one of the students into the kitchen to fetch a plastic bag.

Zoran set out a stack of bamboo colanders, and the student returned with the bag. Through the clear plastic, the contents looked like gray hoses, except that they had eyes. According to the label, the eels had come from Korea.

"Go on," Zoran said, "take them out of the plastic. I don't want to get my hands on those things!"

The student cut open the bag and caught a whiff. "Oh, man!"

Kate wrinkled her nose.

"Now," Zoran continued, "what's the first thing we need to do with them? *Wash!* They are slimy. Then we salt them, then fillet. Do *not* throw away the head. We'll use them—you'll see."

Zoran ripped open the package and emptied the eels into a large steel pan, along with their gooey white slime.

"Usually *anago* live in the bottom of sandy crevices. See, look at these teeth." He pulled open an eel's mouth. "They can be mean.

In Japan, when the yakuza kill you, they take your body to an eel farm and dump it in." When divers discover human corpses in rivers, eels are often nibbling on them.

Zoran gestured at the pile of eels. "Come on! I don't want to get my hands all bloody slimy!" Nobody moved. "Come on! We haven't got time, let's go!"

In the comic book *Sushi Chef Kirara's Job,* the young female chef Kirara impresses a male colleague by grabbing up slimy seawater eels and handling them without a trace of disgust. At the California Sushi Academy, one of the students now heeded Zoran's call and slowly stepped forward. It was Kate. She started lifting eels out of the pan. One by one, her classmates followed.

Each eel was a foot and a half long. They were thin and flat. They had dark brown backs, little fins behind the head, and white spots along the sides. They tapered to a pointy tail. Kate saw they'd been gutted. Whoever had packaged and frozen the eels in Korea had done the worst work already.

Zoran lifted one of the eels and laid it on his cutting board. Using his fillet knife he sliced off the dorsal fin that ran the length of the back. He cut off the head, the front fins, and the stomach lining, and he pulled out a few bones.

The students imitated Zoran. The greatest challenge was slicing off the long dorsal fin. It turned out to be a painstaking job. They hunched over their cutting boards.

In the kitchen, Zoran set a wide pan on the big burner and sautéed the eel heads in oil. Once they were nice and brown, he transferred them to the broiler. When the students finished filleting they filed into the kitchen. Zoran mixed water, sake, mirin, soy sauce, and sugar, and heated it on the stove. The students lowered their ribbons of eel flesh into the pot.

When the eels had cooked, Zoran hefted the steaming pot and deposited it on the kitchen table, next to a bowl of ice water. The students gathered round. Suddenly the situation looked unpleasantly familiar—rather like the time they had tenderized snapper skin.

This time, Zoran soaked his hands in the ice bath for a moment, then dunked them straight into the steaming water. He removed a ribbon of cooked eel. He held it gently, supporting it so the fragile flesh wouldn't fall apart. He laid it carefully in a tray. His hands were bright red. Steam billowed off them.

"Your turn," he said. "Hands in the ice, then pick up the *anago,* place it on the tray, and make sure they're *flat.* The meat is soft— that's why you must use your hands. They've got to be laid flat."

Marcos stepped forward. He'd been out late at a concert the night before, and was only just waking up. He soaked his hands in the ice water for a moment. Then he jabbed them into the pot and grabbed a steaming piece of eel. Now he was wide awake. He winced, then hurled the eel out onto the tray as if he were tossing a ball in a rugby match.

Kate stepped forward. When her hands hit the hot water, she yelped and chucked the eel out even faster than Marcos.

"Are you *kidding*?!" she blurted, shaking her red hands. "This is madness!"

The next student took his turn. He flinched and dropped his eel back into the pot. It broke in two. Another student went. He held on, and rotated over to the tray, yelling in pain the whole time—"Ugh! Argh!" Both students danced on their feet and shook their arms.

Zoran pulled out two more eels. He rearranged the students' pieces on the tray and yelled at them.

"Guys, which part of *flat* don't you understand?" Several ribbons of eel remained in the pot. "Come on, come on!" Zoran bellowed. "Get your five grand worth!"

The students struggled with the eels while Zoran dashed to the broiler and retrieved the heads. When the pot was empty of eels, he dropped the heads into the broth.

"We'll boil this for thirty minutes," he said. After that he would show the students how to make eel sauce. Americans love eel sauce—possibly because it's full of sugar. Most of them have no idea it contains eel brains.

"The thing about Western customers," Zoran complained, "is that you make them eel sushi with sauce already on it, and they *still* put it in the bloody soy sauce!"

Half an hour later, Zoran called the students back to the

kitchen. To the broth with the boiled heads he added more sugar, more sweet mirin, and corn syrup. Average sushi restaurants use mass-produced eel sauce. The better restaurants make it themselves, and the best have their own secret recipe.

"Then we simmer it for five to six hours," Zoran said.

He herded the students back to the classroom to set up the Monday lunch counter.

They opened the doors at noon. It was a gorgeous sunny day, and a warm breeze blew in. Disco played on the sound system. Soon the bar was full of customers and the students were busy making sushi.

Zoran strolled over to a stool on the far side of the classroom and sat down, one foot resting on the floor, the other dangling off the stool. He leaned his back against the wall. It was the first time he'd stopped moving all day. It was the last time he would see his students standing behind the sushi bar, serving customers.

Zoran watched Kate. She stood next to Takumi. She joked and laughed with the customers, while Takumi kept quiet. Together, they delivered a beautiful platter to a woman at the bar.

The woman sucked in her breath. "You guys do a great job!"

Someone switched the music from disco to funk. Kate goaded Takumi, trying to get him to dance. Finally he relented. He held a piece of sushi over his head and squeezed it while gyrating his hips, doing a sushi-making dance. Kate and the customers clapped. Takumi collapsed into embarrassed laughter. None of them had any idea that shy, quiet Takumi used to sing and dance in front of crowds of fans for a living.

Monday was the Hama Hermosa chef's day off. As usual, the restaurant was closed for dinner that night. Toshi and the other chefs took Zoran out for a meal before his return to Australia. Everyone was sick of sushi. They went out for Korean barbecue. They gathered around a communal fire in the center of their table and seared slabs of beef and pork, smoke billowing toward the ceiling.

37

TENTACLES OF
THE DEEP

*W*hen Kate had stepped up to the classroom table and grasped the slimy eels in front of her classmates, she had done so with an increasingly nuanced appreciation for levels of disgustingness. By now she had encountered enough blood and guts in the kitchen to keep things in perspective. Slimy eels were gross, but compared with the other things she'd run into recently, they weren't that bad.

In fact, Kate had been developing a list of disgustingness rankings. So far, the most disgusting thing all semester had been the live shrimp she'd ripped in half. Second-most disgusting was the huge smelly yellowtail with the load of salami-size guts. She still hadn't decided on third-most disgusting. Zoran was about to provide her with a couple of prime candidates.

"What is *octopus* in Japanese?" he asked the next morning. He answered his own question. "*Tako.* Is octopus poisonous at all?" Again he answered his own question. "Nope."

Yet some fishermen in Japan claim that on rare occasions, octopus accumulate nerve poison in the tips of their tentacles, similar to the poison in toxic blowfish. Jirō Ono, one of the most respected sushi chefs in Japan, never serves the tips of octopus legs.

"Octopus sushi is very hard to make," Zoran said. "The cutting technique is called *namagiri*—the 'wave cut.' That helps it stick to the rice. If you cut it too thick, it won't stick to the rice, either. Thin cuts are necessary for *tako* sushi."

Thin cuts are also necessary because octopus flesh is so chewy. Octopus and squid are invertebrates, so they have no bones. To compensate, they hold their muscles together with a tough matrix of reinforced collagen—three to five times more collagen than fish. The muscle fibers of octopus and squid are also thin and densely packed, and the animals don't store fat. Instead, they continue to build muscle, growing larger and larger the more they eat.

Octopus and squid once possessed shells. A few hundred million years ago, they looked much like today's nautilus, a cousin of the octopus and squid that still lives in a shell and that uses a bubble of gas inside the shell to stay afloat. Octopus, squid, and nautilus are called cephalopods, which means "head-foot."

Shells offered early cephalopods some protection. But new predators evolved, notably sharks and bony fishes, that drove cephalopods into deeper water. If a nautilus swims too deep, the pressure of the water overwhelms its gas bubble and its shell implodes. Shells turned out to be a liability.

The ancestors of octopus and squid lost their shells and gained the ability to escape into the depths. Instead of floating on a bubble of gas, they evolved into muscular swimmers, moving by squirting water through a siphon and, in the case of squid, flapping their fins like wings. All that swimming required more food, so they evolved into hunters with keen senses and fast reflexes. Transformed into aggressive predators, some of them returned to shallow water and multiplied.

From the refrigerator, Zoran produced a black lacquer tray. In the center sat a bundle of tightly curled pink tentacles, covered with white suction cups.

Zoran had tried to buy a live octopus, but outside of Tsukiji Fish Market in Tokyo, live octopus are hard to come by. Most sushi chefs buy their octopus pre-cooked, like this one. Japan consumes about two-thirds of all octopus caught around the world. Many of

them come from West Africa. But the best sushi chefs insist on pur-
chasing octopus alive so they can prepare it themselves. Had Zoran
succeeded in acquiring a live octopus, it would almost certainly
have taken first place on Kate's disgustingness list.

For starters, by the time a live octopus goes on sale, the fish-
erman or fishmonger has usually sliced out the animal's internal
organs. Despite losing its guts, the octopus continues to move
around in its tub of water. This is possible because each of an octopus's eight tentacles possesses its own brain. These ganglia receive
a single command from the primary brain—such as "grab that
crab"—and then execute an entire subroutine of action independent of the primary brain's control. The tentacles require their
own brains because their movements are so complex. Lacking a
skeletal structure, each tentacle is capable of infinite degrees and
directions of movement.

Jirō Ono, the respected sushi chef in Japan, sets the bar for
sushi preparation techniques. After he returns to his sushi shop
with a still-moving octopus, he gouges out the eyes with a knife.
Then, to soften the animal's tough flesh, he gives the octopus a
full-body massage.

The animal continues to writhe under Ono's hands as he mas-
sages it, and after about ten minutes the octopus oozes slime from
its skin. Gradually the tentacles stop moving. Ono gently cleans
off the slime and continues the massage for another thirty minutes, until the tentacles become fully relaxed and no more slime
appears.

Now that he has softened the octopus's tissue, he hangs the
animal by its head from a hook and dips the tentacles repeatedly
in boiling water, until the legs spread out and curl up, as he puts
it, like a flower. Then he drops the whole animal in the water and
boils it for about fifteen minutes.

In the comic book *Sushi Chef Kirara's Job,* during a televised
cooking contest, Kirara prepares a live octopus using a similar
technique. The judges and audience regard the process with revulsion, but Kirara defends the technique as the only way to tenderize
the flesh.

Less often, sushi chefs serve raw octopus as well, a preparation
called *nama tako.* Zoran had returned a few times from the fish

markets in L.A. with a long, slippery raw octopus leg. Before serving it, he pounded it with a peeled giant radish. The pounding and the natural enzymes in the radish helped soften the flesh.

Now Zoran picked up the pink cooked octopus and pressed his hands into the animal's head. Out popped its beak-like mouth.

Kate's head snapped back.

Zoran shoved it toward Marcos and yelled. "Alien!"

He laughed and tossed the bundle of curled tentacles and suckers onto his cutting board. He decapitated it with a couple of quick incisions, then whacked two of the tentacles off the bundle of legs. He pressed one of the spirals of pink and white flesh to the cutting board and sliced into it on an angle. As he cut, he twisted his wrist from side to side, so that his knife traced a zig-zag through the flesh. He pulled off the slice—it was an oval strip of milky-white flesh encircled by a deep purple rim. He showed the students the wave pattern he'd created across the surface. Then he tipped his knife toward the ceiling and tapped the slice all over with the heel of the blade, poking small dents in the rubbery flesh. Finally, he squeezed it onto a *nigiri*.

"When you go to get a job," Zoran said, "if I were testing you, I'd ask you to make *tako* sushi."

He set the octopus aside.

"Also, we have squid."

"*Ika*," Zoran said, using the Japanese word for squid. "Not calamari—completely different! They are ugly. But very good to eat. Though not much taste."

Like fish, cephalopods counteract the osmotic pressure of the salty ocean by filling their cells partly with free amino acids, but mostly with the amine TMAO, which is tasteless. Another component they contain in substantial amounts is taurine, popularly thought to impart strength and virility, and often obtained from ox bile. Taurin was an ingredient in the Red Bull and Monster Energy drinks that Kate liked to sip in class.

"How many legs does *ika* have?" Zoran asked.

Kate guessed twelve. Marcos said eight.

"You'll see in a minute," Zoran said. "*Ika* is so chewy that we score the piece in a cross-hatch pattern. Today we're going to do a sashimi arrangement. See how you guys do."

Zoran darted into the kitchen and returned with five packages. He handed out four of the packages. He ripped the last one open and extracted a squid. Its skin was a fine patchwork of small brown dots.

Cephalopods have the most extraordinary skin in the animal kingdom. Squid skin contains tiny elastic sacs full of different pigments, as well as arrays of tiny mirrors. In a relaxed state, the sacs are closed and don't reveal the color inside. By contracting certain muscles, the squid can expand some sacs and not others, and flip their mirrors on or off, revealing a wild array of patterns and colors. Most cephalopods are able to take a quick look around them and instantly transform their skin to match the colors and patterns of their surroundings, for camouflage. In the excitement of mating, squid also flash dramatic patterns and colors across their bodies. Some species even light up. Japanese researchers have used squid skin as a model for a new polymer for computer display screens.

"How many legs did you say they have?" Zoran counted out eight. Two appendages remained. "These two aren't legs, they're tentacles."

Squid hunt by lunging at crustaceans and fish, grabbing them with their two long tentacles and wrapping up the struggling prey with their eight legs. The legs are covered with bowl-shaped suckers armed with tiny teeth that dig into the prey. There is no escape.

The mouth of a squid, like that of an octopus, is located in the center of the legs and is nearly identical to a parrot's beak. The squid uses it to chomp bites out of its immobilized prey. Like bears feasting on salmon, squid in a school of fish often take only a few bites before tossing away one fish and snatching another.

"We cut below the eyes to get the tentacles off." Zoran sliced off the two tentacles and tossed them in the trash. He cut off the legs in pairs. He yanked out the head and guts, then he grabbed something else—he tugged and tugged. Finally, out popped a transparent spear. This was all that remained of what had, hundreds of millions of years ago, been a shell. A squid was, in a sense, a highly sophisticated clam, turned inside out.

He peeled the brown skin from the body, using a towel for grip. All that remained was a glistening white piece of flesh, shaped like a cone. He sliced the cone open and spread it out to make a flat triangle.

"Now, remove all the skin on the inside." He wiped it off with a towel, then cut off the bottom edge and carefully pulled away the inner skin. "It's up to you how to divide it into slices for sushi, to get the best yield."

Humans aren't the only ones who like to eat raw squid. Sharks devour squid. Salmon eat squid and octopus. Swordfish have a unique approach to catching squid. They race into a school of squid and slash around wildly with their bills, then swim back through the carnage, gobbling up parts. Squid themselves even eat squid.

Mackerel eat small squid, and tuna eat big ones. Large tuna are one of the few fish in the sea fast enough to overtake big squid as they jet away. In Japan, some sushi connoisseurs believe that the best tuna are caught in the northern Japan Sea, where the tuna feast on squid instead of fish, giving the tuna's flesh a unique taste.

Squid are one of the few marine creatures that humans appear not to have wiped out by overfishing. Probably that's because humans have wiped out huge numbers of the fish that eat squid. According to some scientists, all wild fish populations will have disappeared by the year 2050. Squid could turn out to be the last wild-caught species that will be served in sushi.

Each student took a squid. Kate stuck her fingers under the edge of her squid's mantle. She twisted, then pulled. The body of the squid broke away from the head and legs, spilling guts onto her cutting board.

Kate pondered this. She examined the tentacles, the big squid eye looking at her, and the spilled innards on her cutting board. Squid, she decided, definitely qualified for the rank of third-most disgusting in her disgustingness list. She felt better already. She'd handled worse. She was becoming a pro.

Kate turned to Zoran and pointed at her tentacles. "Cut below the eye?"

Zoran nodded. "Yup."

Kate set her blade on the squid's head, just below the eye. She stuck out her lower lip. She started to cut, but stopped and yelped. "Ew!" She took a deep breath and forced herself to continue. But she couldn't watch. She turned and looked off into space while slicing through the rest of the squid. She'd sharpened her knife again, and it severed the squid easily.

Zoran showed the students a shrink-wrapped package.

"Most sushi bars use this—frozen *ika,* already prepared, already scored. Squid's not so popular for Western customers. They don't usually order it too much. But if you have really fresh squid and you serve it to them, they love it."

While the students worked on their squid, Zoran constructed an ingenious platter of squid sashimi. It had layered square towers, rolled spirals, draped sheets, and clever garnishes. Where his earlier sashimi displays had resembled Zen gardens, this one was an avant-garde sculpture park.

The students practiced making platters of their own. Kate puttered with her squid. She used the white body flesh to squeeze together two *nigiri,* and then she hid slices of perilla leaf between the squid and the rice. She built three more *nigiri,* each topped with bunched perilla leaf and the tip of a squid tentacle, tied down with a belt of nori. She scored another section of flesh and rolled it into a spiral around a bunch of perilla. She arranged her work on a ceramic platter in an asymmetric formation. She added a bit of radish sprout for garnish and stepped back.

It was gorgeous. It was *Japanese*-style gorgeous. Kate had combined her own aesthetic imagination with Japanese tradition and achieved the sushi Zen that had been eluding her. She couldn't put her finger on it, but she knew that she had produced something at a new level of mastery.

She stayed after class and sharpened her knife.

Upstairs in the restaurant offices, the news was not good. Toshi had called together all his chefs for a staff meeting. Afterwards the men filed out, looking grim. Not enough customers had come back, and not enough of Toshi's charisma had returned. The restaurant was losing too much money to stay in business.

38

GIANT CLAM

On Wednesday, Zoran began class with an announcement.

"You have a test on Friday," he said. That would be his last day. "You'll be tested on knives, uniform, sashimi, and *nigiri*." Toshi would administer the test.

Kate's knife-sharpening skills had improved. She'd achieved an element of Zen with her sashimi. The question that remained—for her and for the rest of the students—was whether their *nigiri*-making skills would pass muster with Toshi. On Friday they would find out.

Zoran moved on to the day's lesson.

"Today we have *mirugai*," he said. "What's *mirugai* in English?" He wrote the English names on the whiteboard: giant clam, geoduck, horse clam.

"These are all the same thing!" Zoran seemed cheerful. "There are probably more names."

Indeed, there are. For example, "Nature's dildo." But Zoran didn't go there. "Guys," he said, "I'm being politically correct today."

From the fridge, Zoran extracted a long, erect, fleshy shaft. One bulbous end was sheathed in a protective shell. Again, Zoran said nothing. Other commentators throughout history have been less restrained. For example, one wrote that "the geoduck looks pretty much like a long, thick, monster cock."

"*Mirugai* are bloody expensive," Zoran said. "Not too many left in Japan now—mostly fished them out. This one is from Washington, farmed."

In the 1970s, the Department of Fish and Wildlife in the state of Washington encouraged people to harvest geoducks because the mudflats of Puget Sound were overrun with the things. But few people were interested in digging them up. The clams fetched ten cents a pound at best.

Originally, Native Americans harvested geoducks, and white settlers did too, using them as cheap chowder meat. A Canadian folk song pays tribute to the geoduck, in the form of a lament from a fellow whose girlfriend has left him after discovering a particularly fine specimen. Among scientists, geoducks go by a couple of different names—usually *Panopea abrupta,* but sometimes also *Panopea generosa.* The folk song makes no mention of which one the lady prefers but the answer seems obvious.

While geoducks may have provided a degree of pleasure, in chowder or otherwise, few people knew them as an expensive delicacy. Then harvesters in Washington heard about sushi. They began shipping geoducks to Japan, and by the mid-1980s, as sushi took root in the United States, prices for geoducks shot up. Poachers supplied a thriving black market and threatened each other with physical violence. In 1998, Washington State authorities clamped down and convicted several criminals for clam rustling.

Aquaculture operations now grow geoducks in large numbers. In addition to the sushi market, buyers from Hong Kong and Shanghai pay top dollar for geoducks for Chinese cuisine. In North America, apart from connoisseurs of sushi and fans of casual West Coast fare, most folks still haven't warmed to the geoduck's charms, at least in the kitchen.

Zoran held up a slip of paper that had been in the bag with the clam. "You must keep this ticket for three months. If someone eats a giant clam and gets sick, and they trace it back to you, you've got a lawsuit coming—unless you have this ticket."

Clams are susceptible to red tides, especially during summer months. These blooms of toxic algae can produce nerve poisons a thousand times more powerful than cyanide. Many clams and related shellfish also lose flavor in summer, as they deplete themselves through spawning. In Japanese, a traditional saying goes, "Not even dogs eat summer clams."

Zoran put the ticket on the table and laid his hand on the huge clam. The shell was nearly 6 inches long and the protruding shaft added another 8 inches. Left alone in the wild, geoducks can live for 150 years and weigh up to 15 pounds. The part that looks like an erect penis is actually a sort of snorkel, called a siphon. The clam lives deep in the mud and sticks its snorkel up to the surface of the mud, where it sucks in food and water and squirts out waste.

"*Mirugai* is not a good product for the sushi bar," Zoran explained, "because it must be alive to be eaten raw. The max shelf life is three to four days. Not many people like the taste. It's a strong, oceany taste. Chewy. Crispy."

Yet in old Tokyo, clams of various kinds were exceedingly popular sushi toppings. While fish and cephalopods balance the osmotic pressure of the sea mostly with the tasteless amine TMAO, along with some amino acids, clams rely completely on tasty amino acids, especially glutamate, which produces the flavor of *umami*. And like cephalopods, clams can't store energy as fat, so any excess food they consume goes to the production of a variety of additional flavor-producing amino acids. Generally, clams are more flavorful than fish. And the saltier the water, the greater the flavor.

"The meat must be firm," Zoran said, "and it should move when you slap it." He laid the clam on his cutting board and slapped the tip of the long siphon. It writhed. "But if you keep slapping and moving, slapping and moving, it will get tired, and die quicker." A few of the male students snickered. "Butter knife is the easiest way to open it," Zoran said. "Watch out—sometimes when you do this they'll pee on you."

He pried the clam open and scraped inside the shell to detach the organs. They looked like bulbous testicles.

"Guts and nuts!" Zoran said, decorum forgotten. He held up

the defenseless clam, the siphon drooping downward. "Can't use these." He ripped off the parts that looked like testicles and tossed them in the trash. The men in the class looked stoic.

In the kitchen, Zoran dunked the clam in boiling water. Marcos winced.

"Is it still alive?" Marcos asked.

"Yup."

After five seconds Zoran yanked it out and dropped it in an ice bath. Back in the classroom, he pulled out a knife.

Zoran held his knife at the base of the siphon and, without apparent empathy, cut the thing right off. He skinned it, then pressed it sideways onto the cutting board and inserted the point of his knife into the end.

"Every time you move it, it gets upset," Zoran said. Even detached, it was still alive. "Don't move it too much. Usually when we serve *mirugai* sushi, we slap it right before serving it, so the customer can see it move."

He made an incision down the length of the siphon to butterfly it open, then carried it to the sink and scrubbed it under running water. "Gotta get the sand out. All mollusks have sand in them. Sand is worse than bones or scales in your sushi."

Back at his cutting board, Zoran sliced the opened siphon into two long halves and loaded them onto *neta* trays. He lifted one of the sections into the air and dropped it on his cutting board. It writhed again. He flipped it upside down and carved off thin slices for sushi. The muscle responded to each pass of the knife, as though it were trying to wriggle away.

"When you try to cut, he's contracting to make it harder for you," Zoran said. "Hell, yeah, it bloody hurts! Shit! He's like, 'What did I ever do to you?'" He tenderized the slice by tapping it with the heel of his blade.

Zoran handed the two halves of the siphon to the students, one half for each side of the table. The students practiced making sushi with the clam. Kate sliced off two pieces and passed it on.

"Who likes *mirugai*?" Zoran asked. Only a few of the students raised their hands. "Wow, that's it?" Zoran said. "Tsukiji Fish Market, 6:00 a.m., a meal of beer and *mirugai*—so good! But you *must* tenderize it. If you don't, you're going to be chewing like a cow."

Zoran eyed the students. "C'mon, taste the *mirugai* if you haven't yet. I don't care if you spit it out. If you're going to be at the sushi bar, you should know what taste you're shooting for."

Kate had no interest in eating an undulating clam that looked like a penis, but under Zoran's eye she sliced a tiny corner off one of her *nigiri*. It felt like chewing on a rubber band. Zoran watched her. She knew he was waiting for her to spit it out. She swallowed.

39

FINAL FISH

The last day of Zoran's marathon of fish lessons dawned crisp and clear. A fresh ocean breeze blew in from the Pacific.

Today the class had arrived at the culmination of contemporary sushi. The Japanese had long disparaged the fish for today's lesson as poor man's food—a *gezakana,* or "inferior fish." Even North Americans had been known to discard trophy-winning specimens of this fish at the town dump because no one would eat it.

But now the fish's status in Japan has risen to *kōkyū sakana*— "high-class fish." North Americans fall over themselves to sell the best specimens to Japan and then buy them back at astronomical prices. At which point, they fall over themselves again to eat them.

"Somebody tell me a type of tuna," Zoran said. He wrote the Japanese word for tuna—*maguro*—on the whiteboard.

"Bluefin," the students called out. "Bigeye." "Yellowfin." Zoran nodded. Sushi chefs serve all three, but bluefin is king.

A bluefin tuna can grow to weigh 1,500 pounds. Bluefin inhabit cold waters and their bodies can be up to 15 percent fat, depending on the region and season. Bigeye are smaller, and live in temperate and tropical waters. Yet they swim deep, where the water is relatively chilly, and thus can accumulate up to 8 percent fat. Yellowfin tuna are about the same size as bigeye. They inhabit warmer waters, and accumulate only about 2 percent fat.

"There's different types of *maguro* meat," Zoran said. He wrote

the English names on the whiteboard, with their Japanese counterparts:

- red meat—*akami*
- medium fatty—*chūtoro*
- fatty—*toro*
- very fatty—*ōtoro*

Toro got its name from "*torokeru*," the Japanese word to describe
something melting. The *chū* in c*hūtoro* means "middle," and the *ō* in
ōtoro means "very."

Apart from the question of fat, all tuna flesh is red meat.
Although some tuna have shiny skin, sushi chefs categorize them
as red fish. Bluefin in particular are the reddest. They are also the
fastest fish in the sea.

Bluefin tuna appeared in the ocean as recently as 1 or 2 million
years ago. For a fish, their circulatory systems have attained a new
level of complexity and sophistication. Like mammals and birds,
bluefin are warm-blooded. Warm-blooded creatures routinely
move and react faster because crucial chemical reactions in the
body can occur more quickly in a heated environment. This is
especially valuable to a predator.

In the cold waters of the ocean, however, retaining body heat
is a challenge. Most of the warmth a fish could generate inside its
body would be lost when the blood is exposed to the cold water,
as the blood passes through the fish's gills to collect oxygen. As a
result, most of the fish in the sea have remained cold-blooded.

To become warm-blooded, bluefin developed an elaborate
counter-current heat exchanger inside their bodies. As warm blood
leaves the bluefin's muscles and heads for the gills to pick up more
oxygen, the veins it travels through run directly alongside the
veins carrying the colder blood returning from the gills. The cold
blood absorbs most of the heat from the warm blood and carries
the warmth back into the body. By the time the low-oxygen blood
arrives at the gills, it's already cold. The bluefin's heat exchanger is
so efficient that it retains 97 percent of the animal's heat.

Bluefin tuna can swim faster, see better, digest more food, and react more quickly than other fish. Scientists estimate that bluefin can swim at speeds of 50 miles an hour. But there's a price. They can cruise at a more leisurely pace, but they must always swim fast enough to ensure a sufficient flow of oxygen across their gills to fuel their system. If they swim too slowly, they will suffocate.

For bluefin, the distinction between fast-twitch muscle and slow-twitch muscle is largely irrelevant. Instead of having a thin ribbon of slow-twitch muscle that runs down each side of the fish under the skin, the bluefin's slow-twitch muscles have migrated inward—where they will stay warm—and have swelled into massive, high-output engines that produce fast-twitch performance.

And unlike most fish, which flex their spines when they swim, tuna remain stiff, directing 90 percent of the thrust their engines generate into the movement of the tail fin alone, rather like a torpedo. The stiffness of the swimming tuna is so well known in Japan that the word *maguro* is used to describe a woman who is stiff during sex.

Bluefin hunt in packs like wolves, in formation. When they locate a school of small fish or squid, fifteen or so bluefin attack together at high speed in a parabola, shaped like a mouth. The parabolic formation acts as a dragnet to concentrate the prey, but it also allows the bluefin to attain higher speeds as they push off each other's wakes.

To supply the vast quantities of oxygen necessary to fuel the bluefin's massive engines, the tuna pumps its muscles and blood full of myoglobin, the iron-red protein that transports oxygen. That's why tuna meat is so red.

When prey are abundant, bluefin store up fat for future use. Fatty cuts of bluefin—*toro*—became a popular sushi topping in Japan beginning in the late 1950s. Sushi chefs cut the highest-grade *ōtoro* from the forward section of the bluefin's belly. *Ōtoro* can be as much as 40 percent fat. Sushi chefs distinguish two types of *ōtoro*. *Jabara*—literally, "snake's stomach"—is the fattiest part, and comes from the bottom of the belly. *Shimofuri*—which means "fallen frost" and can refer to any red meat marbled with fat—is rarer, and comes from the upper belly.

"Now, *toro* doesn't just mean from the belly," Zoran said. "You can get *toro* from other parts of the fish." He drew a diagram on the board.

Sushi chefs cut the mid-grade fatty cuts, *chūtoro,* from the rear and upper sections of the belly, but also from the upper and outer portions of the back. This meat is 15 to 20 percent fat.

Toward the center of the fish, insulated by the fat, resides the *akami,* or red meat, the primary engine that continuously drives the fish through the water. Chefs find that the best-tasting *akami* lies between halfway and two-thirds of the way to the tail. Here, the muscle gets more exercise than the muscle toward the head, but contains less fiber than the muscle at the tail.

Hard-core sushi aficionados will still choose a good piece of red meat over *toro.* They consider the fattiness of *toro* to be too simplistic a pleasure. By contrast, appreciating a fine cut of *akami* takes experience.

Either way, getting a fine cut of tuna from the sea to the sushi bar isn't a simple matter.

"Ninety percent of tuna," Zoran said, "when they catch it, they bleed it, take the head off, and flash-freeze it."

Like salmon, much of the tuna at the sushi bar has been frozen, but with more elaborate technology—even when sushi chefs say it is fresh.

Regular freezing inhibits bacteria, which is good, but it creates other problems, particularly in the form of ice. During regular freezing, the water in animal flesh migrates out of the cells and forms ice crystals between them. Since water expands when its molecules rearrange themselves into ice, crystallization can crush nearby cell structures, turning the flesh mushy. Also, when the proteins inside the cells lose their watery environment, they unfold and bond to each other, forming a tough, spongy mass.

To prevent this, the Japanese fishing industry has developed shipboard "superfreezing" techniques for tuna so that fishing boats can remain longer at sea. Fishermen pack the tuna in artificial snow and then immerse them in liquid nitrogen, which rapidly reduces the core temperature of the fish to −70°F. The water molecules don't have time to migrate and crystallize, so the cellular structures and proteins are protected. The goal is not much different from that of cryonics—the science of deep-freezing human bodies in the hope of future revival. The flesh of superfrozen tuna can taste and feel almost completely fresh for up to two years after harvest.

At Tsukiji Fish Market in Tokyo, the daily tuna sale begins around 5:00 a.m. in a brightly lit hanger. The concrete floor is hidden by a layer of swirling mist. Visible in the mist are rows upon rows of frosty white pods. They look like a field of alien eggs, fresh from some sci-fi cryonic freezer and ready for hatching. These are flash-frozen, high-quality tuna, solid as rocks. Their fins, gills, and guts have been removed, but otherwise they are intact.

"There are some tuna that do come in fresh," Zoran told the students. Some of the best come from New England. "They are in coffins and are ridiculously expensive. How much do you think tuna costs?"

"Thirteen dollars a pound?" Marcos said.

"Thirteen dollars a pound?!" Zoran yelled, incredulous. "At Tsukiji in 2001, one 445-pound *maguro* sold for $173,000!"

"Wait," Marcos said, not comprehending. "A hundred and seventy-three dollars?"

"One hundred seventy-three *thousand* dollars," Zoran said. That worked out to nearly $400 per pound. To be sure, that had been an absurdly extravagant bid, for the best of the best—a winter bluefin caught in the waters near Japan, a type of fish that accounts for less than 1 percent of the global tuna catch. Moreover, the purchase had been the buyer's way of celebrating the first day of business in the new millennium, with an ostentatious show of wealth.

Even the ridiculously expensive fresh tuna, though, have a drawback—it's possible for them to be *too* fresh.

After an animal dies, its muscles still live. Muscle cells contain a local supply of fuel, in the form of crystals of stored sugar called glycogen. Enzymes in the muscle continue to use and break down this fuel. Eating a fish too soon after death is like eating it while it's still alive. The muscles are still functional. They are firmly bound together and remain relatively tasteless because the proteins have yet to disassemble into amino acids. Fancy restaurants and sushi shops that serve "fresh kill" sushi from tanks of live fish are not doing their customers any favors. The only sea creatures worth eating straight from the fish tank are eels, squid, and some shellfish—such as giant clam.

When the glycogen fuel runs out, the muscles finally fail, and the fibers lock into place. The muscles become hard and stiff, and are even worse to eat. This state is called rigor mortis.

But the enzymes in the muscle keep functioning, and begin to digest the proteins that make up the muscles themselves. The meat softens, and the proteins break down into the smaller compounds that provide flavor, such as glutamate and IMP. Beef doesn't become soft and flavorful until it's been sitting around for a couple of weeks after slaughter. Beef producers often age their meat even longer, to allow more IMP to develop.

Fish generally need between eight and twenty-four hours after death to develop flavor. Fish flesh ages much more rapidly than the flesh of terrestrial animals—and spoils more quickly—because fish are cold-blooded. The enzymes in fish function well at temperatures similar to those in a refrigerator. By contrast, the enzymes of warm-blooded mammals slow down when the flesh cools.

Bluefin tuna, however, are warm-blooded and very large, so after they're killed they take longer to age than other fish. Generally, bluefin don't reach peak flavor until about a week after death. The Japanese have a nickname for bluefin—*shibi*. It means "four days." In the age before refrigeration, when someone caught a bluefin, he buried it in the ground for four days before eating it.

For the sushi chef, bluefin epitomize the fundamental contradiction of serving raw fish. If the meat doesn't age long enough, it won't develop sufficient taste. But once rigor mortis is past, the meat rapidly loses firmness and texture. With fish, it is nearly impossible to achieve perfect flavor and perfect texture at the same time. The sushi chef is locked in a delicate dance of timing with armies of enzymes. Instead of cooking, he practices the art of compromise.

There are other challenges to tuna. If a big tuna puts up a long struggle before death, its core temperature can rise so high immediately after death that its meat can literally cook itself, denaturing the proteins even before rigor mortis sets in.

The myoglobin in tuna flesh is also highly susceptible to oxidization. When a molecule of myoglobin loses an electron, it turns from bright red to brown. Much of the tuna served at sushi bars in the United States is red only because distributors have gassed it with carbon monoxide, which creates carboxymyoglobin, another bright red molecule. The Japanese government has outlawed this practice, fearing that it could mask spoiled fish.

However, the greatest challenge regarding the bluefin doesn't involve killing them but, rather, keeping them alive. Bluefin mature slowly. That means fishermen can easily decimate bluefin populations. Demand for sushi has taken a severe toll on bluefin around the world, though just how badly they are overfished remains a subject of debate. Environmental groups now recommend that people avoid eating bluefin altogether.

Bluefin ranching operations capture bluefin from the ocean and fatten them in large pens for high-profit, year-round harvesting. In Australia, tuna ranchers have become some of the country's richest men. But ranching does nothing to reduce pressure on the wild population—it may even make the situation worse. In contrast, bigeye tuna mature faster and so their populations are more resilient to fishing, as are yellowfin.

Meanwhile, researchers are learning to breed bluefin in captivity, and are even considering the use of surrogate parents for bluefin to increase production of bluefin eggs. So far, scientists have succeeded in implanting primordial trout cells into female salmon, causing the salmon to produce not salmon eggs, but trout eggs. When fertilized by trout sperm, the trout eggs from the salmon grow into healthy trout. This could be good news for trout populations. Salmon reach sexual maturity more quickly than trout, so as surrogate parents, they can produce trout eggs more quickly than trout can.

The researchers have suggested that the same sort of arrangement could produce bluefin eggs. Either way, the mass production of factory-farmed bluefin, from egg to fattened adult fish, may yet replace the supply of both wild and ranched tuna—a sad fate indeed for such a majestic, free-swimming fish.

What type of fish might qualify as a surrogate mother for a giant bluefin?

Bluefin's little cousin, the mackerel.

40

CARVING THE MOUNTAIN

"Now," Zoran said, "how are you going to get a 445-pound tuna into the *neta* case?"

Giant tuna are the biggest of the tubular fishes. For the purposes of sushi, filleting a tuna proceeds according to the "five-piece breakdown." Only the tools are different. At the fish markets, professional cutters first attack the huge fish with industrial table saws and knives the size of swords.

"No one buys a whole tuna—too much meat," Zoran said. "You can ask for sections: semi-back meat, midsection meat, belly meat. You can ask for just *toro*—for seventy or eighty dollars a pound. Or you can ask for a whole side of fish, including *toro*, in which case the price comes down."

For today's class, Zoran had purchased an entire quarter fillet. He stepped to the refrigerator. He looked over his shoulder at the female student who was pregnant.

"You know, bluefin is the worst to eat if you're pregnant. They have the most mercury."

In the 1950s, around the quiet bayside town of Minamata in southern Japan, cats began dancing uncontrollably in the streets. Soon hundreds of people suffered from numb limbs, slurred speech, constricted vision, and uncontrollable movements. Some people's bodies became locked into contortions; other people tore at their own skin. Women gave birth to a generation of crippled children.

Eventually the "disease" was traced to fish. The fish were full of mercury. A nearby factory had been dumping its waste in the bay.

Today, coal-burning power plants emit much of the mercury produced in the United States. Airborne mercury can travel from a factory smokestack halfway around the world. Underwater volcanoes also pump mercury into the sea.

Like PCBs, mercury spreads upward through the food chain and "bio-accumulates" in high-level predators. Bluefin tuna are the highest-level fish predator of all. Women who are pregnant, or who could become pregnant, shouldn't eat bluefin, nor should children, and others need to limit their intake. Even canned tuna poses hazards.

"Do we have bluefin today?" the pregnant woman asked.

"No, we can't afford bluefin!" Zoran said. "I got bigeye. I might even get in trouble for that."

Zoran pulled out a 3-foot-long package wrapped in white paper. It had been flown in from Hawaii. He peeled away the paper, then a layer of green cellophane.

"Like Christmas!" he said.

Inside lay a dark red hunk of muscle. The long piece of meat bulged near the center and was tapered at one end. It was triangular in cross section—13.8 pounds of solid flesh.

"It smells," Zoran said. "Can you smell that? I can. The skin's still on." He unwrapped it all the way. "Oh, good tuna." At the bottom, against the skin, it had a nice pale fatty belly.

"Normally only the head chef cuts tuna," Zoran said. At Hama Hermosa, not even Zoran was allowed to cut much tuna for the sushi bar. The job belonged to Tetsu, and sometimes fell to the other chefs who had more experience than Zoran. Today provided a rare opportunity for Zoran to work with a full fillet of tuna. He would surrender most of that opportunity to his students.

Zoran grabbed a *neta* tray and set it atop the meat, the end of the tray flush with the head edge. He reminded the class that a *neta* tray was three palm widths long. He removed the tray and measured off three four-finger widths, then lowered the blade of his knife onto the fillet. He pressed the knife into the flesh and sawed gently straight down. At the end, he exerted extra pressure and cut through the skin. He lifted the huge hunk of meat onto a metal tray.

Zoran handed the knife to Marcos. "Your turn."

Marcos measured off three more palm widths. He took a breath and cut straight down. Everyone watched.

"Good," Zoran said.

Zoran retrieved his knife and made the third and last cut. By now he'd entered the tapering tail section, so the hunk was squatter and smaller. After that, only a little triangle of meat remained, just a few inches long. Zoran explained that toward the tail, the meat contains more fiber and fetches a lower price. He stowed the hunks of meat on the metal tray.

Zoran hefted the first hunk back onto his cutting board. The cross section was the shape of a rugged mountain peak. Across the wide base of the mountain, flat against the cutting board at the bottom, the flesh against the skin was pale pink and full of fat, especially on the end near the belly. Rising toward the summit the meat turned darker red, and lines of muscle fiber traced U-shaped curves through the cross section like geologic layers.

On one side, the peak was so purple that it was nearly black. This was the core of the tuna's oxygen-burning, heat-generating machinery, where huge quantities of myoglobin proteins had concentrated.

"Bloodline," Zoran said. "If you leave the skin and bloodline on, the next day it will stink."

He carved the dark edge of flesh off and chucked it in the trash. Then he turned his knife flat and sliced off the rest of the summit.

Zoran held up this piece of dark red meat. It had been the innermost edge of the tuna's muscle, snug against the spine.

"Very soft meat," Zoran said. "Usually not good for sushi. Okay for *tekka-maki*"—thin tuna rolls.

Zoran examined the flattened mountaintop. He peered at a circular irregularity in the surface of the meat.

"Tuna get a kind of ringworm," Zoran said, pointing. "You don't want to serve that. Right around the ringworm the meat gets watery."

Parasitic worms don't make it into tuna as often as they do into smaller fish because tuna tend to swim in deep water, far from shore. But sushi chefs have to stay on guard. Zoran cut out the worm and tossed it in the trash.

The next step was to slice the hunk of meat into smaller blocks for the *neta* case. This presented fresh challenges. A sushi chef wants some blocks to consist entirely of fatty flesh, or *toro,* for which he can charge more. He wants other blocks to consist entirely of plain old red meat, or *akami,* which sell for less.

Moreover, when the chef cuts his little slices off at the sushi bar, he wants the little slices to come out in a nifty rhomboid shape with lots of pretty fiber lines running across it from side to side, rather than a few long lines running end to end.

To achieve these goals required reverse thinking. Sushi chefs had settled on some informal rules. As usual, they involved measuring things with fingers.

Zoran measured down the side of the truncated mountain in three-finger increments. The slabs of *neta* he was aiming to cut stood vertically inside the cliff face. Three fingers would be a little shorter than, say, salmon *neta,* but later, when he cut slices from the *neta* for *nigiri,* he would cut on a diagonal so they would measure the standard four fingers. Diagonal slices of tuna were more attractive than simple rectangles.

Satisfied, he inserted his blade sideways into the mountainside, three finger widths from the top, and cut horizontally across the mountain. He removed this block, leaving a flat expanse where the mountaintop had been. He repeated the procedure. The next block he cut off closer to the base; it was wider.

A final block remained, roughly three fingers high. The belly edge was pale and riddled with fat—*toro* material. The rest was pink with some fat—good *chūtoro.*

The horizontal blocks were still too big for a *neta* tray. Zoran sliced straight down into the last block, measuring off the width of one thumb each time. This was a little shy of the two-finger width of a *nigiri* slice, but the chef would slice the *neta* at an angle from vertical. The slices would come off wide enough, and again, they would look more attractive.

Zoran cut the new *neta* free from the skin. They were the right length, thanks to the initial cuts. Some were all *toro,* some were all *chūtoro*. The upper-level blocks would be *akami*. The grain of the muscle fiber ran across each *neta* from side to side.

Zoran pointed at the leftover skin. Bits of flesh remained on the fibrous surface.

"That's where your spicy tuna comes from," he said. Later, someone would scrape the meat off with a spoon.

Two big hunks of tuna remained. Each was a formidable mountain of flesh. Zoran placed one on the cutting board of the student next to Kate. The other he placed in front of Kate.

"Okay," Zoran said, "now it's your turn." He paused, his face serious. "*Please* ask me if you need help." Bigeye was not the best tuna, but today's fillet was still worth $200. "This is the time where I need you to not be shy, and call me if you need help."

Kate stood in front of her mountain of meat. Nothing so big had ever sat on her cutting board. She looked at the huge hunk of tuna, then she looked at Zoran, and then she looked back at the huge hunk of tuna.

In the comic book *Sushi Chef Kirara's Job,* the young female chef Kirara never works with large hunks of expensive tuna. She deliberately avoids them. She is trying to restore the traditional sushi of old Tokyo to its former glory, and she prefers to work with the more modest fish and shellfish that were popular before the rise of tuna. Kirara's arch-rival in the sushi-making competitions—the muscle-bound male chef Sakamaki—shows off by cutting the largest and most expensive blocks of tuna he can find.

Kate lifted her knife and whittled at the bloodline down one side of the meat. She peeled off a piece of the purple goo. The bloodline was deep and irregular, and she'd only removed the outside edge. Zoran stepped in and carved out the rest. Then he left her alone.

Kate cocked her head to the side and sliced horizontally into the summit, removing the peak of soft meat. That was the easy part. She measured three fingers down. She took a breath.

Kate sliced into the mountain from the side again. She cut carefully, moving her knife in a straight horizontal line. The block of meat came off. She laid it to the side. She handed the rest of the mountain to the next student.

Zoran examined what remained of the block.

"Oh," came Zoran's voice, "that's not straight." He shook his head. "Oh noooo."

Kate had cut in a horizontal line, but had not held her knife flat. The tip had been lower than the handle. The top of the decapitated tuna mountain was not level.

"Oh dear," Zoran said, shaking his head some more, "it's going to be hard to fix *this*."

Kate shrank down inside her chef's jacket.

"Sorry," she said, her voice tiny.

While the students practiced with the hunks of tuna, Zoran marinated the soft top cuts of inner flesh in soy sauce, just as nineteenth-century street vendors had done. When all the students had taken a turn at cutting, he told them to spend the rest of class practicing their sushi and sashimi for tomorrow's test.

Zoran stood silently at his cutting board. He squeezed together simple, perfect tuna sushi—*nigiri,* and thin rolls wrapped in nori—using the marinated meat. He arranged his red, white, and black sushi on a black lacquer tray. The display was simple, a tribute to the Japanese art of food.

The students' trays filled with *nigiri* and sashimi. Except for one. Kate's tray was empty. She wasn't practicing for the test. She was in the kitchen, cooking sweet egg omelet.

Zoran peered into the kitchen.

"You been in here with your eggs the whole time?" he asked.

"Yeah," Kate murmured.

Zoran looked at the floor, turned, and walked away.

41

SUSHI KUNG FU

On the day of the test, Kate steered her Mustang into the lot behind Hama Hermosa at 8:00 a.m. She'd already had a tough morning. She hadn't gotten to sleep until 1:00 a.m. She'd rolled back out of bed at 4:20 a.m., bought gas, hit Starbucks, and arrived at the Laundromat a little after 5:00. When she yanked her chef's jacket from the dryer, she saw that a big brown smudge still marred the front.

In the parking lot at Hama Hermosa, she saw Jeff, the restaurant consultant, sitting in his car and talking on his cellphone. He noticed her and waved. He pointed at his cellphone and asked Kate to come back in a few minutes. She nodded and carried her gear inside.

Finally, Kate thought. She was going to find out once and for all about the nightclub job. In the ladies' room, she stared into the mirror at the smudge on her jacket and at the dark circles under her eyes.

When she returned to the parking lot, Jeff shook his head. The way he put it was that the nightclub simply hadn't gotten back to him.

'But you're a hot commodity!' Jeff said. He sped away.

Kate stood in the parking lot, gazing after him.

In the classroom, the students laid their equipment out for inspection. Zoran strode in and checked knives, tapping the blades on his thumbnail.

"Fingernails and hands, please!" he yelled. The students held out their hands and Zoran circled the table. Several of the students had bleached and ironed their jackets. Zoran glanced at the brown smudge on Kate's jacket and guffawed. Kate pressed her lips into a flat line.

Toshi rushed in and clapped his hands. "Let's go!"

The students stepped into position. Toshi strode to the head of the table with his clipboard of scoring sheets in hand. He looked down the table. With the restaurant in danger of closing, the school was in danger of closing, too. Right now, this class of students was all Toshi had left. He issued a single instruction.

"*Katsura-muki.*"

Column-peel. In unison, the students reached for a chunk of giant radish. Toshi lowered his glasses onto his nose. He rounded the corner of the table and watched Kate. A few weeks ago, this would have unnerved her. But now, she just kept peeling. Toshi scribbled on the clipboard, then moved down the table.

One by one, the students folded their sheets of radish onto their cutting boards and began slicing them into slivers. Silence gave way to tapping as their knives hit the wood. Each student slowly accumulated a mound of white shreds.

Toshi returned to Kate's station and watched.

"Not like this," he said softly. She stopped working. He imitated her posture. He faced the table straight on, slouching, with his hips square to the cutting board. He shook his head.

Toshi took a step back with his right foot. Now he stood at a 45-degree angle to the cutting board.

"Like *this.*"

He spread his legs, planted his feet, dropped his stance, and flexed all his muscles. He sucked in a deep breath, and belted out a cry like a warrior. "*Huuuggghh!*"

The other students looked up, startled. Toshi grabbed Kate's knife and chopped so fast that the knife sounded like a machine gun.

"The power enters your arm from the stance," Toshi yelled,

"and goes into the knife!" He stopped cutting. "You gotta have good posture." He looked around the room. "The stance."

Kate nodded slowly.

Marcos might as well have just viewed a martial-arts film. Eyes wide, he turned back to his cutting board. He lowered himself into an athletic pose and began slicing, trying to match Toshi's speed. Toshi wandered over to watch him. Suddenly a burst of crimson flooded across Marcos's white sheets of radish. He dropped his knife and grabbed his hand. Toshi peered at the blood and then looked Marcos in the eye. "Is your finger gone?"

Marcos smiled through the pain. "No." He rummaged in his bag for a Band-Aid.

Toshi turned to the rest of the class. "Stop!" he bellowed. "One step back!"

The students moved away from the table. Toshi fingered each student's shreds of radish, then he inspected the floor for dropped food. He scribbled on his clipboard.

"Okay," Toshi said. "Sashimi. Three-point presentation. Tuna."

Zoran opened the fridge and pulled out the blocks of bigeye he'd cut yesterday. The assignment was simple. Nine slices of tuna, arranged in three groups on a plate, plus garnish.

"You have five minutes," Toshi said. "Go."

Zoran clicked the stopwatch. Everyone squished three mounds of shredded radish onto their plates and propped a perilla leaf against each mound. Soon everyone was cutting fish, drawing the blades down through the blocks of flesh to create neat dominos of dark red meat. Kate fell behind.

In quick succession the students finished and stepped away from the table. Zoran glanced at the stopwatch, then at Kate's plate, then back at the stopwatch. The digits on the readout raced past the five-minute mark. The instant Kate plated her final slice of fish, Zoran clicked the stopwatch. "Time."

Toshi made his rounds, grading each student's plate and making suggestions. He reached Kate's station last.

"Your slices could be higher," he said. "But it's good!"

Kate cocked her head and studied her plate.

"Okay, everybody, nice cutting!" Toshi said. "What's next? Sushi! I want to see your sushi!"

They rushed to grab trays of salmon, snapper, and shrimp.

"Come on, come on!" Toshi yelled. "Let's *go*! Everybody ready?"
They weren't. He bellowed at the top of his lungs. "Come *on*!"

The students finally stood ready.

"I need to see six pieces—*nice*." Toshi paused. "Go!"

But he stopped them after only two *nigiri*.

"Just practice," Toshi muttered. "I'm not going to test." He leaned on Zoran's cutting board. "How many days have you been doing *nigiri*?"

"Every day," someone said.

Toshi frowned. "Shame on you guys. You guys make good rolls. But *nigiri*? No good. Just practice."

It took Kate a moment to realize that it wasn't just her. Toshi was criticizing the whole class.

Toshi strolled around the room, watching the students squeeze sushi. They stood with their elbows tight against their sides, their backs slouched, the wads of rice held up to their faces. Each *nigiri* took them nearly a minute to complete.

Toshi shook his head. Then, suddenly he smiled.

"When you make sushi, it's magic!" he said, his eyes twinkling. "Show the magic!"

Toshi stuck his hand in Marcos's rice canister. Intrigued, the students put down their sushi and watched. Concealing the rice with his fingers, Toshi held his hands away from his body. It was as if, when he opened his hands, a white dove might flutter out. With a flourish he executed several quick squeezes and turns, like a magician shuffling cards. It took less than ten seconds. He opened his palm to reveal a perfect *nigiri*.

"*Not* like this," Toshi said. He held his palm flat and turned and squeezed the clump of rice in plain view, his movements plodding and deliberate. He jabbed his hand into the rice again. He opened his palm and pointed.

"It's already sushi!"

He had already formed a *nigiri*, with one hand.

"Look at my hand here."

The students gathered around. He showed them how to form the rice into a *nigiri* by pressing it in the crook between the base and middle knuckles of his fingers. Then he continued the final formation of the *nigiri* with both hands. His fingers moved so fast that it did look like magic.

There is an old Japanese haiku, "With the movements of witchcraft and sorcery, squeezing sushi rice." A nineteenth-century Japanese observer wrote that the hand movements of the sushi chef were like those of a ninja.

In the comic book *Sushi Chef Kirara's Job,* when the young female sushi chef Kirara competes against her muscle-bound male colleagues, each chef squeezes out *nigiri* with his own martial-arts style, such as Flying Swallow, Stone Pagoda, and Dragon in the Clouds.

In fact, real sushi chefs in Japan employ different styles of *nigiri*-making technique, called *waza,* depending on the chef's lineage. The real styles have less whimsical names than those in the comic book—True Hand Flip, Little Hand Flip, Sideways Hand Flip, Upright Flip, and Thumb Nigiri.

In the comic book, Kirara's teacher instructs her to tap into a higher power when she squeezes *nigiri.*

"The squeezing process can be done with just one hand," he says. "But when you connect each grain of rice, you have to use both your hands. When both hands meet, you look as if you are praying toward the gods, don't you? You must form *nigiri* with technique, not physical power. If you can do it, the spirit of sushi will arrive in your hands."

"The spirit of sushi?" Kirara asks.

"In your connected hands, a spirit arrives, and sushi is born."

Meanwhile, in preparation for the sushi competition, Kirara's arch-rival Sakamaki prepares by meditating under a freezing waterfall, like a samurai before battle. He arrives at the sushi bar dressed in a ninja's chain mail.

In comparison, Toshi wasn't asking his students for much.

"I want you to make ten pieces," Toshi said. Again he sidled up to Kate, watched, and then stopped her.

Once more Toshi settled into his fighting stance. Like a ninja reaching for a throwing star, he reached into her canister for a ball of rice.

"*Huuuggghh!*" Toshi's hands flew across his body, his fingers a blur of cryptic movements. With his shaven head, he could have been a Buddhist warrior-monk performing magical mudra. There is a Zen temple north of Tokyo that contains a stone statue of a Buddhist sushi sage, his hands pressed together, squeezing *nigiri,* just as Toshi was doing now. Toshi opened his hands and out popped a perfect *nigiri.* He flexed all his muscles, and grunted again.

"You understand?" he asked, looking at Kate. "You see?"

Kate nodded. She bent her knees, flexed her muscles, and grabbed some rice. "*Arrgh!*"

42

MORTAL COMBAT

That night, Friday, was Zoran's last night working at Hama Hermosa. Just before the restaurant opened, Tetsu, the head chef, slipped away and returned with a present for Zoran in a Tupperware container. He peeled off the lid to reveal white goo with orange streaks.

"*Nare-zushi*," Tetsu said. "Sushi's ancestor."

Tetsu had mixed slices of raw fish with radish, ginger, and carrot—ingredients known to possess antiseptic properties. He'd splashed in sake and stirred in cooked rice. He'd tucked the mixture in the back of the walk-in and left it there to ripen—for five months. This was a version of sushi in its original form.

Zoran perked up. "I've never had that before." He plucked out a glob with his chef's chopsticks. He raised the chopsticks toward his mouth. Tetsu lifted a hand to stop him.

"I'm not responsible if you get sick," Tetsu said.

The whole point of packing fish with fermenting rice had been to keep it edible. As the rice had fermented, it had created lactic acids, which in theory had retarded the growth of harmful bacteria. Tetsu had drawn on more than a thousand of years of wisdom, and he had the advantage of refrigeration. But in the modern era, offering homemade food five months old to a friend requires a waiver.

Zoran gave his assent and stuck the goo in his mouth. He chewed. "Tastes like cheese."

By 6:30 p.m. the dining room was nearly full and the sushi bar had several customers. Behind the bar, the ticket printer spit out table orders.

Kate walked out from the kitchen wearing her chef's jacket. She stood in the hallway by the rear entrance to the sushi bar and rested her elbows on the pickup shelf. From there she could see into the workspace behind the sushi bar and watch the chefs from behind.

A party of four sat at the bar. They were regulars, and they knew all the chefs. They greeted Tetsu and Zoran and asked Tetsu for *omakase*.

The ticket printer chattered again, spitting out more tickets. The chefs grabbed ingredients, pressed rolls, and squeezed out *nigiri*. Zoran noticed Kate and pointed at the avocado in his hand. She ran back to the walk-in and returned with an armful of avocados. Zoran grabbed them and turned back to his cutting board. Kate retreated to the hallway.

A customer ordered a round of drinks for the chefs. The Mexican busboy squeezed into the chefs' workspace and delivered a beer to Tetsu and a Diet Coke to Zoran. The busboy beamed and yelled, "*Kanpai!*"

Tetsu chugged the beer and knocked out another platter of *nigiri*. The ticket printer chattered and spit out more order tickets. Tetsu still hadn't had a chance to deliver an opening appetizer to his *omakase* customers.

Zoran gulped his Diet Coke and squeezed together a big platter of rolls. He rushed it to the pickup shelf. He slipped on a wet spot on the floor and nearly dropped the plate. He cursed. Kate shrank back. The ticket printer continued spitting out orders.

In the confined space behind the sushi bar, the chefs spun, ran, sliced, and squeezed. An assistant chef hunted in the lowboy by Tetsu's knees while Tetsu slashed through blocks of fish with his knife just above the other chef's neck, at the same moment that the Mexican dishwasher lugged in a heavy tub of clean plates. The kitchen chef popped in and out every few minutes to deliver items from the stove or fry station. Waitresses slipped into the workspace to pester the chefs on the status of their orders. Kate tried to stay out of everyone's way.

Tetsu delivered the opening volley of his *omakase* to the group of regulars. While they consumed their first course, he lifted the intercom handset and called in an order for a cooked course from the kitchen.

That bought him time to attack an enormous table order for *nigiri* in the row of order tickets. He ran his eye down the ticket, memorized it, and sliced the first round of fish he would need.

He stepped back on his right foot and settled into a stance for sushi combat, just as Toshi had demonstrated to the students that morning. He dipped a finger into a bowl of water, rubbed his hands together quickly, and clapped twice. He flexed the muscles of his stocky frame, then reached his right hand into his canister of rice. His hand flew out of the canister. His finger flashed into a dish of wasabi as it passed. His left hand snatched a slice of fish off his cutting board. The right-hand finger brushed down the under-side of the slice and left a pale green streak. A cylinder of rice, just formed in his right palm, impacted the slice of fish on the palm of his left. In a blur of flicks and pulses, his hands swept in a wide arc across his chest and down to his left hip, his upper body twist-ing around to the left, his legs dancing through a series of small kicks. His hands landed over a clean plate and out popped a per-fect *nigiri*. The entire process had taken seven seconds.

That was too slow. Tetsu's hands flashed out again, already forming the second *nigiri,* repeating the process exactly as before. His legs danced, his torso twisted, and his hands flicked across his body in a wide arc as he added more speed. Another perfect *nigiri* popped out onto the plate.

Tetsu leaned over the fish case for another block of fish. Every few minutes he leaned back to pluck more tickets from the printer. He kept his legs spread in combat stance the entire time, leaning only his upper body to and fro at steep angles, as though dodging bullets.

The customers poured Tetsu more beer. He stopped and chugged it down. He nodded politely and whipped his hand back to the rice canister. He completed the enormous *nigiri* order, chugged another glass of beer, and moved on to rolls. Zoran was also fighting through a stack of table orders and serving customers at the bar. He grabbed the blowtorch and blue flame hissed across an order of flounder fin muscle.

The customers ordered more drinks for the chefs. A woman in Tetsu's *omakase* party shot Zoran a smile.

"We love you, Zoran," she said.

Zoran gave her a nod. "Thank you." He continued to work, then broke the news that this was his last night. She was crushed. He downed more Diet Coke and pressed together another roll.

The kitchen chef rushed past Kate and squeezed behind the bar to deliver the second course of Tetsu's *omakase*. Someone else rushed past and maneuvered inside to deliver deep-fried shrimp to Zoran for a roll. The busboy delivered more beer for Tetsu and another Diet Coke for Zoran. Somebody jostled Tetsu. Luckily, he was not holding his knife, but the roll he'd been arranging was knocked into disarray. The customers raised their glasses, the chefs raised their glasses, and everyone yelled, "*Kanpai!*"

Tetsu chugged his beer and held his glass upside down over his head, empty. He went back to work and knocked one of his chopsticks off the counter. It clattered to the floor and rolled away. Zoran danced around it as it passed. Tetsu grabbed a pair of disposable bamboo chopsticks and kept working. He spun and grabbed four platters and four sauce dishes from the back shelves. There was a clatter and they started to fall. He dropped his body toward the floor, and in a juggling act caught them all. He sucked in his breath. "That was close."

By now Zoran had burned through most of his vegetables and garnishes. He poked his head into the hall and sent Kate to the walk-in for supplies. When she returned, the other chefs sent her back for additional items.

As Kate returned this time, Zoran burst out from the bar. He pushed past her, lugging his empty rice canister. Moments later he thundered back through, hugging a full canister to his chest. "Coming through!"

Kate backed away. She turned and pushed through the saloon doors into the drink station, and then on into the back sushi bar, where it was quiet. She took a slow, deep breath.

Officially, the back bar was closed. But Toshi was there, serving a leisurely meal for a couple of Japanese friends—another sushi chef and his wife. Toshi sipped a Scotch and joked. Takumi helped out, chatting with Toshi's friends. Toshi saw Kate. He smiled and motioned for her to join them.

At the front sushi bar, mayhem gave way to murder. Tetsu returned from the walk-in clutching a handful of shrimp, with legs flailing and tails snapping. One by one he ripped them in half. He peeled the shells off the tails, and the muscles pulsed with contractions until he butterflied them open with his knife.

A customer purchased a big bottle of sake for everyone at the bar, customers and chefs. The entire row of customers at the bar and the chefs all raised their glasses.

"*Kanpai!*" everyone yelled.

The customers at one table and then another raised their glasses. "*Kanpai!*"

As they all brought their glasses to their lips, an abrupt silence descended on the dining room. Zoran bellowed into the silence.

"Happy Friday!" he yelled. He wasn't smiling. When Zoran next turned to look for Kate, he saw that she was no longer there.

The group of regulars who'd been eating *omakase* paid their check and departed. Immediately a new group took their place—a couple and two daughters wearing glitter on their faces. They'd been waiting for Zoran. They knew he was leaving. Another couple sat down and requested *omakase* from Zoran, too. He lined up six plates and squeezed on mounds of wasabi and pickled ginger.

More customers streamed into the restaurant. A posse of young women in tight skirts jostled in the foyer, followed by more couples. The ticket printer kept spitting out orders. The chefs grabbed tickets and squeezed out more rolls, knocking sheets of nori on the floor. Parties piled up, waiting for tables. Customers at a table demanded that Tetsu come out to drink sake with them. He joined them and gulped down a glass. "*Kanpai!*"

When Tetsu returned, the husband of the family poured him

more beer. Zoran reached for his glass to join them in another toast, but his second glass of Diet Coke was already empty.

"My bloody customers, and I don't even get a drink?" He ran out of the bar. He returned with a full glass. The family and chefs raised their glasses. Zoran thrust his Diet Coke high overhead and glared out at the entire dining room.

"*Kanpai!*" Zoran thundered. "*Kanpai!*" His face glistened with sweat.

People throughout the entire restaurant raised their glasses and shouted, "*Kanpai!*"

At the back sushi bar, Toshi had encouraged Kate to chat with the customers. She'd had a wonderful time, talking with them and joking with Toshi and Takumi. Finally, Toshi brought the leisurely meal to a close. Kate said goodnight. She sailed off to the ladies' room and slipped out of her uniform into a pair of pants and a tight shirt.

Meanwhile, at the front sushi bar, the chefs were running out of fish. Zoran sprinted to the walk-in. He returned with a 2-foot slab of salmon draped across his arms. He cut it into chunks at his station, his knife flying.

Kate emerged from the ladies' room. But instead of leaving, she returned to the hallway, and leaned her elbows on the pickup shelf behind the front bar. She watched Zoran work. She wanted to say good-bye, but she wasn't sure how. After a few minutes he noticed her.

"Hang out, sweetie," he whispered, "don't leave."

Zoran manhandled a couple of rolls to completion. Then he leapt up the two small steps from the floor of the sushi bar and into the hall. His hands were covered in fishiness. He straightened his arms and pressed them against the sides of Kate's body, his fingers clenched in fists so they wouldn't touch her. He gave her a squeeze, like a piece of sushi, and then let her go.

"Take care, sweetie."

He rushed back behind the bar.

43

DRUNKEN MASTER

At midnight the dining room was nearly deserted. The toasts had continued until the end. Now, one last group of customers lingered at a corner table.

Behind the sushi bar only Tetsu remained. The other chefs had cleared the fish cases, cleaned up, and scattered. Tetsu had stayed behind the bar to stow a few final odds and ends. He saw a full glass of beer in a corner of the counter. He called out to the table across the room. "*Kanpai!*" Without waiting for an answer he chugged the beer and flipped the glass upside down. He wiped his mouth. "I feel terrible."

The back room was empty and dark except for a row of lights shining onto the back sushi bar. Behind the bar stood Takumi, illuminated like a solitary actor on a stage. Next to him was a steel canister of leftover sushi rice.

Takumi planted his right foot back, so he stood at a 45-degree angle to the counter. He settled into his stance. He dipped his fingers in a bowl of water, clapped, and jabbed one hand into the rice. He brought his hands together. He squeezed and turned, squeezed and turned, and deposited another rectangle of rice onto the countertop. The countertop was littered with the rectangles of rice he'd already made, forty or fifty of them, laid out in long rows like tombstones.

Takumi kept replaying the scene from that morning. He pictured Toshi at the classroom table, whipping out *nigiri* like a kung-fu magician.

Takumi jabbed his hand into the canister for more rice.

The swinging doors banged open. Tetsu stumbled into the workspace behind the back bar. He leaned heavily on the counter and eyed Takumi's technique. Like the other students, Takumi still held the *nigiri* close to his face.

Tetsu grunted and spoke. "Nobody wants to eat sushi made by somebody who is all hunched over like that. It's unappetizing. You have to make it look dramatic. That way they'll want to eat it."

Tetsu straightened. "You need to decide on a motion that's comfortable for you. Hold your arms up, and keep your arms out from your sides. Keep them loose. If your arms are too tight, you're going to wear yourself out."

Tetsu stuck his hand in Takumi's rice canister and rolled a cylinder of white grains.

"Use your thumb to punch a hole in it," Tetsu said. That was another trick of the sushi chef. Indenting the clump of rice at the beginning of the process introduced air and empty space into the interior of the *nigiri*, so it would disintegrate easily in the mouth when eaten.

Tetsu was unsteady on his feet, but he closed the cylinder around the hole, bent his fingers at right angles, and pressed the cylinder into a perfect rectangular packet. All this happened with one hand, still in the rice canister.

"After a while it becomes unconscious," Tetsu said. His eyelids drooped. He looked like he was about to become unconscious.

Tetsu snapped the rectangle of rice in half and showed Takumi the cross section. The center was an airy space of loose grains, while the edges were firm walls of packed rice.

"You need to make them with your whole body," Tetsu said. He teetered toward the counter and picked up an imaginary slice of fish with his left hand. He brought his hands together. As he squeezed and turned the *nigiri*, he drew his hands in a sweeping arc across the front of his body, just as he had earlier behind the sushi bar.

"From start to finish, you should use the same set of motions every time. When you reach the end of your routine, your *nigiri* will be done." He plopped the rectangle of rice on the counter, adding to Takumi's graveyard.

Takumi nodded.

"You also need to be able to adjust your *nigiri,* depending on the customer and the situation," Tetsu went on. The sushi chef's job wasn't simply to make sushi. A good chef had to make snap judgments about every customer who sat at his sushi bar.

"Maybe they want a quick lunch," Tetsu said. "If so, you make them nice, fat *nigiri* with more rice. If they're here for a leisurely dinner, you only want to put a slim little pack of rice under each piece of fish—and even less if they're drinking sake. You learn to tell by watching their faces if they've come to drink or to eat.

"And, of course, for a man, you usually make the *nigiri* a little bigger, and for a woman, a little smaller. But it's different in every case. Look, if a big, fat guy sits down at the sushi bar, you figure he likes carbohydrates, right? So you make his *nigiri* with more rice. But you also have to figure out what kind of mood they're in, and what's their purpose in coming to the sushi bar that day."

Tetsu chuckled. "With American customers, it's different. You've got to judge how much experience they have eating sushi. A lot of Americans dip the rice side of their *nigiri* in the soy sauce instead of the fish side. Well, of course, in that case a properly made *nigiri* will just fall apart. So you have to squeeze the *nigiri* together much more firmly for them. But if you do that to Japanese people, they're going to tell you your sushi sucks—it's too hard and doesn't melt in your mouth."

This was a practice that the venerable sushi chef in Japan, Jirō Ono, followed when he encountered a Western customer. "For foreigners, I make the sushi so hard that Japanese customers would refuse to eat it," Ono once told an interviewer. It's likely that many American sushi enthusiasts have never experienced a proper *nigiri.*

A customer who chooses to use chopsticks instead of his fingers will also require a firmer pack of rice.

Takumi stared down at his rows of rice rectangles. "So it's really about adjusting to the needs of the customer?"

Tetsu nodded. "That's the sushi chef's job. You've got to figure out what the customer's needs are and adapt."

Tetsu drifted away. Takumi reached for more rice and went on practicing.

After a while Tetsu returned. He'd changed out of his uniform. The aura of sushi master had vanished. He leaned against the counter looking like an oversized schoolboy. His stocky legs stuck out of a pair of shorts and he wore a baseball cap turned backwards.

Takumi dipped his fingers in the bowl of water and clapped. Tetsu stopped him.

"Too much water." Tetsu said. He told Takumi never to dip both hands into the bowl of water. "Too much water, and your *nigiri* will fall apart."

Tetsu demonstrated. He wetted just the index finger of his right hand. With that one wet finger, he painted a circle of water onto his left palm. Then he rubbed his hands together as if lathering them with soap, spreading a thin sheen of moisture across his skin. He cupped his right hand and knocked it twice against his left palm.

"I do it exactly like this, every time," Tetsu said.

Now that his hands were primed, Tetsu reached into the rice canister, formed a rectangle, and picked up another imaginary piece of fish with his other hand. He pressed both hands together and carried them across the front of his body in an arc—squeeze, turn, squeeze, turn—and banged out another *nigiri*.

He repeated the water routine, dug in the canister for more rice, and swept his hands through the air. He banged out another, and another.

"It should never take you more than ten seconds to make a *nigiri*," Tetsu admonished. "And when you're busy, you've got to do it in five." He blasted through the routine again. "So count to five while you're making each one. As soon as you put your hand in the rice, start counting and move your body through that whole set of motions—in five seconds. The *nigiri* has to be finished by the end."

Tetsu raced himself. "Five seconds!" His hands were flying now in a blur across his body. "Four seconds!" He deepened his stance. He dipped his finger in the water, rubbed, and clapped. The hands flew. "Three seconds!"

He left Takumi to race himself, and went on home.

Takumi tried to master Tetsu's tricks, slowly at first—the water, the hollow rice rectangle, the sweeping arc. *It's just like making pasta,* he thought.

He speeded up. He jabbed his hand in the rice and rushed through the motions, trying to complete his *nigiri* by the count of 5. He succeeded only in ripping it to shreds. He peered down at the disintegrated pile of loose white grains in his palm and laughed.

He tried again, and again, and the faster he went, the more the rice simply fell apart. He laughed again. He stopped and surveyed the array of white rectangles on the counter. There must have been sixty or seventy.

Suddenly Takumi grew sober. The rice was sacred. Seven deities in every grain. A single *nigiri* contained five or six hundred grains. Takumi stiffened, then bowed formally to the pantheon before him.

He apologized to the rice. He must redeem these deities, Takumi decided. He must master the art of sushi. He wiped his arm across the countertop. A quarter of a million little gods fell into the trash.

Weeks 9 and 10

44

EGGS AND OVARIES

The last few weeks of the semester passed in a pleasant blur. With Zoran's absence, it felt as if a weight had been lifted. Tetsu took over the class. He didn't speak a lot of English, but he got by.

One day, Tetsu told Marcos he was a good student. Marcos walked around in shock. Tetsu let Kate indulge her creativity. He taught the class how to make Japanese desserts, and he let Kate play with her cookie cutter, punching colorful heart shapes out of Japanese seaweed Jell-O.

Tetsu taught the students how to speak sushi-bar lingo. Sushi chefs use their own words for everything. Soy sauce is *murasaki*, which means "purple." Wasabi is *namida*, which means "tears." Nori is *kusa*, which means "grass." Pickled ginger is *gari*, which supposedly is the sound pickled ginger makes in your mouth.

Tetsu warned the students to use this lingo only when behind the bar. "If you're a customer at the sushi bar, you shouldn't use these," he explained. "Some customers think they know sushi and use these, but it sounds ridiculous. This is just for employees to use with each other."

Tetsu taught them how to cook rice the old-fashioned way— in a pot on a stove—"in case your rice cooker broken." He told them that when he was a boy in rural Japan, his grandmother had cooked rice in an iron bucket over a wood fire.

They practiced their basic sushi and sashimi skills. Under strict orders from Toshi, Tetsu used the last half hour of every class for *nigiri*-squeezing drills, including posture. Takumi's posture quickly improved.

Toshi himself taught a few classes. He spent three days teaching the students how to taste different types of premium sake. Everybody got a little tipsy. On the day Marcos turned 18, Jay brought a chocolate cake with cherry filling to class and everyone sang "Happy Birthday." They ate the cake with chopsticks.

Without Zoran around, discipline went out the window. But in a way, he no longer needed to be there in person. Kate and Marcos both heard his voice in their heads every time they did something dumb. Kate called it the "Ghost of Zoran Past." Every few days Marcos would sidle up to Kate, adopt an Australian accent, and yell, "Kate, you're *terrible!*" and Kate would throw her head back and laugh. As the semester wound to a close, they realized that Zoran had taught them almost everything they really needed to know before he left.

One morning Tetsu arrived at class with a Tupperware container. He peeled off the top and revealed a mass of plump orange spheres: salmon eggs.

Cheaper sushi restaurants purchase their salmon eggs salted and marinated, but better restaurants prepare them in-house. The standard marinade includes the usual suspects—soy sauce, mirin, sake, and dashi. Tetsu fingered the eggs. They were covered with a tacky residue.

"Need to clean them," Tetsu said.

He ran warm water over the eggs in a strainer and rubbed them with his fingers. The water turned milky white. The smell of the ocean wafted up.

Salmon invest a lot in their roe, which is why salmon eggs are bigger than other caviar. A single salmon egg contains enough food to feed the embryo for an entire winter and on into early spring, as the embryo becomes a baby fish. Marcos plucked one of the orange orbs from the mass, held it up to his face between his thumb and finger, and inspected it like a jewel.

Tetsu lowered the strainer into a bowl of saltwater and picked away bits of white membrane.

"You need patience," Tetsu said. He quit and handed the strainer to one of the students.

When the student had finished, Tetsu salted the eggs in a brine solution. A bit of salt plumps each egg and causes enzymes inside to digest proteins, generating more flavor-enhancing amino acids. Salt also causes enzymes to strengthen the egg's shell, making the eggs firmer and therefore more fun to eat. After salting, Tetsu would leave the eggs to drain overnight. Tomorrow he'd marinate them for two or three hours.

Before the arrival of sushi, Americans mostly used salmon eggs as bait, to catch fish. The Japanese have been eating the salted ovaries of salmon and trout for more than a thousand years. But it was the Russians who pioneered the eating of loose salmon eggs as caviar in the 1830s. The Japanese word for salmon caviar used in sushi, *ikura,* comes from the Russian word for caviar, *ikra.* Today, in Russia's Kamchatka Peninsula just north of Japan, the black-market trade in illegal salmon eggs is worth $1 billion a year. Bears are also fond of salmon roe. They will suck out the eggs—20,000 of them in a full female—and leave the mother fish lying dead.

Salmon eggs are a recent addition to sushi. The respected Tokyo sushi chef Jirō Ono began serving them in the early 1980s, at the request of a customer. Now salmon eggs are so popular that Japanese food scientists have perfected techniques for manufacturing fake ones from vegetable oil.

Next, Tetsu brought out a small wooden tray loaded with pale yellow slabs that looked like cat tongues.

'*Uni,*' Tetsu said.

Sea urchins—called *uni* in Japanese—share 70 percent of their genetic code with humans. Nevertheless, there are significant differences. For example, humans and most other multicellular organisms develop "mouth first"—the first hole in the embryo becomes the animal's mouth. By contrast, sea urchins develop "ass first."

Until recently, Japanese people and Americans both despised sea urchins. Sea urchins commit a terrible crime—they eat kelp. In Japan, kelp is a sacred source of *umami*, necessary for making dashi. Japanese kelp harvesters destroyed sea urchins. In America, meanwhile, factories used kelp to manufacture agar for petri dishes. In southern California in the 1960s and 1970s, dive clubs and local authorities sponsored underwater urchin-killing parties. Scuba divers would swim around smashing urchins with hammers to save the kelp forests for the factories.

Kelp and urchins have been locked in battle with each other for eons. Vast armies of urchins swarm across the sea floor, advancing at speeds of up to 20 inches a day and chewing up all the kelp en route. In response, kelp have evolved a diabolical weapon to defend themselves against the urchin hordes. Kelp produce a protein that tricks at least some female sea urchins into believing that a male sea urchin has already fertilized their eggs. As a result, the female urchins stop making babies.

In Japan, sometime after the seventeenth century, people in a region called Hokuriku on the northern coast of Japan's central island, came to appreciate the taste of sea urchins so much that they started harvesting urchins instead of destroying them. Since urchins eat kelp, they are loaded with the same delicious IMP that gives kelp its flavor.

Inside a sea urchin, the edible portions are the urchin's gonads—either its ovaries or its testes, depending on gender. It's difficult to tell which is which because the male and female sex organs look almost exactly the same. These gonads can occupy up to two-thirds of the urchin's body. They are delicious, not only because they are loaded with tasty amino acids and IMP, but also because they are composed of 15 to 25 percent fat. The French have long cooked with urchin gonads, adding them to scrambled eggs, soufflés, and sauces.

In 1975, a young scuba diver in southern California named Dave Rudie heard that instead of smashing sea urchins with a hammer, he could make seven cents a pound selling them to a man from Japan. Rudie began collecting urchins from the bottom with a garden rake. Soon he was processing urchin gonads in his garage and selling them to sushi bars in San Diego. Now, his company,

Catalina Offshore Products, is the premier American urchin supplier, selling high-grade California urchin to sushi bars around the
country. His urchins are known at Tsukiji Fish Market in Tokyo as
the best outside Japan.

Tetsu taught the students how to wrap a strip of nori around
the edge of a rice *nigiri* to hold salmon eggs or sea urchin gonads
on top. The Japanese refer to these *nigiri* whimsically as *gunkan*—
which means "battleship"—because supposedly they look like little
boats.

The following night, Toshi served customers at the front bar.
Takumi worked next to him. By now Toshi knew that this might be
one of the last nights he would ever stand behind a sushi bar.

Despite several busy evenings in recent weeks, Hama Hermosa
had still been losing too much money. Toshi had decided to shut
the restaurant for good. He wasn't sure what would happen to the
academy. American sushi, it seemed, had left Toshi behind.

A young lady sat down at the bar. She wore a shirt with a deep
V-neck revealing an ample bosom. She leaned forward, her elbows
on the bar. There were certainly things Toshi would miss about
being a sushi chef. He turned to Takumi and spoke in Japanese.

"Working at the sushi bar really is the ideal angle for viewing
breasts."

Takumi bowed his head and laughed quietly into his chest.
Toshi looked at his Japanese student for a moment.

"If you were in Japan," Toshi said, "you sure as hell would not
be standing at the bar making sushi already."

Takumi had been studying sushi for less than three months. In
Japan, a traditional apprenticeship would have taken him years.
And he was already nearly 40 years old.

Takumi nodded. "I'd be in the back washing dishes."

"Your life would be over before you had the chance to make
sushi," Toshi said.

New customers arrived, including a gorgeous brunette whose
tight T-shirt barely contained her breasts. She sat in front of Toshi.
He sighed and turned to Takumi.

"I can't help it. When a cute girl sits down at the bar, I always want to make her something special. I've always given the cute girls the special cuts of fish." He shook his head. "It's sushi-chef discrimination."

Toshi's eyes wandered toward the T-shirt. The woman was talking with her friends and remained oblivious.

"Damn," Toshi blurted in Japanese, "*look* at those breasts! They're perfect!"

Takumi turned away, his body shaking with laughter. Toshi kept talking. "When I see tits like that, sometimes my dick gets hard and pushes up my cutting board."

Takumi ducked below the counter and held his stomach. Toshi looked down at his work, but his eyes kept wandering back to the breasts. "God, I can't stop looking at them."

Next a blond woman wearing a cowboy hat sauntered in and sat at the bar. Her low-cut strap top barely contained the generous landscape of her chest.

Toshi turned to Takumi, eyes wide.

That weekend, Toshi catered another film set. He took Takumi along.

They had competition. Next to the sushi stall was a truck with a grill serving barbecue. Fragrant smoke billowed across the sushi stall.

At lunchtime the film crew mobbed the sushi stand. Grips jostled each other to get their serving of raw fish and rice.

Takumi was averaging seventeen seconds per *nigiri*. Still too slow. Next to him Toshi knocked out each *nigiri* in five seconds flat. Takumi deepened his concentration and picked up his pace. Ten minutes later he hit twelve seconds per piece.

After an hour, the crowd thinned and Toshi slowed down.

A grip strode past. "Thank you, guys, that was fantastic. I came back for seconds twice." Two more grips stopped by and thanked them, too.

The barbecue truck had gotten only a handful of customers.

Toshi threw together a few final plates of sushi and carried them next door to the barbecue truck. He returned with a couple of Styrofoam clamshells. He and Takumi sat in the van with the doors open and the air-conditioner blasting. Toshi shoveled seared steak and potatoes into his mouth with a plastic fork.

"Man," he said in Japanese, "American food is good."

Weeks 11 and 12

4 5

LAST DANCE

The academy had scheduled a special final student sushi bar. Again, Kate invited her mother and brother. She planned to serve them *omakase*—chef's choice.

That morning the students rushed around the kitchen making preparations. Kate sharpened her knives.

When Kate's mother and brother arrived, she took her place behind the bar.

"We'd like *omakase,* please," her mother said. Kate had coached them beforehand.

Kate nodded. She peered into the fish case.

"Well, let's see, I could make you tacos," Kate said, smirking. Her mother looked confused. Kate laughed. "*Tako,*" she explained, "is Japanese for 'octopus'!"

Her mother frowned. Kate thought for a second. She pulled a tray of albacore tuna and sliced off five neat pieces. She squeezed a bunch of shredded radish onto a plate. She pressed a perilla leaf on top and laid the slices of fish in a slanted row. She straightened up and eyed the platter. She stuck a blue cocktail umbrella in the radish. She handed the plate across the fish case. Her mom smiled.

While they were eating the sashimi, Kate broiled slices of eel in the toaster. She rolled the eel into a pair of hand rolls with crab and cucumber, and squirted on eel sauce—her own concoction. She handed them across the fish case.

Kate built a spider roll. She loaded the standard deep-fried soft-shell crab on the rice, but altered the recipe and layered in cilantro and shredded radish. She chose a wide white plate, arranged the roll elegantly, and handed the plate to her mother and her brother.

Kate pulled a tray of flatfish and cut off two quick slices. She straightened up, lifted her elbows and hands away from her body, and squeezed together a pair of *nigiri* as if she were performing for a crowd, just as Toshi had demonstrated. She dripped lemon juice on the *nigiri* and handed them across the fish case. Her mother bit down, chewed, and nodded. "That's good."

"Now I'm going to invent a Kate roll!" Kate said.

She loaded spicy tuna, avocado, eel, cucumber, and shredded radish on a pad of rice and nori and tucked it in tight, just like Zoran had taught her.

On the last night of Hama Hermosa's existence, Toshi strode into the dining room at 5:15 in his white jacket. He switched on the lights over the front sushi bar and surveyed the row of sea creatures in the fish cases.

There were beige ribbons of eel, tight purple curls of octopus, and orange flaps of shrimp. There were tan blocks of albacore, red bricks of tuna, pink strips of fatty tuna, and translucent sheets of flounder. There was a pale shaft of giant clam. There were orange trapezoids of salmon embedded with zigzag lines of fat, and wedges of yellowtail with maroon triangles of dark muscle. It was like an anatomy booth at a museum of natural history, except that visitors were encouraged to eat the exhibit.

Toshi took his station behind the bar. His wingmen flanked him. On his left stood Tetsu. On his right, Takumi.

Zoran's departure had left a gap in the lineup of chefs and Takumi had stepped into it. Toshi had begun to delegate parts of his *omakase* to Takumi. He had imagination, whimsy, and creativity. That could only be good for sushi, but none of it would matter if Takumi couldn't bring himself to perform for customers, just as he once had for fans. He still acted shy and reserved behind the sushi bar.

The restaurant manager propped open the front door. As the sun sank over the Pacific Ocean across the street, light streamed into the dining room. The colors in the fish case blazed and the white tablecloths glowed. Minutes later the sun dropped below a building and the vibrant colors vanished. A fly buzzed around the sushi bar. Takumi swatted at it with a towel.

Toshi went to the kitchen and entered the walk-in. He sorted through plastic food-storage tubs, now mostly empty, and consolidated the remaining items. He peered into corners of the cavernous refrigerator and extracted a potato growing sprouts and a banana that had turned black. He emerged and hugged himself. "Brrr."

Toshi returned to the sushi bar, and a few minutes later three customers walked into the restaurant.

"*Irasshaimase!*" the chefs yelled.

It was Kate, dressed up for dinner, with a couple of friends. Toshi narrowed his eyes and scowled at her. She wrinkled up her nose and scowled back. The scowling intensified. Then they both laughed. Kate led her friends to the bar and they ordered sake. Tetsu began squeezing out *nigiri* for his student.

Then, several of Toshi's most loyal customers came in and sat at the bar. One woman had been eating Toshi's sushi for twenty years. They all tried to act upbeat, but Toshi could see that they were sad. He served them *omakase,* punctuated by frequent, poignant toasts.

But it was Takumi who delivered a special dish of deep-fried tofu to Kate and her friends. Kate's eyes popped open.

"For us?" Kate asked.

Takumi nodded.

Kate smiled, then wrinkled up her nose and scowled theatrically again, this time at Takumi. He took the bait and scowled back. He even growled. Kate laughed. He beat his chest and growled again, pretending to be King Kong.

"What about Dancing Sushi Chef?" Kate asked.

Takumi froze. Slowly he raised one arm and danced a little disco, gyrating his hips. Kate applauded.

Takumi went back to work and Kate went back to chatting with her friends. Two Japanese men and a young Japanese woman came to the sushi bar, and Toshi commenced a new *omakase* for them. Takumi helped.

Takumi was fond of squid. For this last evening at the restaurant, he'd prepared a dish that drew inspiration from Italian cooking. He served it to the Japanese customers, explaining that it was calamari marinated in lime juice and dill. The young woman watched Takumi closely while he spoke. She and the two men tried the squid and pronounced it delicious. Takumi bowed his head, looking pleased, and continued to chat with them. The woman kept watching Takumi, her brow furrowed.

Kate and her friends finished their meal and left. Toshi juggled dishes for his different batches of *omakase* customers. He tossed eel in the toaster and leaned on the lowboy. He sighed. In English he muttered, "Sake made me tired." A minute later he got confused and served several dishes to the wrong customers. He shook his head and berated himself in Japanese. "No good."

After a while Toshi delegated the rest of the *omakase* to Tetsu and Takumi, and simply stood in the center of the bar, chatting with his customers and watching people come and go from the dining room. When the American *omakase* customers had finished their sushi, Toshi disappeared into the kitchen and returned carrying plates of sherbet for their dessert. He'd decorated each plate with a crisscrossed pair of little flags. One was the Stars and Stripes, the other was the Rising Sun.

The American customers said their final good-byes, leaving the Japanese customers alone at the bar. The young Japanese woman couldn't stop looking at Takumi. She covered her mouth with her hand, as Japanese women often do when embarrassed, and spoke up.

"I feel like I've seen you before somewhere," she said.

Takumi laughed. "Really?"

"Yes," she said. Her face brightened. "Do you work part-time at some *other* sushi restaurant?"

Takumi laughed again. "No, no." He glanced down at his cutting board. "I used to do a little part-time work, ah . . . on TV."

The woman giggled and held her hand over her mouth again. "Really?"

He nodded. He was smiling. He stuck his hand in the canister of rice, then straightened up. He lifted his elbows and hands away from his body and performed for the customers, squeezing sushi in an arc across his body.

The woman watched. She still couldn't place him. She seemed to be trying to remember when on television she'd last seen a sushi chef who looked like this man.

New customers came in and sat at the bar. Toshi turned away, picked up the intercom, and called to one of the students, who was interning in the kitchen. A moment later the student appeared, looking startled.

Toshi smiled. "You make sushi now. Get your knife."

The student returned and took Toshi's place behind the bar. He turned to the customers and suggested a few dishes. Toshi stood back and watched him work. A few minutes later, when no one was looking, Toshi closed up his knife case and slipped away.

Later that night, after all the customers had left, after all the creatures had been cleared from the fish cases, the floors had been mopped, and the countertops wiped clean, Takumi and Tetsu stood alone in their chef's whites under the bright spotlights in the empty sushi bar.

Takumi poured two cups of sake. Then he poured a third cup. Takumi believed that a spirit resided in every object and creature in the world. Tonight the life of this sushi bar and its spirit had come to an end, and it was time for the chefs to express their thanks.

Takumi and Tetsu clinked cups, tipped back their heads, and drank. At the same instant, Takumi flicked the third cup, and thousands of droplets of fermented liquid rice, swimming with little gods, flew through the air and fell across the sushi bar like rain.

46

DELI

The semester at the California Sushi Academy came to a close with a series of three practical exams. The students were tested on the preparation of cooked appetizers, sushi, and sashimi. The final written exam would come a few days later.

After their last practical exam, Kate and Marcos hopped into the Mustang and set off for a last lunch at the Jewish deli downtown. Heavy fog billowed in off the ocean, blanketing Hermosa Beach in the gray hues of a Japanese ink painting.

"I'm sad it's over," Kate said.

"I'm really sad I'm leaving Hermosa," Marcos said. "I really like it out here."

Kate decided to treat herself to a cigarette, and cracked open a pack of Marlboros. "I *am* looking forward to getting some sleep. Seems like I haven't slept in three months. Always thinking about something. The Laundromat. Where's my textbook? Where's my hat? I'm going to be late."

She was silent for a few minutes. "I still hear Zoran's voice in my head whenever I do something stupid."

Marcos nodded. "Me, too."

Downtown L.A. came into view. The glass towers punched high into the air through a film of brown smog. An hour later, in the same booth at the deli as before, Kate ordered a big piece of chocolate cake for dessert.

"I wonder what Zoran is doing right now," she said. She chuckled. "Probably wrestling a kangaroo."

She took a bite of cake and stared out the window. After a moment she spoke again.

"The best thing I learned this summer," she said slowly, "was that I could stick with something, even through all my doubts."

A jar of red licorice sat on the deli counter. Kate remembered that Jay had said Zoran liked licorice. She asked the waitress for a few sticks. She offered one to Marcos.

"No, thanks. But Zoran would like it."

Kate nibbled on a stick.

"Even though he was really mean to me," she said, "he was also really nice to me, the bastard. On the sashimi test, he called time *right* when I put down my last cut of fish."

They settled their check and wandered outside. Mexican women sat on the curb in the hot sun, waiting for a bus. Marcos and Kate strolled down the street and found a quiet curb of their own. They sat and smoked cigarettes. Kate turned her face to the sun.

"Sushi is the first thing I've gotten excited about in a long time," Kate said. She took another drag on her cigarette and blew out the smoke. "I needed this. I think it's given me confidence."

47

SUSHI MASTER

Toshi peered out the window of the Boeing 737. Green fields came into view as the plane sank toward Sacramento. Stretching north through the Sacramento Valley are half a million acres of rice paddies. Ninety-five percent of the rice are the short-grain and medium-grain Japonica varieties used for sushi.

A trade group called the California Rice Commission had contacted Toshi months ago. They'd been planning a "Sushi Masters" competition in Sacramento, the first of its kind. The commission had invited Toshi, as CEO of the California Sushi Academy, to serve as presiding judge. Tonight, he and five other judges would confer the title of Sushi Master on one of eight sushi chefs nominated from around the state.

The event would also honor the first sushi chefs and restaurateurs in L.A.'s Little Tokyo in the 1960s and 1970s—or at least, those that were still alive and could be located. Katsu Michite, the chef whose restaurant Toshi had frequented when he'd gotten his first job in Malibu, would be there, along with other stalwarts of traditional sushi in the United States.

Rumor had it that some of these men looked down on Toshi as an opportunist who lacked proper credentials. Worse, Toshi could assume that they already knew what had happened—that after losing his first restaurant, he'd now driven his second restaurant into the ground. Never mind that without chefs like Toshi, who'd thrown tradition to the wind, average Americans might never have warmed to sushi, and there might not even be a Sushi Masters event to honor the founding fathers of American sushi.

When the plane touched down on the tarmac, Toshi looked stoic. Earlier that day at the academy, he'd administered a final practical exam for his students. After the exam, Toshi and Jay had driven straight to the airport. Toshi had scarfed down a cheese pizza at the departure gate.

Downtown in Sacramento, they entered a vast four-story atrium. A long table with black-and-red tablecloths stretched through the middle of the hall, and in the center towered a four-foot ice sculpture, in which was embedded a bright red Japanese character: "sushi."

The private opening ceremony for the pioneer chefs was already under way. Toshi adjusted his gray suit jacket and red tie. Nearby stood a cluster of Japanese men in black suits. A lone woman in an elaborate kimono provided the only color.

Toshi scanned the group, keeping his distance. He identified Rocky Aoki, the founder of the Benihana chain, whose tight curly hair and dark glasses made him look like a member of the yakuza. Near Aoki stood the silver-haired president of the Mutual Trading Company, Noritoshi Kanai, the first person to recognize that Americans might actually eat sushi. Toshi's eyes landed on his old mentor Katsu, and then on Teruo Imaizumi, a chef who'd been present at the creation of the California roll; he was in a wheelchair.

The president of the rice commission, Tim Johnson, was giving a speech, pausing every few sentences so his words could be translated into Japanese.

"A hundred years ago, we had the first successful rice crop in California, after fifty years of trying. It was short-grain Japonica rice." Johnson gestured at the Japanese men in black suits. "You allowed our industry to begin, and you have allowed our industry to thrive."

Frank Rehermann, chairman of the commission and a rice grower himself, took the podium. He was a big, balding man. He doubled over in an awkward Japanese bow, directed at the men in black suits.

"*Konnichiwa*," he said. "One-third of California rice sales are to Japanese customers in the United States. A fifth of our crop is exported to Japan. People here took great risks in gambling to bring sushi to the United States, at a time when most of us didn't even know what sushi was." He bowed again, this time deeply. "*Dōmo arigatō.*"

The sushi pioneers in their black suits applauded stiffly. A few of them delivered speeches. One admitted that he still couldn't understand why Americans had adopted sushi at all. He called it a "miracle."

Hardly.

Toshi had heard enough.

Minutes later, a commission official rushed Toshi into a silent conference room. The shades were drawn. Toshi glanced around the table and took a quick inventory of the other judges.

One was Japanese—the president of a Japanese restaurant association. The rest were Caucasians—a state senator whose district included Little Tokyo, a writer for a food magazine, and a chef-instructor from the Culinary Institute of America. One more judge, an executive chef at a trendy group of grills, bars, and cafes in Sacramento, was on his way.

"This is the judges' war room," the official explained. "The chefs' war room is in there." He gestured at a set of closed doors. Behind those doors, in a large hall, eight sushi chefs were completing their preparations.

"Toshi is our consulting judge," the official said. "If any of you have any questions about how to grade something, please consult with Toshi." He handed out clipboards with scoring sheets and gave each judge a calculator.

The competing chefs would be required to create three presentations. The first would be a traditional platter of *nigiri* sushi and Japanese-style thin rolls. The second would be an American-style creative roll of their own devising. The third would be a "governor's roll"—containing a selection of Arnold Schwarzenegger's favorite sushi ingredients. The "Governator's" list included sea urchin gonads.

The sound of taiko drums thundered through the wall. Guests had begun to arrive. The commission was expecting 250 luminaries and VIPs to attend.

"Things are getting started," the official said "The competition begins at six o'clock. The chefs have forty-five minutes."

Toshi wandered back out to the atrium and found Jay. They sidled up to the hors d'oeuvres. Toshi surveyed the food.

"Sushi again?"

Jay snickered. "See, aren't you glad we ate at the airport?"

The chef-instructor from the Culinary Institute of America conferred with Toshi on scoring standards. A few minutes later, the eight contestants took their stations along three walls of the hall. The commission had chosen them based on popularity. Each chef had earned a top ranking in California's largest newspapers and dining guides. Of the most popular sushi chefs in California, only two were Japanese. Another two had Chinese roots. Three appeared to be Latino and one was Caucasian.

A commotion drew Toshi's attention. A camera crew pointed bright lights on one of the chefs, while a man with a microphone interviewed him. A crowd gathered. Toshi strolled over and maneuvered his way to the front.

It was the younger of the two Japanese chefs, Taro Arai. Arai's restaurant was here in Sacramento, and he was a local sushi celebrity. He was tall and ebullient, with an orange headband, highlights in his hair, a flashy baseball jersey, and oversized black shoes with enormous silver buckles. He beamed at the camera as he answered questions. He was clearly the crowd favorite.

Toshi was looking not at Taro Arai but at his table. It was a jumble. Vegetables and sauce containers were strewn across the surface, along with Arai's extra-long black-handled sushi knife and his Razr cellphone. Toshi shook his head and clicked his tongue.

A thunderous drum roll signaled the start of the competition and the eight chefs burst into action. The man with the microphone ran from table to table and delivered play-by-play updates over the PA system.

Jerry Warner, the Caucasian chef, had not set any ingredients out on his table, which stood nearly bare. He produced a single cucumber and commenced the process of column-peeling it, just as Toshi's students had learned to do. The TV camera and announcer swung by Warner's table for a moment and then hurried on, returning to Taro Arai's station across the room. The crowd followed. Warner kept his gaze on the knife and cucumber.

At Arai's station Toshi stood directly in front of the young Japanese chef, inches from his table, and stared at his cutting board. Arai's long knife flashed around the cutting board so fast that bits of food seemed to scatter and vaporize. Every few seconds, Arai glanced up and fired another winning smile into the crowd while he worked, never ceasing to slice, peel, chop, and squeeze. He squeezed *nigiri* so fast that his hands were a blur—each packet of fish and rice popped out from his fingers in under five seconds.

Toshi scribbled on his scoring sheet and moved on. At several stations he deducted points simply because the chefs wore watches and rings. Not even his students committed such blatant violations of basic hygiene. One chef even wore a chef's jacket with fancy pinstripe sleeves that scraped the food as he worked. Toshi was flabbergasted.

Toshi arrived at Jerry Warner's table just as the first drumbeat thundered through the hall, marking ten minutes. Toshi watched Warner slice a block of yellowtail. Warner's workspace was immaculate. Toshi returned to Arai. Jagged cuts of vegetables and fish and half-finished rolls lay scattered across his table. Arai slapped slices of whitefish onto a mound of rice and tossed on elaborate garnishes of sauces and multi-colored fish eggs. He kept smiling at the crowd of onlookers.

The second drumbeat sounded. Toshi completed another circle. He deducted more points from the other chefs, this time for using their bamboo mats upside down, for not squeezing their cucumber rolls tight and square, and for letting onions and avocado slices come in contact with plates and work surfaces. The third drumbeat sounded. Toshi visited Warner again. Warner was plating his completed sushi. Otherwise, his table was empty and spotless. Toshi returned to Arai. Arai's table looked like a grocery store hit by a typhoon.

The final drumbeat sounded. Each chef set out three plates. Toshi ignored the sushi. He strode behind the tables to scrutinize the floor and shelves at each station, checking for neatness, organization, and dropped food.

Jay rushed over to Toshi. "They need you in the war room."

Toshi shook his head. "I need more time."

When he was ready, Toshi joined the other judges. As the double doors closed behind him, the noise of the crowd faded to silence. The judges hovered over two tables against the wall. The contestants' plates of sushi were laid out like a buffet. The chef-instructor from the Culinary Institute of America, Ken Woytisek, loomed over one of the tables in his starched white chef's jacket. He was looking down at Taro Arai's plates.

Woytisek was an imposing man, with a high receding brow and a sharp nose. He taught classes on Asian cuisine. He'd traveled to Japan, India, Vietnam, Thailand, Korea, and China. Toshi approached and stood beside him. Woytisek turned to Toshi, pointed at Arai's sushi, and said, "What's all this shit?"

Toshi chuckled and nodded. He strolled down the table, raised his clipboard, and started deducting more points from other contestants. He sampled a couple of the rolls and skipped the rest. He sat down, punched the keys of his calculator, and handed in his scoring sheets.

Toshi turned to Woytisek. "Messy chefs!"

"I wasn't impressed with what I saw out there," Woytisek said. "Nor with what I tasted." Woytisek noted that only the elder Japanese chef had prepared a bucket of water and washed his hands.

Toshi nodded. "I would never let my students make sushi that way."

"They haven't been trained properly," Woytisek said.

Toshi nodded again. He handed Woytisek his business card. Woytisek offered one of his own.

"The best part of the day," Woytisek said, "was meeting you."

In the cab on the way back to the airport, Toshi and Jay reviewed the outcome. The awards had played out as Toshi had predicted. The judges had shut Taro Arai out of every category. There was such a thing as a sushi chef performing too much.

None of California's most popular sushi had much impressed the judges, and in the end, the title of Sushi Master had gone almost by default to the chef whose traditional platter was the simplest, and whose fundamental sushi-making techniques had somewhat resembled those of a traditional Japanese chef. Neither Toshi nor Jay found it ironic that the chef who'd earned the title of Sushi Master was a white guy named Jerry Warner. It confirmed everything that they believed about sushi in America. And it reminded Toshi of why he ran the California Sushi Academy. Toshi believed that anyone could become a sushi chef. Hell, *he* had become a sushi chef.

On the plane, Toshi ordered a Scotch and leaned back in his seat. Twenty-five years ago, he'd broken with tradition and introduced sushi to Americans, American style. He'd helped sushi grow deep roots in his adopted homeland. Tonight, he had seen how badly sushi in America now needed discipline. Ken Woytisek had put it exactly right. California's most popular sushi chefs hadn't been properly trained.

As the plane descended over L.A., Toshi gazed down at the lights of the sprawling city. Maybe American sushi still needed him after all.

48

PIZZA PARTY

Friday morning, Kate walked into the empty dining room at Hama Hermosa in flip-flops, her lovely brown hair dangling loose for the first time all semester. The other students trickled in. Without their white jackets and hats they looked like ordinary civilians. Only Marcos, in a tight black T-shirt, looked more mature and handsome than he had in his rumpled chef's gear.

Takumi, though, was wearing his chef's jacket. He'd been kneading pizza dough and simmering tomatoes in the kitchen.

They sat at tables in the dining room and Jay passed out the final written exam. Kate signed her name at the top and decorated it with a love heart. The students bent over their tests.

The dining room had been stripped bare. The artwork was gone. Nail heads protruded from the walls. In the foyer, the shiny gold Buddha had vanished. The only decoration that remained was Phil Jackson's signature on the wall.

When Takumi completed his test he rushed back to the kitchen. He donned an apron and poured himself a glass of red wine. He sprinkled flour on the counter and leaned into his pizza dough with the heels of his hands. He wore a baseball cap, backwards, emblazoned with the Japanese character "sushi."

One by one, the other students finished their tests. A group of them went out for ice cream and strolled in the sun near the beach, while Jay tallied up the students' scores for the semester.

Around noon, the restaurant manager shoved the dining room tables together to form a large rectangle. He spread out white tablecloths, and Toshi set out silver wine chillers loaded with ice and expensive bottles of sake.

The students reconvened and welcomed family and friends. Marcos's mother had flown in from Colorado. Soon Takumi carried in platters of pizza, spaghetti, and risotto from the kitchen, and the kitchen chef brought in chicken wings and pork stew. Jay had brought ribs.

Jay called the group to attention.

"I was really surprised by your sashimi test," Jay said, referring to a section of the practical exams. "Everyone has really improved." He paused. "I'm really proud of you guys."

Jay held up a sheaf of papers, one for each student showing his or her total score for the semester and where they ranked. "These don't show who got what score, except for your own."

Toshi grabbed the papers. "I can tell who was Marcos and Katie!"

Everyone laughed, even Kate.

Toshi grew serious and called out names, one by one. Each student stood up, and Toshi presented the new graduate with a diploma, a class photo, and a scorecard. The students applauded each other. When Toshi got to Kate, he gave her a hug. When he called out Marcos's name, Marcos looked surprised. "I graduated?" He raised his fist.

Toshi handed out awards, one for the student who earned the highest score in the class, and another to Takumi, who came in second. Then Toshi announced a special award.

"Kate!"

She stood up and he handed her a stuffed kangaroo—a mini Zoran.

Next, Toshi delivered a short speech.

"This week I went to the Sushi Master's competition. I was not very impressed. I was wondering why I had to decide a Sushi Master from them. My students were better." The class cheered and Toshi nodded. "They were messy. So remember what I told you. Keep clean, keep your cutting board clean. Okay, that's it."

Toshi asked each student to give a speech, too. When it was Kate's turn, she stood up and cleared her throat.

"I wish I'd prepared something!" She paused. "Oh, wait." With a flourish, she pulled a piece of paper from her pocket. Everyone laughed. "First," she said, dabbing her eyes like a swooning movie star, "I'd like to thank the Academy!" More laughter.

Kate grew serious. "I had a really good time with you guys, especially being one of two girls." In the end, Kate did feel like one of the guys, and it was clear that her classmates had accepted her. "I'll miss you," she said.

When it was Takumi's turn, he hooked his thumbs on the straps of his apron and bowed. "Thank you very much," he said. He hesitated. "I have to study English more. Thank you very much."

"Let's toast," Jay said, "to the thirtieth class of the California Sushi Academy."

After the formalities, Kate gave each of her classmates a manila envelope. Inside was a note, plus an enlargement of a photo her mom had taken of the group during the student sushi bar.

Toshi shouted out to the group. "Okay, let's eat!" He paused. "Ah, we have no sushi today."

There were chuckles. Everyone dug in, happy to be eating cooked food.

Soon, Marcos said his good-byes. Kate gave him a hug. Toshi clapped him on the shoulder and shook his hand. "Good luck."

Toshi sat down and munched on a piece of Takumi's pizza. He snorted a happy laugh.

"Good class," he said. "Good teamwork." A few minutes later he slipped away.

Takumi sat in a booth with Tetsu. Takumi would board a plane for Japan in a few days. He looked forward to seeing his wife and daughter, but he dreaded arriving at Tokyo airport. The paparazzi would no doubt be waiting. Takumi hoped to return to America someday, perhaps to open his own restaurant.

Kate hung around until the party petered out. Finally she said her good-byes and went home. She came right back the next day.

Kate had completed all her intern hours, but Jay was teaching a final civilian class and Kate wanted to help out. She ladled out sushi rice with the bamboo paddle. She fetched plates, cut nori into half-sheets, and helped the beginners with their basic cucumber rolls—the *kappa-maki*.

While they worked, Jay tried to convey the importance of the cucumber roll to the group. "If you screw up a *kappa-maki* in a job interview," Jay explained, "it's like having an accident during a driver's test."

Kate nodded and pursed her lips. "That damn *kappa-maki* was my nemesis."

Before the end of class Jay delivered a few final words.

"Everyone take a good look at Kate. She may be serving you sushi someday."

Kate held out her hands, flipped them like a magician performing for a crowd, and smiled.

The class dispersed. Sunshine streamed through the skylights, illuminating Kate's white jacket. She stood where Zoran used to stand, at the head of the table, and made herself a spicy tuna roll, the motions now familiar and comforting. When she'd finished, she wrapped up the leftover sushi rice and spicy tuna mix so she could take it home and practice. She wiped down the classroom table until it was spotless. She put away a few odds and ends. Then she stood still and looked around the room.

The room was silent. The floor freezers and the fridge sat unplugged, their doors propped open. The classroom shelves were empty. Kate gazed at the corkboard on the wall. Some Polaroid photos that the students had taken of each other hung from pushpins. The photos had already yellowed, as if they were a hundred years old.

She peered into the front sushi bar. The lowboy fridges under the counter sat silent, their doors propped open, too.

"So empty," Kate murmured. "So weird." She gazed at the empty fish cases.

Jay stood in the hallway and watched her, his shoulder against the wall. She strolled back into the classroom and ran her fingers down the length of the long steel table.

"Well, I guess this is it," she said. She glanced once more at the place she had stood for twelve weeks. "Good-bye, table." She waved, then turned away.

On the service shelf in the hall sat a stack of plates bearing the logo of the California Sushi Academy. She looked at Jay.

"Can I take a plate?"

"You want a CSA plate?"

"Yeah."

Jay nodded "Go ahead."

She hugged the plate to her chest.

"Oh," Jay added, handing her a book. "Something for you from upstairs. A sushi cookbook."

"Thanks, Jay."

"Work hard, make us proud."

"I will. Monday, I'm going to start looking for a job."

Epilogue

49

HOMECOMING

*W*hen Kate returned to her apartment, she was sniffling. By Monday she had the flu. She lay around feeling wretched. One day she got a call from Jeff, the job guy and restaurant consultant. He told her that a shopping mall near Beverly Hills had launched an upscale food court with a sushi bar. It was no nightclub, but they were looking for chefs.

The manager drove down to Torrance to interview Kate at Starbucks. He looked Asian, but she wasn't sure if he was Japanese. The place was scheduled to open November 16—Kate's twenty-first birthday. Kate was willing to wait if it meant getting a job in the area. Jeff had recommended a few of the other students from the class for jobs there, too. It would be like old times.

November 16 turned into December. Kate sat around her apartment with nothing to do. She got depressed. The one bright spot arrived in her computer's inbox, from Australia. An e-mail from Zoran, saying hi.

The sushi bar finally opened the second week of December. Kate drove to the mall. With traffic, the commute was two hours each way.

The manager ran the operation like a sushi-roll factory. Kate and two of her classmates were the cheap labor. They squeezed out California rolls and spicy tuna rolls a hundred at a time, and stuffed them in fridges for the lunch rush. This was not how Kate had been taught to serve sushi. She rarely interacted with customers. She never received any tips.

Every day Kate dragged herself out of bed at 5:00 a.m., arrived at the mall by 8:00 a.m., and worked a ten-hour shift. The shifts grew longer. One day she was in the middle of a fourteen-hour shift when a woman took a bite from one of the mass-produced California rolls and complained. 'This is rancid!'

Kate wasn't surprised. The roll wasn't fresh. Before Kate could say anything the manager interceded. He blamed Kate, and apologized to the woman. 'I won't let you pay for anything that she made that you don't like.'

Tears welled up in Kate's eyes, but she held them back. The manager told her to step outside and have a smoke. It was her only break all day.

By the weekend Kate was sick again. On her way to work she called in and asked if she could switch days. On the phone, she got the feeling that they didn't care that she was sick, and that she was expendable.

She turned the car around. She called one of her classmates and told him not to expect her at the mall anymore. He quit a week later. When Kate received her paycheck, it was less than half of what they owed her. Her sushi diploma hadn't even earned her the minimum wage.

Kate rifled through her collection of photos and found a picture of herself that she liked. It made her look tough. She stuck the picture on the dashboard of her Mustang.

Then Kate drove around Torrance. She stopped at every sushi place she found, walked in, and asked for a job. The Asian sushi chefs just looked at her funny. She walked back out and sat in the car for a minute and stared at her picture. Then she drove to the next place and did it again.

By mid-January Kate was out of money and sinking back into depression. She lost her appetite. Her weight was down 10 pounds. She conceded defeat, loaded up her belongings, and drove back to San Diego. She couldn't afford an apartment so she moved in with her grandparents. She drove down to Mexico to visit friends and sit on the beach for a week and think.

Kate had worked a lot of different jobs. She had never liked anything as much as interacting with customers at the sushi bar. Staring out at the Pacific Ocean, Kate decided she hadn't come this far to give up sushi. She drove back to San Diego with a plan.

First, Kate swallowed her pride and went to work at the surf shop owned by her ex-boyfriend. It was only to pick up extra cash. Luckily the ex-boyfriend was away.

She still had the picture of herself stuck in the dashboard of her car. She drove up and down the boulevards of Pacific Beach in San Diego. She'd never seen so many sushi restaurants. A one-mile stretch contained Haiku Sushi, Mika Sushi, Kabuki, Tokyo House, Zen Five Sushi, Mister Sushi, Reggae Sushi, and Pacific Beach Sushi. Surely, one of them would need a chef. She walked into each restaurant and introduced herself. These Asian sushi chefs looked at her funny, too. Pacific Beach Sushi offered her a job as a waitress.

Then Kate noticed a brand-new restaurant off the main drag called Wasabi Sushi. A "Help Wanted" sign hung in the window.

She took a deep breath and strode in. Customers sat at the sushi bar. Kate introduced herself to the Asian man behind the bar and explained that she was a graduate of the California Sushi Academy, and that she was looking for a position as a chef. The man listened to her pitch. He offered Kate a piece of advice. 'Girls can't be sushi chefs.'

She walked back out and sat in her car and stared at her picture. It no longer helped.

In the comic book *Sushi Chef Kirara's Job,* the young female chef Kirara is full of confidence when she enters the televised sushi-making competition "Sushi Battle 21." She advances to the final showdown, where she faces her muscle-bound arch-rival, the male chef Sakamaki. Whoever wins five battles first will win the overall competition.

Kirara loses her first three battles against the huge man. Her confidence is destroyed.

Kirara's teacher tells her to stop focusing on her outward technique. Instead, her teacher says, Kirara must show the judges her soul.

Two weeks later Kate's grandmother handed her a newspaper with three classified ads for sushi-chef positions. Kate dutifully called all three and left messages.

She was driving around town running errands when her phone rang. She spoke with a man named Jack. He told her to stop by the restaurant.

'Right now?'

'Yeah, sure, right now.'

Kate swung the car around and pulled into a half-finished retail development near the football stadium. She found the place. It was next to a McDonald's. It was called Oki Ton Japanese Bistro.

In the entryway hung an elegant kimono. Kate peered inside and saw a thick wood sushi bar topped with a serving step of black granite and a row of shiny black fish cases. From the ceiling hung yellow paper lanterns and sloping sections of pale wood, evoking the roof of a Buddhist temple. Standing in the middle of it all was a tall man with a pointy chin, a long sharp nose, and salt-and-pepper hair. He wasn't Asian. Actually, he looked Italian. This was Jack.

Jack told Kate the manager would return in a few minutes. Perhaps the manager would be Asian. When the man arrived he looked like Jack. He held out his hand. His name was Arbie. He was Jack's brother.

Jack and Arbie Kenefick were Bostonians with Irish-Italian roots. They had recently returned from a couple of decades in Japan. Their goal was to serve Japanese food in the United States in a more authentic fashion than the Japanese did. When they saw Kate, they thought she might be able to interact with American customers more easily than someone who wasn't American. The result would be an experience closer to what a Japanese customer at a sushi bar experienced in Japan.

Arbie chatted with Kate for a few minutes.

'Why don't you come in the day after tomorrow and do prep,' Arbie said. 'We'll see what you can do.'

Oh crap, Kate thought, *they're going to make me cut cucumbers!* She was out of practice. She knew what would happen if she screwed up a cucumber roll in a job interview.

When Kate returned two days later, she hunted down prep work like a tuna hunting squid. She washed and cooked rice. She prepped crabmeat and spicy tuna mix. She quartered avocados. She stirred water into the wasabi powder. She cut cucumbers. Out of the corner of her eye she watched the guys—the other chefs, the dishwashers, even the delivery men—and did everything they did.

Arbie watched Kate. He told her to come in for a few more days. Finally, he took her aside.

'You need practice,' Arbie told her. 'But you're a hard worker. We'll keep you.'

The head sushi chef, a strict Korean named Randy, gave Kate a simple black chef's coat with Chinese buttons and stationed her in a corner of the sushi bar, away from the customers, where he pelted her with roll orders during lunch and dinner. She improved her cutting technique, and wrapped pink ribbons around the handles of her knives so everyone would know which were hers. She kept them sharp.

Randy and the other sushi chefs started teaching her things. Soon Randy asked for Kate's help in decapitating fish and descaling them in the kitchen. Cutting up fish suddenly seemed important in a way that it hadn't at the sushi academy. Kate's customers would actually be eating these fish. She paid more attention to the work.

After a week or two, Randy gave Kate her own station at the sushi bar, where she could interact with customers. The other sushi chefs didn't speak much English, but customers could get into real conversations with Kate, and she was fun to talk to. She would suggest things for them to try and recommend sushi that wasn't even on the menu.

At first the customers said, 'Wow, a girl sushi chef!' Now they walked in and said, 'Hey Kate, how's it going?'

Sometimes her regular customers would buy Kate a beer. She didn't even like beer, but those beers tasted delicious. After three weeks, the other chefs started splitting their tips with Kate. When customers settled the check and got up to leave, Arbie always asked if they'd enjoyed their meal. Sometimes Kate overheard what they said. 'Kate is great! We're coming back!'

One day in March, Kate took a break between lunch and dinner and hopped in the Mustang.

She cruised past all the sushi restaurants that had turned her down. She drove by her ex-boyfriend's surf shop. Then she gunned the Mustang past Wasabi Sushi, where the Asian man had told her that girls couldn't be sushi chefs. She shook her fist out the window and yelled, "I'll see you in hell!"

Kate drove back to Jack and Arbie's restaurant and took her station behind the sushi bar. At five o'clock people began streaming in. By seven the place was packed. Arbie turned down the lights. The yellow paper lanterns glowed overhead. Customers filled the sushi bar.

A gentleman strolled into the restaurant and sat in front of Kate. She engaged him in conversation while squeezing out *nigiri* for his dinner.

The man leaned back in his chair and watched her. He said something and smiled. Kate laughed. The sound soared across the room, like a flying fish breaking the surface of the sea.

ONE YEAR LATER

𝒟uring the summer of 2006, Kate was still working as a sushi chef in San Diego. She subsequently decided to advance her chef training further by applying to the San Diego Culinary Institute. Marcos was working as a sushi chef in Colorado, and planned to attend college. In Tokyo, Takumi was working as a chef at a Korean restaurant, with the goal of continuing to expand his culinary horizons. Fie returned to Denmark, where she endured a difficult year of discrimination by Asian chefs at a sushi restaurant. Eventually, however, she was offered the position of head chef, as well as a job filming a Danish sushi-making instructional video.

In Los Angeles, Toshi reopened the California Sushi Academy at a new location near Marina del Ray, north of Hermosa Beach, and Zoran returned to the academy to teach in the fall of 2006. Jay teamed up with his friend Jeff, the restaurant consultant, to found a new consulting company called ZeroSushi, with the goal of helping restaurant owners with no prior experience in sushi enter the business.

Volume 13 of the comic book *Sushi Chef Kirara's Job* was released in October 2006, with Kirara having fallen behind in the sushi-making competition. On the last page of the volume, she switches—like a kung-fu warrior—to a new sushi-making stance and announces that she is about to unleash a secret weapon.

For more on the story of sushi, and for photos of some of the people and events described in the book, please visit www.TheZenOfFish.com.

Appendix

HOW TO EAT SUSHI

Many Americans walk into a sushi restaurant and opt to sit at a table because they find the sushi bar intimidating. Sitting at a table feels familiar, as does ordering from a menu. California rolls and other American-style sushi rolls are often the preferred items simply because the diner knows what to expect.

Turning one's back on familiarity and choosing to sit at the sushi bar requires courage, but the experience is more interesting. For starters, most of the sushi that traditional chefs serve at the bar is not rolls, but *nigiri*—hand-squeezed rectangles of rice topped with fish. *Not* knowing what to expect, either with the ingredients or the order in which they are served, is part of the fun.

Americans can take solace in the knowledge that they are not alone. Many Japanese people also find the sushi bar intimidating. In 2005, a pair of Japanese comedians, known for their irreverent cultural commentary, produced a video called *Sushi: The Japanese Tradition*. The video has become popular on the Internet, in both the United States and Japan. "Sushi," the narrator says, "is a snack that represents Japan." When the narrator utters the next sentence, the astute viewer gets his first clue that something is up: "Most Japanese people eat at a sushi bar every day." Japanese viewers find this amusing, since quite the opposite is true. Many Japanese people—especially women—seldom eat at sushi bars because they are frightened of them, just as many Westerners are.

As the video progresses, it pokes fun at the insecurities of the average Japanese person about proper behavior in a sushi bar. The video provides instructions on how to act. In the process, it plays on the obsession most Japanese people have with social etiquette.

For example, the video explains that when entering a sushi bar, a patron must place his hand on the curtain over the entrance at a point 3.2 inches from the corner, at an angle of 48 degrees, before flipping the curtain out of the way. Inside, he must demonstrate his fine manners, and his sensitivity to social obligation, by bowing to other patrons and asking if the empty seats at the bar are available. At the bar, he is instructed to pour exactly 20 cubic centimeters of soy sauce into his dish. He must address the chef only as "chief." In addition, he must never ask the chef about himself because all sushi chefs have a secret past. Here, the chef glowers menacingly at the camera while slowly polishing the long blade of his knife.

Japanese viewers recognize all this as satire. But some have worried, in their comments on the Internet, that Westerners might take the video seriously. After all, Westerners are even less familiar with sushi-bar etiquette than are the Japanese. For starters—as the video points out—there are no waiters, waitresses, or menus at a traditional sushi bar. So how do you even order?

In reality, when a customer sits down at a sushi bar in Japan, he or she generally utters one of three words to begin: "*okimari*," "*okonomi*," or "*omakase*" (the latter is pronounced oh•mah•ka•say). The ordering will proceed differently depending on which of these three approaches the customer chooses.

The first option, *okimari*, literally means "it's been decided." The customer uses this word to indicate that he has chosen to eat the shop's standard "set meal," a sushi sampler at a fixed price. The chef chooses the contents and serves the sushi to the customer all at once.

The second option, *okonomi*, literally means "as I like it." The customer uses this word to indicate that he knows what he wants. He asks the chef for different kinds of fish, one by one, as he eats. The order in which the customer requests different types of fish is not crucial, but most sushi connoisseurs begin with leaner, lighter-tasting fish and progress toward fish with stronger flavors and higher fat content. At most sushi bars, when the customer asks for an order of a given sushi topping, the chef makes two *nigiri*.

Japanese customers seldom eat more than two *nigiri* topped with any given fish, before moving on to a different topping. For most Japanese, the point of sushi is to enjoy the variety. *Okonomi* customers who order only high-end items such as fatty tuna, sea urchin, and rare clams can, of course, expect their bill at the end of the evening to be higher than average.

The third option, *omakase,* literally means "I leave it up to you." This is an invitation to the chef to impress the customer with his finest ingredients, served in the order the chef believes will best highlight the flavors of the toppings. The chef may include other small dishes to augment the sushi. Generally, when a customer orders *omakase,* this indicates that he is not overly concerned about the price of the meal and is prepared to accept a certain level of expense.

Regardless of how the customer orders, some sushi experts suggest that it is the customer's responsibility to know the price range of a particular sushi bar before walking in the door. And because the selections of fish at a high-quality sushi bar vary by the day, the customer must be willing to trust the chef's calculation of the cost of the meal. It's bad form to quibble.

Sometimes the customer comes out ahead. In Japan, traditional sushi chefs are famous for calculating each customer's bill from memory. In an interview, one of Tokyo's most respected sushi chefs, Jirō Ono, admitted that he frequently forgets to charge customers for very fatty tuna, one of the most expensive items he serves. He laughed and told his interviewer that the amount of money he'd forgotten to charge customers over the years probably added up to eight or nine thousand dollars.

In the United States, many sushi restaurants have introduced menus and clear pricing because that is what Americans expect. But while menus may make American customers more comfortable, menus can also have the effect of discouraging customers from asking the chef about the other items currently available.

There is another approach to ordering. The customer can simply ask the chef what he recommends. The satirical video *Sushi: the Japanese Tradition* suggests that many sushi ingredients come from endangered species that have been illegally harvested, so the chef won't tell you about them unless you ask. At this point in the video, even most Western viewers will recognize the video as satire, as pictures of sea turtles, exotic lizards, and panda bears flash across the screen. The customers in the video say to themselves, "I know nothing," "It's none of my business," "It's the chef who's bad," as they swallow pieces of sushi. "Thinking these thoughts," the narrator comments, "is the Japanese people's way of allowing everyone to enjoy a wide variety of protected species." The joke is funny. But considering the plight of the bluefin tuna, for example, it is actually this portion of the satire that rings most true, and not just for Japan.

Next come the mechanics of eating the sushi once it's been ordered. A few inches above the counter at most sushi bars there is a narrow shelf, which the chef can easily reach. If a customer orders *okonomi* or *omakase,* the chef places a rectangular stand, usually made of wood, on the shelf. The stand will be empty, except for a mound of pickled ginger. (Only in the United States do chefs also add a mound of wasabi.) This rectangular stand is called a *geta* because it looks like a traditional Japanese wooden sandal by the same name. The customer should leave the *geta* on the shelf, where the chef can reach it. The chef will place orders of *nigiri* on the *geta.* If he serves *nigiri* with more than a small dab of sauce, he will most likely serve them on a plate, so the *geta* will remain clean.

Most sushi bars put out bottles of soy sauce, as well as a small dish for soy sauce for each customer. The better sushi bars augment the soy sauce with dashi broth, sake, and mirin to produce a "house" soy sauce, or *nikiri.* The best sushi chefs often add their own sauce or seasoning to the fish before serving it, and instruct the customer not to add extra soy sauce. Some sushi connoisseurs forgo soy sauce in any case, preferring to concentrate on the subtle flavors of the fish.

As for wasabi, chefs in Japan don't serve extra wasabi on the side because they put what they consider the proper amount in the *nigiri* itself, between the topping and the rice. Generally, the chef increases the amount of wasabi with toppings that have a high fat content. Many Americans have developed the habit of stirring extra wasabi into their soy sauce. Chefs and most Japanese diners frown on this practice. It's better for the customer to ask the chef to adjust the amount of wasabi inside the *nigiri* to match the customer's preference. Americans stir the wasabi into their soy sauce to increase the level of spiciness. Ironically, however, wasabi (and the green horseradish that passes for wasabi) rapidly looses its spiciness and flavor when immersed in liquid.

A good *nigiri* ought to melt in the mouth, so chefs prefer not to pack the rice too firmly. Most connoisseurs pick up sushi with their fingers, since chopsticks are likely to break apart a loosely packed *nigiri*. Some people claim that chopsticks are preferable because the flavors of the different fish linger on their hands, preventing full appreciation of each separate topping. But most sushi bars provide each customer with a damp cloth, and wiping one's fingers between each type of *nigiri* should be sufficient to keep the flavors separate. Likewise, the purpose of the pickled ginger is to cleanse the palate between different types of fish. The ginger shouldn't be eaten as an appetizer, but it is fine to ask for more if the supply on the *geta* runs out.

Methods for eating *nigiri* with one's hands vary from person to person. One option is as follows. The diner presses his thumb and middle finger lightly against the sides of the *nigiri*, at the rectangle's midpoint. He extends his index finger along the top of the *nigiri*, down its length. The grip is a bit like the grip he would use on a computer mouse. Holding the *nigiri* lightly, he lifts it off the *geta*. He curls his index finger, pulling the far end of the *nigiri* upward and toward him with the tip of the finger. He allows the rectangle to rotate 180 degrees "head over heels," while continuing to hold it between the thumb and middle finger, so that it is now upside down. This allows the diner to dip the fish side of the *nigiri* in the soy sauce, rather than the rice side. If the diner dips the rice side of a loosely packed *nigiri* into the soy sauce, the *nigiri* will disintegrate in the soy sauce dish.

Chefs who see customers using chopsticks or dipping the rice side in the soy sauce will pack the *nigiri* more tightly than is ideal. Even when a customer doesn't dip the *nigiri* in soy sauce, many prefer to turn the *nigiri* upside down so that the fish touches the tongue first, but that is a matter of preference. If the customer isn't using soy sauce, it's perfectly acceptable to put the *nigiri* in the mouth fish side up.

Either way, a *nigiri* should always be eaten in one bite. It should also be eaten as soon as the chef serves it, so that it can be enjoyed at the proper temperature, with the rice still slightly warm. Traditional sushi rolls—with the seaweed on the outside—should also be eaten right away, before the seaweed gets soggy. If the chef serves a platter, the rolls with seaweed on the outside should be eaten before the *nigiri*.

The etiquette for eating sashimi—slices of raw fish without rice—is a bit different. Sashimi should always be eaten with chopsticks. (It is bad form to rub the chopsticks together before use. The assumption that the chopsticks contain splinters is an insult to the chef.) Chefs serve a small mound of wasabi on the side with sashimi. To avoid losing the spiciness and flavor of the wasabi by mixing it with liquid, the customer should dab a bit of wasabi directly onto the slice of fish with his chopsticks, then dip a different corner of the fish in soy sauce. The garnishes that come with sashimi—usually a green perilla leaf and shredded radish—are meant to be eaten and provide digestive benefits.

Opinions among sushi experts vary as to whether to ask the sushi chef about his "secret past," as the video jokingly says. Most believe that what makes sushi unique is the intimacy that develops between the chef and his customers. Becoming acquainted with a particular chef, and returning to his sushi bar repeatedly, is one of the best ways for a customer to broaden his horizons. The chef is likely to serve his most interesting and highest quality ingredients to his regular customers. That said, a few sushi experts argue that the customer ought to keep a respectful distance from the chef.

Either way, most experts agree on one thing. Customers who show off their sushi knowledge at the sushi bar are tiresome. Chefs appreciate customers who would rather eat sushi than talk about it.

ACKNOWLEDGMENTS

J owe an enormous debt to Harold McGee, whose masterpiece, *On Food and Cooking: The Science and Lore of the Kitchen,* was my primary source for basic food science; I relied heavily on the book. For the history and culture of sushi, I relied primarily on the work of several Japanese scholars and writers, including Naomichi Ishige, Mitsuru Nakamura, Shinzo Satomi, and Masuo Yoshino.

It was my good fortune that Jay Terauchi answered the phone when I first telephoned the California Sushi Academy (CSA). Jay immediately understood my intent and was a steadfast and sensitive advocate for my research during the three months that I became a perpetual presence at the school and restaurant. On numerous occasions he explained my presence to the chefs, instructors, students, and restaurant staff and encouraged them to put up with my intrusion and to answer my questions. He also reminded me to be sensitive to their needs, and to the logistics of a cramped and busy workplace where extremely sharp knives, shooting flames, and vats of hot oil were constant features. Along with Jay, Jeffrey Nitta engaged me in hours of conversation about sushi in America and was a source of thought-provoking ideas, background information, and fascinating stories.

Toshi Sugiura generously gave me the run of his school and restaurant. I can imagine no other sushi chef who would let a reporter don a chef's jacket and stand behind the sushi bar with a notebook during dinner service—not just once, but nearly every night.

The students and instructors at CSA in the summer of 2005 hadn't signed up to be written about. As I became a fixture in their classroom, they were extraordinarily tolerant of my presence.

I am especially grateful to instructor Zoran Lekic and students Kate Murray, Takumi Nishio, and Marcos Wisner, who ended up becoming the focus of the classroom scenes in the book. I also owe special thanks to the other instructor, Tetsuya Tsumoto, and the students not mentioned by name in the book: Jenard de Castro, Reo Julyant, Shane Koenig, Elena Puig, Karen Saito, and Fabiel Yepo. In addition, Fie Kruse was a keen observer of the chefs and students—and of herself. I appreciate the candor with which she shared her thoughts.

After getting to know me and coming to understand my intent, the people I describe in the book signed release forms that gave me the freedom to write about them honestly. I am grateful.

The rest of the staff at CSA and the Hama Hermosa restaurant during the summer of 2005 also have my appreciation, including Takashi Koike, Wataru Shiratori, Danica Yamasato, Caitlin Earl, Kimiko Masuda, Tricia Watters, Sheila Hwang, and Filipé Sanchez. Restaurant manager Susumu Jimbo deserves particular thanks for fielding my numerous requests for fish-market invoices and other restaurant and school documents, and also for several informative conversations.

Nikki Gilbert, a graduate of CSA and owner of the Sushi Girl catering and teaching operation spent an evening showing me around Venice Beach, telling me her story and bringing to life the glory days of Toshi's old restaurant, Hama Venice. Tali Sever and Philip Yi, both CSA veterans, spent part of an afternoon with me at their store, Sushi Central in Culver City, sharing tales of the academy and sushi in America and Japan. Thanks also to Tracy Griffith for sharing her CSA stories.

Beth Horan and Paul Buttner of the California Rice Commission kindly made the arrangements necessary for me to report from behind the scenes at the 2005 Sushi Masters competition in Sacramento. Dave and Kathy Rudie of Catalina Offshore Products in San Diego showed me their sea-urchin operation and discussed the history of sushi in southern California. Ted Wakeman and Bridgett Klingler at Pacific Farms in Florence, Oregon, talked with me about wasabi in America and showed me their former farm and current processing facility. Clark Sayer of Clark Sayer & Associates taught me about the science of wasabi. Nach Waxman at Kitchen

Arts and Letters in New York City was a stimulating source of ideas, encouragement, and reference materials. These people and many others related to the world of sushi assisted me in a variety of ways. They all have my profound gratitude.

My editor at HarperCollins, Hugh Van Dusen, has been able to envision my books as completed works before I can. His belief in my book on sushi was ardent from the beginning, and it never wavered, in spite of repeated delays, changes of direction by the author, and down-to-the-wire suspense with the approach of deadlines. Marie Estrada at HarperCollins provided sanity, camaraderie, advocacy, understanding, and humor as she helped get me through the entire process. Over the past few years the enthusiastic support from the staff at HarperCollins, including in particular Jane Beirn, but also the many others who work behind the scenes, has been a dream come true.

Stuart Krichevsky also saw the book's potential more clearly than I could at the beginning, and his patience and thoughtful prodding as I struggled to articulate the book's direction and purpose were a tremendous help. Stuart helped keep me on track, both as my agent through the formalities of publishing and as an astute counselor who helped me clarify my approach to the subject matter. Shana Cohen at the Krichevsky Agency was also a steadfast source of friendship and information and has my thanks as well.

At the Boston Law Group, the sage advice of Sean Ploen bolstered me at crucial moments in the creation of this book. I also wish to thank the community of editors and writers connected with the *Atlantic Monthly* magazine, as well as my teachers and colleagues at the Nieman Conference on Narrative Journalism.

My research assistants Sakiko Kajino, Jennifer Esch, and Jenny Mayo made the timely completion of this book possible, and amplified the depth and breadth of its contents. I made a point of using my Japanese language skills for both the oral and textual portions of the research for this book, and I translated two of the Japanese books that I used as references. However, the sheer volume of material available in Japanese prevented me from perusing it all myself, and Sakiko Kajino, a graduate student in linguistics at Georgetown University, became my other set of eyes for Japanese-language information on sushi. Sakiko's enthusiasm was unbounded, her ability to locate exactly what I was searching for was uncanny, and her contribution to the book was enormous. Jennifer Esch, a brilliant undergraduate at Harvard University with a sure-fire instinct for weird and wonderful science, did most of the hunting through libraries, databases, journals, and scientific texts for the morsels of biological, behavioral, and ecological drama that helped bring the book alive. Jenny Mayo, a graduate student in nonfiction writing at Johns Hopkins University and herself an accomplished journalist, performed the many hours of meticulous legwork behind the survey of Midwest American sushi that appears in Chapter 20. I am deeply indebted to all three of my assistants; the book is far richer for their contributions. In addition, the book could not have been completed on time without the heroic efforts of Dolores Young and her team at ACE Transcription Service, whose ability to read my handwritten notes bordered on the supernatural.

In a category of her own is Jennifer Hammock. She worked as a research assistant, gathering biological, behavioral, and ecological information on the creatures in the book. Even more important, she worked closely with me as a freelance editor on the manuscript during the crucial first two drafts. She suggested radical improvements to both the narrative and the explanatory material, and accomplished the seemingly insurmountable task of carving an unwieldy manuscript down to size. She was a solid pillar of good sense, rational commentary, and exceptionally careful editing. More generally, throughout the year that I was researching and writing the book, she was a source of scientific education and helpful conversation. The book is far better for her involvement.

Sarah Corson performed several meticulous edits to subsequent drafts of the book and improved the readability of the text immensely. I am indebted to her for this, and for a lifetime of encouragement and wise counsel in the use of the written word for effective communication. Dick Atlee and Michael Vazquez generously read the manuscript and made numerous helpful suggestions as well. My brother Ash Corson also provided valuable comments on the manuscript while writing his own book. Moreover, without Ash I might never have managed to spend three months at CSA. He allowed me to encamp in his little apartment in L.A. with my suitcases and stacks of notebooks, and he was always ready to lend a car, bicycle, and sympathetic ear as I pursued sushi and its practitioners into uncharted territory.

My family, friends, and advisors helped me through a challenging year with this book, and I'm thankful for the presence of all of them in my life.

My previous book, *The Secret Life of Lobsters,* was about one creature, and that was daunting enough. This book is about—at last count—approximately thirty plants and animals (not including the humans), plus a set of foreign culinary traditions dating back more than a thousand years. While I have received a huge amount of help with this book, any mistakes it contains remain my responsibility.

SOURCE NOTES

$\mathcal{T}$he scenes described in the book that occurred during 2005 and 2006 are based on firsthand reporting by the author (as detailed in the Author's Note at the beginning of the book) unless a scene is noted below as a reconstruction based on interviews. Chapters that relied on no additional sources other than firsthand reporting by the author are not included below. The references in the notes below are listed in approximate order of importance for each subject. The references indicate items that are listed in the Bibliography, unless otherwise noted. For Bibliography items, the primary author's name is given, plus page numbers for the longer documents; if the item has no author listed, the first word or two of the item's title is given instead. Many of the books and other documents referenced for *The Zen of Fish* were in Japanese, and were translated by myself or my research assistant Sakiko Kajino of Georgetown University. California Sushi Academy is abbreviated as "CSA" throughout.

1. SUSHI SCHOOL

Reconstruction of week 1 of summer CSA class, 5 July 2005–8 July 2005: interviews with Kate Murray (10 and 23 Aug. 2005, 29 Sep. 2005, 24 Mar. 2006), Jay Terauchi (23 Sep. 2005), Jenard de Castro (18 Aug. 2005), and Toshi Sugiura (23 Sep. 2005); also, diary entry for 11 July 2005 by Jenard de Castro. **History of Hama Venice and CSA:** Tamamura 256–260; Louie; interviews with Toshi Sugiura (21 Sep. 2005), Jeffrey Nitta (21 July 2005, 9 Sep. 2005), and Robert Stanfield (25 Aug. 2005). **CSA student nationality and employment data:** Louie; "Sushi Academy." **Boisterous sushi chefs of old Tokyo:** Omae 86; Ishige 227–228. **Other CSA students attending sum-**

mer 2005 semester: interviews with Reo Julyant (23 Sep. 2005), Shane Koenig (25 Aug. 2005), Fabiel Yepo (10, 11, and 23 Aug. 2005), Elena Puig (13 Sep. 2005), Marcos Wisner (16 July 2005, 17–22 Aug. 2005), Karen Saito (16 July 2005), and Jenard de Castro (18 Aug. 2005). **Japanese swords and knives:** Ishige 206–213; Satō 53; Nagayama, Kokan 3, 44; Klippensteen 13–20; "Hōchō-shiki."

2. EATING TO LIVE

Kate's personal history and decision to attend CSA: interviews with Kate Murray (10 and 23 Aug. 2005, 29 Sep. 2005, 24 Mar. 2006) and Jay Terauchi (23 Sep. 2005). **Short story "Sushi":** Okamoto 31–60.

3. MOLD

Reconstruction of CSA visit to miso factory on 8 July 2005: see "1. Sushi School" above; also, author visit to Miyako Oriental Foods miso factory and interviews with factory staff Terry Shimizu and Joe Arai (22 Mar. 2006). **History and science of miso and soy sauce:** Shurtleff (1983) 28–29, 212–231, 248–254; Shurtleff (2004); Ishige 39–40, 113–117; Hosking 211–214, 220–221; interview with Terry Shimizu (22 Mar. 2006). **Lack of dairy in Japan:** Ishige 58–62. **Enzymes:** Thain 239–241; McGee 809; Radzicka. **Glutamate:** Thain 307; McGee 175, 271, 806; Steingarten 91–99. **Fermented fish paste:** Ishige 36; McGee 235. **Buddhism and Japanese vegetarianism:** Ishige 45–58. **Vinegar and acetic acid:** McGee 772–775.

4. TASTE OF THE SEA

Dashi, kelp, and bonito flakes: Ishige 219–224; Hosking 200–203, 206–208; McGee 237–238, 334. **Bonito and ATP:** Naruse 96–97. **Nikiri sauce:** Nagayama, Kazuo 247; Nakamura 65; Sakaguchi 176; interview with Fie Kruse (19 July 2005). **MSG, IMP, and umami:** McGee 342; Steingarten 91–99; Zhao, G.Q.; Zhang, Y.; Nelson, G.; for a fascinating essay on the history of MSG, see Sand. **Reconstruction of week 2 of summer CSA class, 11 July 2005–16 July 2005:** interviews with Kate Murray (10 and 23 Aug. 2005, 29 Sep. 2005, 24 Mar. 2006). **Big Mac sauce ingredients:** "McDonald's."

5. LIKE THE VOMIT OF A DRUNKARD

Sushi rice at body temperature: Satomi 244–245; Nakamura 31–32; Tamamura 261–262. **Jay's personal history, his views on sushi in America, and his observations on CSA students:** interviews with Jay Terauchi (16 July 2005, 23 and 24 Sep. 2005). Wasabi science: McGee 415–418. **Correct and**

incorrect use of wasabi: Ikezawa 157–159; Nakamura 69–71; Nagayama, Kazuo 241. **Function of pickled ginger:** Nakamura 72. **Sushi-eating etiquette:** Omae 16; Nakamura 60–61; Nagayama, Kazuo 9. **Calories:** California roll and cheese pizza purchased from Trader Joe's in Washington, D.C., on 27 Oct. 2006. According to the labels: California roll, 600 calories; two slices of pizza, 620 calories. **Varieties of sushi:** Nakamura 43–48; Omae 110–113; Tsuji 285–289. **Apprenticeships and rice cooking:** Omae 86; Tsuji 272–273. **Early Japanese diet and agriculture:** Ishige 8–17; Kiple 132–148. **History of sushi and its fermentation process:** Ishige 35–43, 230–231; Nakamura 9–10, 13–14; Yoshino 15–20; Omae 104; Ōba 12; Sakaguchi 174–175; McGee 234, 291–293, 808; Purves 29–30. **Garum:** Ishige 36; McGee 235. **Vomit of a drunkard:** Nakamura 15. **Taxes:** Nakamura 11; Yoshino 19. **Etymology of "sushi":** Nakamura 13–14; Yoshino 20. **Rice vinegar:** Sakaguchi 175; Nakamura 12; Omae 98–99; Naruse 58–59; McGee 775 (for sake, 755–758). **California Rice Center prices:** "Rice." **Toxic bacterium:** McGee 475.

6. SEVEN GODS IN EVERY GRAIN

Rice enrichment, biology, milling, history, and nutrition: "Cereal"; Juliano chap. 6; McGee 461–462, 472–474; Kiple 132–148; Ishige 17–32; Fletcher; "Milling"; interview with Yasuo Sasaki of Japan Food Corp. Int'l (12 Sep. 2006). **Sushi apprenticeship:** Omae 86–90. **Religion and rice:** Tamaru 80–81; Omae 21; interview with Takumi Nishio (15 July 2005); e-mail interview with Sakiko Kajino of Georgetown University (4 July 2006). **Rice starches:** McGee 457–458. **Grain size and brands:** interviews with Jay Terauchi (15 July 2005), Marcos Wisner (21 Sep. 2005), and Elizabeth Horan of the California Rice Commission (13 Sep. 2005); Hama Hermosa brand was Tamanishiki, see "Premium." **Rice more important than fish:** Satomi 243. **Qualities and types of rice; blending:** Satomi 243–247; Naruse 40–47; Nakamura 30–32; Omae 56. **Miora:** "Suihan"; Araki; Purves 121–122, 738, 993. **Rice preparation and cooking:** Ishige 202–206; Naruse 50–52; Nakamura 56; e-mail interview with Fie Kruse (3 Nov. 2006). **Vinegar and sugar:** Nakamura 29–32, 55–57; Naruse 53–54; Satomi 248–249; McGee 296–298; interview with Robert Stanfield (25 Aug. 2005).

7. L.A. STORY

History of Japanese Americans: Takaki 180–219. **History of Japanese food and sushi in the U.S. and of Mutual Trading Co. and Noritoshi Kanai:** Tamamura 223–233; Nakamura 157–162; "History of Japanese Foods"; "History: Pioneers"; Fasman; Miller; Sindler; interview with Sharon Perazzoli by my research assistant Jenny Mayo of Johns Hopkins University (26 July 2006); O'Connor. **Healthy diet and omega-3s:** Nakamura 158–161; Nestle 184–185; U.S. Senate. **Toshi's personal history:** interviews with Toshi Sugiura (21 and 23 Sep. 2005), Jeffrey Nitta (21 July 2005, 9 Sep. 2005), Jay Terauchi (21 July 2005); Susumu Jimbo (20 July 2005, 17 Sep. 2005), Nikki Gilbert (26 Mar. 2006), and Danica Yamasato (16 and 21 July 2005); Tamamura 256–258; "Rosanzerusu"; Huneven.

8. BATTLE OF THE SEXES
Kirara comic: Hayakawa; scene with Sakamaki: v. 1 206; scene with hardened woman: v. 4 188–190. **Discrimination against women:** Ishige 228; Nakamura 60; Louie; Weiner; Yuyama 13–20, 23–26, 56, 114–119; Kim. **Conveyor-belt sushi:** Nakamura 37; Tamamura 41–42, 114; "Shufu." **Decline in traditional sushi business:** Yuyama 19; "Gaishoku Sangyō." **Western-style sushi bars in Japan:** Nakamura 173–176; "Hūdo." **Female chefs leaving for U.S.:** Louie. **Toshi establishing CSA:** interview with Toshi Sugiura (16 July 2005); Louie; Fasman. **Tracy personal history:** interview with Tracy Griffith (25 Mar. 2006); Griffith 5–11. **Other female CSA graduates:** interviews with Nikki Gilbert (26 Mar. 2006), Tali Sever (22 Mar. 2006); Louie; Kelly; Baggett. **Fie Kruse personal history:** interviews with Fie Kruse (18 and 20 July 2005, 26 Aug. 2005, 4 Sep. 2005), Jenard de Castro (18 Aug. 2005), and Tetsuya Tsumoto (12 Sep. 2005). **Sushi in Europe:** Tamamura 36–39, 117–120, 124–128.

9. HOLLYWOOD SHOWDOWN
History of tuna in sushi: Nakamura 35–38, 92; Sakaguchi 179–180; Yoshino 113–120; Bestor (2004) 142. **Spicy tuna:** Nakamura 170; interviews with Toshi Sugiura (16 July 2005) and Jay Terauchi (15 July 2005). **Fake wasabi:** interview with Ted Wakeman of Pacific Farms Wasabi (27 Feb. 2006). **Party at Paramount Pictures:** Concern Foundation's Stampede to Conquer Cancer, 16 July 2005; "Block Party"; Peters. **Sushi robots:** Tamamura 247–248; "Sushi, Omusubi"; Bestor (2004) 162; Omae 108. **Transformation of sushi into Edo street food; invention of *nigiri*; early toppings:** Jansen 127–128; Nakamura 16–27, 76–80, 95; Ishige 106–109, 122–124, 227–231; Satomi 139; Sakaguchi 175–176; Yoshino 58–66, 70–71; Omae 24–52, 105–108, 112–113; Tamamura 114, 215–216; Ema 208–210. **Spread of Edo-style sushi throughout Japan:** Nakamura 32–34, 40–41; Sakaguchi 179; Satomi 250; Tamamura 113; Yoshino 73–74; Uchida 53–57. **Regional varieties of sushi in Japan:** Nakamura 43–48; Omae 110–113. **Marcos personal history:** interviews with Marcos Wisner (16 July 2005, 17–22 Aug. 2005). **Kate at Chuck E. Cheese:** interview with Kate Murray (27 Aug. 2005).

10. CHEF'S CHOICE

Sushi bar ordering etiquette: Nagayama 9; Omae 20–21; interviews with Jay Terauchi (15 July and 9 Aug. 2005). **Kaiseki:** Ishige 88, 99–101. **Textbook quote; order of meal courses; sake; chopsticks:** Tsuji 45–52; Ishige 175–179, 189–193. **Sake as profit generator:** interview with Toshi Sugiura (19 Sep. 2005). **Disposable chopsticks:** "Rising Costs"; "Chopstick Inflation"; e-mail interview with Sakiko Kajino of Georgetown University (29 Aug. 2006). **Examples of multi-course** *omakase* **sushi:** "Uma-yasu no Sushi." **The rise of high-class sushi and the transition from street stall to restaurant:** Nakamura 19–25; Yoshino 67–71; Omae 108; Tamamura 41–42; Ishige 112–113; Jansen 116–121. **Anti-bacterial plastic leaves:** Naruse 80; "What is Wasaouro?"

11. INSIDE THE ROLL

Sushi rolls in Japan vs. in the U.S.: Nakamura 68–69, 73, 165–169; Tamamura 241–242; Tsuji 288; "Uma-yasu no Sushi." **Inside-out roll construction:** *Basics of Sushi.* **California roll:** Tamamura 234–235; "History: Pioneers"; Nakamura 162. **Avocado:** McGee 337. **Inside-out rolls to hide seaweed; reports about "black paper":** Nakamura 73, 175. Tamamura 200–201. **Paper-making and nori:** Uchida 135. **Global seaweed consumption:** Kiple 232–233, 1850; Guiry; McGee 341. **Nori and laver, Kathleen Drew-Baker:** Guiry; Chen; Nishizawa; Nelson, W.; Nagayama 245; Satomi 206–209; Nakamura 73–74; Omae 101–102; Tamamura 199–201; McGee 343; "Girl from Leigh"; "Seaweed." **Thin rolls:** Nagayama 193–211; Tsuji 303; "Kappa"; "Tekka-maki"; Shinmura 472; Matsumura 479. **Sushi roll from 1776:** Yoshino 310. **Teenage Mutant Ninja Turtles as** *kappa*: *Teenage.* **Bromophenols:** McGee 192. **Japanese tourists:** interview with Jeffrey Nitta and Jay Terauchi (21 July 2005).

12. PUTTING ON THE SQUEEZE

Neta: Shinmura 1866; e-mail interview with Sakiko Kajino of Georgetown University (6 Aug. 2006). **Converting sea creatures to** *neta*: Satomi 177–204. **CSA** *nigiri* **technique:** *Basics of Sushi.* **Qualities and styles of** *nigiri*: Naruse 14–17, 22–23; Yoshino 78–80; Nakamura 57–61; Omae 67.

13. FAST FOOD

Crisp nori: Nakamura 73. **Big roll:** Tsuji 300–302. **Quest for speed, different approaches in Japan vs. in the U.S.:** Nakamura 186–187; Tamamura 241–242, 248–249, 263–264.

14. AMERICAN STYLE

Jeff's personal history: interviews with Jeffrey Nitta (21 July 2005, 9 Sep. 2005). **Jay's personal history:** interviews with Jay Terauchi (16 and 21 July 2005, 23 and 24 Sep. 2005). **Inflexibility of Japanese chefs in U.S. and influx of non-Japanese Asian chefs:** Jeff's comments echoed in Tamamura 201–202. **Americanization of sushi:** Jeff's comments echoed in Kessler. **Masa:** Platt.

15. SHOW TIME

Nozawa "the sushi Nazi": interview with Jay Terauchi (19 July 2005); author visit to Sushi Nozawa (19 Sep. 2005). **Takumi's personal history:** interviews with Takumi Nishio (20 July 2005; 11, 12, 16, and 23 Sep. 2005); e-mail interviews with Sakiko Kajino of Georgetown University (12 Aug. 2006, 1 Sep. 2006); "Pātonā."

16. FRUITS OF THE SEA

L.A. fish-market items available and purchased on 22 July 2005: author visit to, and inventory and price-list printouts and invoices from, International Marine Products, Inc. and Ocean Group, Inc. (22 July 2005). **Tetsu's personal history:** interview with Tetsuya Tsumoto (12 Sep. 2005). **International Marine Products:** "About Us." **Tsukiji Fish Market in Japan:** Bestor (2004) 1–90; Corson, "Tsukiji"; author visit to Tsukiji Fish Market (18 Mar. 2004); interviews with Zoran Lekic (17, 19, and 22 July 2005).

17. BLOOD AND GUTS

Textbook on grilling: Tsuji 174–182. **Fish evolution:** Moyle 221–243; Purves 617–625. **Lack of ovens:** Tsuji 175. **Anatomy and the science of cooking:** McGee 129–134, 146–150, 187–192, 778; Sakaguchi 117–118, 162–166. **Kirara fish-cutting scene:** Hayakawa v. 1, 181–182. **Smell:** Engen; "The Power of Smell." **Mackerel:** McGee 202.

18. EAT THE PIE

Headbands and other styles of sushi-chef apparel: Ishige 228; *Restaurant Supply* 173–180.

19. THE BIG TEST

Sweet egg omelet: Nakamura 39; Omae 19, 51.

20. SUSHI NATION

Jeff's observations on developments in American sushi: interviews with Jeffrey Nitta (21 July 2005, 8 Aug. 2005, 9 and 23 Sep. 2005, 22 Mar.

2006). **Howard Dean:** Ehrenreich. **Starbucks and Blockbuster in Iowa:**
Lozano; Google Maps at http://local.google.com. **Data on restaurants
serving sushi:** During the summer of 2006 my research assistant Jenny
Mayo of the Advanced Program in Writing at Johns Hopkins University
collected data on restaurants and supermarkets selling sushi in 14 Midwestern states. Mayo gathered initial lists of food establishments from
online restaurant guides and phone books for each city. She telephoned
each restaurant to confirm its status, then checked each restaurant's
incorporation data as filed with the state government. Only restaurants
that Mayo could identify in state government databases are listed here, so
actual numbers are undoubtedly higher. Incorporation data provided an
approximate but not exact guide to the dates when restaurants opened.
Mayo also interviewed restaurant owners and food critics about sushi in
many of the states she surveyed. **Waterloo, IA:** Ericson. **Sioux City, IA:**
Crawford. **Indianapolis, IN:** Lloyd. **Chicago, IL:** phone interview with restaurant critic Phil Vettel of the *Chicago Tribune* (24 July 2006) by Jenny
Mayo; LaMorte. **Dallas/Forth Worth, TX:** Stuertz. **Wal-Mart:** Halkias.
Advanced Fresh Concepts, Genji Express, and Sushi Avenue: Company
Web sites (accessed 31 Oct. 2006) http://www.afcsushi.com, http://www.
genjiweb.com, and http://www.sushiavenue.com; Tamamura 214–216;
Kessler; Moskin "Sushi." **Total number of sushi restaurants and take-out
outlets:** phone interviews with Laura Murphy of the California Rice Commission (31 Aug. 2006) and David Kudo of All Japan News Inc. (31 Aug.
2006) by Jenny Mayo. **Nationalities of chefs:** Naka; phone interviews with
restaurant critic Dennis Ray Wheaton of *Chicago Magazine* (26 July 2006)
and with staff at sushi restaurants in several Midwestern states (various
dates, summer 2006) by Jenny Mayo; Takamura 201–203. **Supermarkets
before restaurants:** Nakamura 161. **Westernization of Japan and Japanese
diet:** Caryl; Lie 76–77; Ishige 155–158, 162–171.

21. MANHOOD OF SHRIMP
Shrimp and crustaceans: McGee 218–222; Yoshino 246; Ōba 202–208;
Koeller; Nagayama 51, 141, 183; Naruse 149; Satomi 189; Otwell; Gar-
rido; Roberts.

22. GETTING FISHY
Mackerel: Nakamura 12–13, 16–19, 24–25, 47, 88–89; Naruse 128. **Ani-
sakis parasite:** Oshima; Akbar; Weir; Sheraton; "Anisakiasis"; "Parasites";
McGee 186–187; Nakamura 89; Roach. **Salting fish:** McGee 212, 231–232.
Smells of fish: McGee 192–193, 205–206; "Trimethylaminuria." **Salting
and marinating:** Omae 104–105; Nakamura 36–37; Sakaguchi 176–177;

Naruse 61, Nagayama 127. **Fish and enzymes:** McGee 189–190, 211. **Mack-erel couriers:** "Saba Kaidō." **Ratio of muscle to body weight:** Tidwell; Blakely; Greenberg. **Three-piece breakdown:** Tsuji 123–127. **Albacore:** Yoshino 122–123; Nakamura 75.

23. RAW DEAL
History of sashimi: Ishige 224–227; Sato 67; e-mail interview with Eric Rath of the University of Kansas (28 Sep. 2006). **Column peel:** Tsuji 138–139. **Radish and perilla:** Nakamura 97–98; Ōba 44; McGee 310, 321–322, 404–405 (see also notes on mustard oils for Chapter 25, "Russian Roulette"). **Food presentation as Zen garden:** Ishige 187–189; Ohnuki-Tierney 206.

24. MACKEREL GAL
Scombroid poisoning: McGee 185; Moskin "Tuna's Red Glare." **Cate-gories of red, white, and blue/shiny:** Yoshino 111; Ōba 94–97; Honda 2–3; Naruse 84–154. **Mackerel gals:** e-mail interview with Sakiko Kajino of Georgetown University (6 Aug. 2006). **Dandy, pimp:** Davidson 467. **Scales:** Moyle 15–17. **Pin bones:** McGee 190. **Box sushi:** Tsuji 295–299; Nakamura 12–13.

25. RUSSIAN ROULETTE
Examples of American-style rolls: Kauffman; Griffith. **Big roll:** Tsuji 300–302; Omae 70. **Most commercial wasabi:** ingredients list is from Waner brand bulk wasabi powder used at Hama Hermosa; most brands are similar. **Wasabi science and history:** McGee 415–418; Bones; Barber, M.; Naruse 78–80; Ishige 227; Ōba 43–45; Nakamura 69–71; Nagayama 241; Hayakawa v. 5 138–139; Ono; "Technical and Medicinal"; *Daiō Wasabi*; interviews with Clark Sayer of Clark Sayer & Associates (26 Mar. 2006 and 4 April 2006). **Roy Carver and Pacific Farms:** author visit to Pacific Farms in Florence, OR, and interview with Ted Wakeman, farm operations man-ager (27 Feb. 2006; follow-up phone interview, 8 Mar. 2006); Sheff; Crain; Uhrhammer; Strauss.

28. COMEDY CLUB
Scene from Kirara comic: Hayakawa v. 4 188–190. **Jay Leno:** Gunther. **Toshi hiring actors and comedians:** interview with Toshi Sugiura (2 Sep. 2005).

30. FROM FRESHWATER
Parasites in salmon: Deardorff; Sheraton; Smith, D.; Frederick; "Para-sites"; McGee 186–187; Omae 24; Roach; "Quarterly Update"; interviews

with state government food safety officials in California (17 Aug. 2006) by my research assistant Jenny Mayo of Johns Hopkins University; "Making Food." **Fish evolution and salmon biology and farming:** Morgan 17–34; Quinn 4–10, 105–129, 141–142; McGee 194, 198–199; Ōba 95; Bestor (2004) 148–149; Hites; Jans; Weber; Purves 617–625; Moyle 2, 24, 221–243; Ade. **Bears:** Gende. **Traditional lean sushi toppings vs. modern fatty ones:** Nakamura 22–23, 35–36, 88–89, 92–93; Nagayama 175; Omae 24, 31, 33; Bestor (2004) 142; Sakaguchi 71–74. **Fish shapes and cutting:** Tsuji 118–131.

31. CONGRATULATIONS FISH

History, names, biology, and farming of sea bream/snapper/tai: Nakamura 22–23, 98–101; Omae 31; Satō 19, 53; Nagayama 49; Ōba 127; Naruse 101–102; Helfman 10–18; Stevens; Marko; *Snapper Aquaculture*; Watanabe, T.; e-mail interview with Sakiko Kajino of Georgetown University (10 Aug. 2006); McGee 197. **Kirara scene with leftover sushi:** Hayakawa v. 1, 34–35. **Muscle types:** Moyle 23–26; McGee 131–133, 184, 188; Helfman 260–262; Sakaguchi 71–72. **Sea bream taste:** Naruse 101–102. *Yuzu* **flavor components:** McGee 374, 378.

32. UNLEASH THE BEAST

Names, biology, and farming of yellowtail: Nakamura 83–86; Naruse 111–114, 159; Uehara; Hernen; Kolkovski; Watanabe, T.; Thakur; "Yellowtail Life Cycle"; Knecht; Mazzola; "Shusse." **Scales:** Thain 636–637; Purves 621; Stern 62–65; Moyle 15–17. **Five-piece breakdown:** Tsuji 123–130. **Wrapping fish in kelp:** interview with Tetsuya Tsumoto (17 Sep. 2005). **Muscle geometry:** Helfman 260–262; McGee 191–192.

33. FLATFISH

Names, biology, musculature, and evolution of flatfish: Bond 232–235; McGee 202–203; Nakamura 23, 80–83, 164; Ōba 143–144; Nagayama 39, 175; Naruse 103–107; Omae 33; Pauly 79–82; Moyle 15–17, 335–340; Helfman 138–139, 268; Okada; Martinez; Ohno; Luckenbach; Sakaguchi 71–80; Satō 71; e-mail interview with Sakiko Kajino of Georgetown University (27 July 2006). **Fish swimming:** Helfman 267; Colgate.

36. SEA SNAKES

History, biology, life cycle, and harvesting of eels: Schweid 12–35, 41–43, 65–68, 89–95, 103; Helfman 224–225; Bond 141; Sakaguchi 163–172; Satō

87, 100; Yoshino 214; Nakamura 26; Ōba 156; Moyle 17; Sbaihi; Tsukamoto; Clarke; Schreiber; e-mail interview with Sakiko Kajino of Georgetown University (27 Aug. 2006). **Kirara eel scene:** Hayakawa v. 8, 133.
Sauce in packaged eel: ingredients list from a common brand (Shirakiku)
of pre-packaged frozen eel from China.

37. TENTACLES OF THE DEEP
Octopus poison: Satomi 87–88; Yoshino 264. **Octopus and squid biology,
behavior, anatomy, and predators:** McGee 229–230; Boyle 15–16, 29–50;
Hanlon 31–43, 69–76; Benjamins; Sumbre; Naruse 136; Nagayama 45,
97; Sakaguchi 159; Satō 179; Yoshino 246; Bittman. **Preparation of live
octopus:** Satomi 196–197. **Kirara scene:** Hayakawa v. 13, 7–64. **Computer
screens:** Ball. **Squid-fed tuna:** Satō 142; interview with Takumi Nishio (17
Sep. 2005). **Overfishing:** Worm. **Hama Hermosa losing money:** interview
with Toshi Sugiura (10 Sep. 2005).

38. GIANT CLAM
Geoduck as phallic object: Dean, Sintax. **History, biology, and harvesting of geoducks:** "Geoduck Program"; Scigliano; Ōba 268–270; Omae
47; McGee 227; *3 Feet Under.* **Folk song:** "(My Gal Left Me for a) Geoduck
Clam" (see Bottomfeeders). **Toxins in clams:** McGee 185–186; Nakamura 95–97; Hackett; Corson "Spreading." **Flavors in clams, popularity
in sushi:** Sakaguchi 116–117, 146–147; Nakamura 95–97; McGee 225–
227; Omae 24.

39. FINAL FISH
Transformation of tuna from low-class to high-class fish: Nakamura
35–38, 90–94; Sakaguchi 179–180; Yoshino 113–120; Bestor (2004) 142;
Bestor (2000). **Types of tuna and their fat content:** McGee 201; Yoshino
122–124; Cascorbi. **Types of tuna meat:** Satomi 99. **Tuna biology and anatomy:** Safina 23, 51–60; Helfman 260–262, 267, 271; Ōba 88–99; McGee
188, 194, 201–202; Satomi 141–146; Naruse 85–89; Moyle 24; Watanabe,
M.; Colgate; Shadwick; Wardle. *Maguro* **to describe stiffness during sex:**
e-mail interview with Sakiko Kajino of Georgetown University (30 Oct.
2006). **Preference for** *akami* **over** *toro*: Nakamura 93. **Freezing:** McGee
205–206, 794–795; Bestor (2000); Bestor (2004) 150; Nakamura 90–94;
Moskin "Sushi"; Knecht; author visit to tuna auction at Tsukiji Fish Market (18 Mar. 2004). **Most expensive tuna:** "One Tuna." **Post-mortem flesh
quality and aging:** McGee 142–144, 189–190, 202–204; Nakamura 90–95,
101–105; Sakaguchi 73–80; Naruse 88–89; Satō 71; Satomi 149; Safina

26. **Kirara scene:** Hayakawa v. 13, 162–163. **Oxidization and carbon-monoxide gassing:** Moskin "Tuna's Red Glare"; McGee 194. **Harvesting and aquaculture:** Cascorbi; Khan; Nakamura 94–95. **Surrogate parents**: Takeuchi.

40. CARVING THE MOUNTAIN

Tuna filleting: author visits to Tsukiji Fish Market in Tokyo (18 Mar. 2004) and Ocean Fresh fish market in Los Angeles (22 July 2005). **Mercury and Minamata**: Nestle 187–202; Roe; Allchin; Smith, W.; Ishimure. **Procedure for cutting a tuna fillet down into *neta*:** also detailed in Satomi 136–138. **Parasites in tuna:** Oshima; Smith, D. **Marinating tuna in soy sauce:** Nakamura 35–37.

41. SUSHI KUNG FU

Haiku about witchcraft: Nakamura 20–21. **Ninja:** Omae 105–106. **Sushi techniques and scenes in Kirara comic:** Hayakawa v. 4 80–81; v. 5 85–86, 120–121, 148, 195; v. 7 133. **Real styles of *nigiri*-making technique:** e-mail interviews with Sakiko Kajino of Georgetown University (10–11 Aug. 2006).

42. MORTAL COMBAT

Nare-zushi: see Chapter 5, "Like the Vomit of a Drunkard."

43. DRUNKEN MASTER

Adjusting *nigiri* to match needs: also mentioned in Nakamura 57–58. *Nigiri* **and techniques**: see Chapter 12, "Putting on the Squeeze." **Jirō Ono:** Satomi 251.

44. EGGS AND OVARIES

Sushi bar lingo: Nakamura 61–67. **Salmon eggs**: McGee 249–242; Quinn 8–10; Sakaguchi 236–237; Satomi 210; Omae 41; "Salmon at Risk"; Gende; interview with Jay Terauchi (7 Sep. 2005). **Artificial salmon eggs:** Tanaka. **Sea urchins**: Ruppert 896–900; Pennisi; McGee 230; Steingarten 435–448; Ōba 236; Nagayama 53; Satō 96; Nybakken 228–230; Nomura; Mattison; interviews with Dave Rudie of Catalina Offshore Products (24 Mar. 2006) and Tetsuya Tsumoto (9 Sep. 2005). **"Battleship" sushi**: Nakamura 34–35.

47. SUSHI MASTER

Rice in Sacramento Valley: press release "Sushi Fact Sheet: Sushi and California Rice," California Rice Commission, 12 Aug. 2005. **Sushi Masters**

competition: "Sushi Masters." **Rumor:** interview with Robert Stanfield (25 Aug. 2005). **Pioneer L.A. chefs:** "History: Pioneers."

49. HOMECOMING

Reconstruction of Kate's job hunt: interview (24 Mar. 2006) and e-mail correspondence (various dates, Oct. 2005–Mar. 2006) with Kate Murray; author visit to San Diego and Oki Ton Japanese Bistro (24 Mar. 2006); interviews with Jack and Arbie Kenefick (24 Mar. 2006). **Kirara scene:** Hayakawa v. 13, 75–104.

APPENDIX: HOW TO EAT SUSHI

Satirical video: "Sushi: Nihon." **Sushi etiquette:** Nakamura 38–39, 58–61; Omae 16–19; Nagayama 5, 9, 241; Satomi 258–262.

GLOSSARY OF SELECTED JAPANESE TERMS

TYPES OF SUSHI ROLLS

futo-maki   big roll: a traditional sushi roll made with a full sheet of nori on the outside and several ingredients inside

hoso-maki   thin roll: a traditional sushi roll made with a half sheet of nori on the outside and a single ingredient inside

kappa-maki cucumber roll: a type of *hoso-maki*

tekka-maki tuna roll: a type of *hoso-maki*

te-maki   hand roll: a quick sushi roll made without a bamboo mat, in the shape of a cone

ura-maki   inside-out roll: an American-style sushi roll made with the nori on the inside of the rice instead of the outside

OTHER TERMS

akami   red-meat tuna cut

ama-ebi   raw sweet shrimp

anago   saltwater eel

buri   mature yellowtail

chūtoro   medium-fatty tuna cut

dashi   broth of kelp and bonito flakes

dōmo arigatō thank you

ebi   boiled tiger shrimp

Edomae-zushi	the fast-food style of sushi from Japan's old city of Edo (now Tokyo) that developed in the 1800s and that has become the predominate style of sushi in Japan and around the globe
engawa	the adductor fin muscle of flatfish, a delicacy in Japan
funa-zushi	an old style of sushi in which carp are packed in rice and left to ferment
gari	pickled ginger
gezakana	low-class fish
hako-zushi	box sushi
hamachi	farmed yellowtail
hikari mono	"shiny things": the category of fish that sushi chefs serve with the shiny skin still attached
hirame	a category of flatfish generally considered desirable for sushi
ika	squid
ikura	salmon eggs
irasshaimase	(pronounced ee•ra•shai•mah•say) welcome
kaiseki	traditional multi-course Japanese meal
kanpachi	lean yellowtail, usually wild-caught
kanpai	bottoms up
karei	a category of flatfish generally considered less desirable for sushi
katsura-muki	column peel, a cutting technique that sushi chefs use on cucumbers and giant radishes
kōji	mold used to ferment food and liquor
konbu	kelp
konnichiwa	hello
kusa	"grass": sushi chef slang for nori
maguro	tuna
makisu	bamboo mat for rolling sushi rolls
mirin	sweet Japanese cooking liqour
mirugai	giant clam
nare-zushi	the original form of sushi, in which fish is packed in rice and left to ferment
neta	seafood toppings used for sushi
nigiri	rectangular, hand-squeezed pieces of sushi

nikiri	the chef's "house" soy sauce, augmented with dashi, sake, and mirin
nori	seaweed sheets made of pressed and dried laver
nyōtai-mori	sushi served atop a naked woman
ohaiyō gozaimasu	good morning
okimari	ordering the set meal, usually a sushi sampler
okonomi	ordering sushi piece by piece
omakase	letting the chef decide what to serve
ōtoro	very-fatty tuna cut
saba	mackerel
sashimi	raw fish (or meat) served without rice
sengiri	julienne
shari	"Buddha's bones," sushi chef slang for rice
shiokara	fish or squid fermented in its own guts
shiso	perilla leaf
sushi	rice seasoned with vinegar, sugar, and salt and topped with, or wrapped around, a variety of seafood and other ingredients
tai	sea bream (also snapper, sea bass)
tako	octopus
toro	fatty tuna cut
umami	savoriness
unagi	freshwater eel
uni	sea urchin

BIBLIOGRAPHY

NOTE: Readers interested in learning to fillet fish, cook rice, and make their own sushi should begin with Kimiko Barber and Hiroki Takemura's book *Sushi: Taste and Technique.* A comprehensive introduction to Japanese cuisine is available in Shizuo Tsuji's book *Japanese Cooking: A Simple Art.*

3 Feet Under: Digging Deep for the Geoduck Clam. DVD. Produced and directed by Justin Bookey, Santa Monica, CA: Coolbellup Media, 2005.

"About Us." International Marine Products. Accessed 30 Oct. 2006: http://www.intmarine.com/aboustus.html.

Ade, Robin, illus. "Salmon & Trout." Poster. *Scandinavian Fishing Year Book.* Hedehusene, Denmark: Urner Barry Publications, n.d.

Akbar, A., and S. Ghosh. "Anisakiasis—A Neglected Diagnosis in the West." *Digestive and Liver Disease* 37, no. 1 (January 2005): 7–9.

Allchin, Douglas. "The Poisoning of Minamata." *Resource Center for Science Teachers Using Sociology, History and Philosophy of Science—Ethics and Health Care.* University of Minnesota, Twin Cities. Accessed 5 Nov. 2006: http://www1.umn.edu/ships/ethics/minamata.htm.

"Anisakiasis." *Public Health Image Library.* Atlanta: Centers for Disease Control and Prevention, 18 March 2005. Accessed 31 Oct. 2006: http://phil.cdc.gov/phil/home.asp.

Araki, Hiroshi 荒木 裕. "Dr. Araki's Dietto no Tame no Hitoguchi Memo" [Dr. Araki's ダエットのための一口メモ Dr. Araki's Bite-

Size Tips on Diet]. *Tōnyōbyō Kaizen Kōnā* [糖尿病改善コーナー Diabetes Improvement Corner]. Nichireku Corporation [株式会社ニチレク]. Accessed 26 October 2006: http://www. nichireku.com/tonyo/index.htm.

Baggett, Marisa. "Graduate Testimonials." *California Sushi Academy.* Accessed 29 October 2006: http://www.sushi-academy.com/ pages/article/graduates_testimonials.html.

Ball, Philip. "Nature Inspires Colour-Change Gel." *Nature,* 8 January 2003.

Barber, Kimiko, and Hiroki Takemura. *Sushi: Taste and Technique.* London: DK Publishing, 2002.

Barber, Melanie, and Michele Buntain. "Wasabi." In *The New Rural Industries: A Handbook for Farmers and Investors,* edited by Keith Hyde, 219–224. Kingston, Australia: Rural Industries Research and Development Corporation, 1997.

Basics of Sushi. Videocassette. Directed by Tommy Sowards. Performed by Andy Matsuda, Venice, CA: California Sushi Academy, 1999.

Benjamins, Steven. "Cephalopod Predators." In *The Cephalopod Page,* edited by James B. Wood. Halifax: Dalhousie University, 2000. Accessed 2 November 2006: http://www.nhm.ac.uk/ hosted_sites/tcp/articles.html.

Bestor, Theodore. "How Sushi Went Global." *Foreign Policy,* November/December 2000: 54–63.

———. *Tsukiji: The Fish Market at the Center of the World.* Berkeley: University of California Press, 2004.

Bittman, Mark. "Octopus Demystified." *The Fish Market,* 16 October 1999. The Splendid Table/American Public Media. Accessed 2 November 2006: http://splendidtable.publicradio.org/ souptonuts/fish_octopus.html.

Blakely, Don. "Cull Cow Body and Carcass Composition." *Beef— Cow-Calf Factsheet.* Toronto: Ontario Ministry of Agriculture, Food and Rural Affairs, November 2005. Accessed 31 October 2006: http://www.omafra.gov.on.ca/english/livestock/beef/ facts/05-075.htm.

"Block Party Participants." *Concern Foundation's Stampede to Conquer Cancer, July 16, 2005.* Concern Foundation. Accessed 7 January 2006: http://www.concernfoundation.org/blockparty.php.

Bond, Carl. *Biology of Fishes,* 2nd ed. Fort Worth: Saunders College Publishing, 1996.

Bones, A. M., and J. T. Rossiter. "The Myrosinase-Glucosinolate System—An Innate Defense System in Plants." *Physiologia Plantarum,* 97, no. 1 (May 1996): 194–208.

Bottomfeeders. *Waterview.* Bottomfeeders and Robert Thoms. Ucluelet, British Columbia: Sundog Studios, 2001.

Boyle, Peter, and Paul Rodhouse. *Cephalopods: Ecology and Fisheries.* Oxford, UK: Blackwell Science, 2005.

Caryl, Christian. "Turning Un-Japanese." *Newsweek International,* 13 February 2006.

Cascorbi, Alice. *Tunas.* 8 vols. Monterey, CA: Monterey Bay Aquarium Seafood Watch, 2003–2004.

"Cereal Flours and Related Products: Section 137.350 Enriched Rice." *Code of Federal Regulations,* title 21, v. 2 (1 April 2003): 384–385.

Chen, Jiaxin, and Pu Xu. *Cultured Aquatic Species Information Programme: Porphyra spp.* Rome: Food and Agriculture Organization of the United Nations, 2005.

"Chopstick Inflation." Steve Herman. *The Marketplace Morning Report* (radio show). Los Angeles: Marketplace Productions/ American Public Media, 3 November 2006.

Clarke, Tom. "World's Eels on Slippery Slope." *Nature,* 30 September 2003.

Colgate, J. Edward, and Kevin M. Lynch. "Mechanics and Control of Swimming: A Review." *IEEE Journal of Oceanic Engineering* 29, no. 3 (July 2004).

Corson, Trevor. "Spreading as Quietly as a Clam: Deadly Plankton Lie in Wait off the Coast of Long Island." *New York Times,* 31 July 2005.

———. *"Tsukiji: The Fish Market at the Center of the World."* Rev. of *Tsukiji: The Fish Market at the Center of the World* by Theodore Bestor. *Gastronomica* 5, no. 5 (Fall 2005): 117–118.

Crain, Liz. "When It Comes to Wasabi, It's Wise to Dig a Little Deeper." *Portland Tribune* [OR], 29 July 2005: B3.

Crawford, Erin. "Iowans, Defend Your State." *Des Moines Register,* 14 April 2006.

Daiō Wasabi Nōjō [大王わさび農場 Daiō Wasabi Farm]. Accessed 1 November 2006: http://www.daiowasabi.co.jp.

Davidson, Alan. *The Oxford Companion to Food.* New York: Oxford University Press, 1999.

Dean, William. "The Sexiest Food in the World." *Clean Sheets: An Online Erotic Magazine,* 17 July 2002. Accessed 3 November 2006: http://www.cleansheets.com/articles/dean_07.17.02.shtml.

Deardorff, T. L., and M. L. Kent. "Prevalence of Larval Anisakis Simplex in Pen-Reared and Wild-Caught Salmon (*Salmonidae*) from Puget Sound, Washington." *Journal of Wildlife Diseases* 25, no. 3 (July 1989): 416–419.

Ehrenreich, Barbara. "Dude, Where's That Elite?" *New York Times,* 1 July 2004.

Ema, Tsutomu, Toranosuke Nishioka, and Giichirō Hamada [江馬 務, 西岡虎之助, 浜田義一郎]. *Kinsei Fūzoku Jiten* [近世風俗事典 Encyclopedia of Early Modern Customs]. Tokyo: Jinbutsu Ōraisha [人物往来社], 1967.

Engen, Trygg. *Odor Sensation and Memory.* Westport, CT: Praeger Publishers, 1991.

Ericson, Jon. "Soho Opens Unique Sushi/Deli Combination." *Waterloo Courier* [IA], 15 July 2005.

Fasman, Jon. "It's Not All Raw Fish." *Intelligent Life.* Special ed., *Economist,* Summer, 2006: 86–87.

Fernández-Armesto, Felipe. *Near a Thousand Tables: A History of Food.* New York: Free Press, 2002.

Fletcher, Anthony. "Buhler Develops Vitamin-Enriching Rice Extrusion Process." *Food Production Daily,* July 10, 2004. Decision News Media. Accessed 26 Oct. 2006: http://www.foodproductiondaily.com/news-by-product/news.asp?id=55229&idCat=23&k=buhler-develops-vitamin.

Frederick, Jim. "Meguro Parasitological Museum." *Time Asia,* 27 June 2005.

"Gaishoku Sangyō Tōkei Shiryō Shū 2005 Nenpan" [外食産業統計資料集 2005 年版 Food Service Industry Statistical Data Collection, 2005 Edition] and "Gaishoku Sangyō Ichiba Kibo 2003–2005" [外食産業市場規模 Food Service Industry Market Size 2003–2005]. *Tōkei Shiryō* [統計資料 Statistical Data], 22 October 2005. Gaishoku Sangyō Sōgō Chōsa Kenkyū Sentā [外食産業総合調査研究センター—Food Service

Industry Comprehensive Research Center]. Accessed 29 October 2006: http://www.gaishokusoken.jp/3421tokeimain.htm.

Garrido, L. R., R. A. Benner, P. Ross, and W. S. Otwell. *Assessing Product Quality, Shelf-Life, and Consumer Acceptance for Freshwater, Farm-Raised Shrimp.* Gainesville, FL: University of Florida Aquatic Food Products Lab, 2000.

Gende, Scott, and Thomas Quinn. "The Fish and the Forest: Salmon-Catching Bears Fertilize Forests with the Partially Eaten Carcasses of Their Favorite Food." *Scientific American* 295, no. 2 (1 Aug. 2006).

"Geoduck Program: Managing a Valuable Natural Resource." Washington Department of Natural Resources. Accessed 29 September 2006: http://www.dnr.wa.gov/htdocs/adm/comm/fs03_159.htm.

"Girl from Leigh Who Became Japan's Mother of the Sea." *Lancashire Evening Telegraph* (UK), 6 May 2003.

Greenberg, Paul. "Green to the Gills." *New York Times Magazine*, 18 June 2006.

Griffith, Tracy. *Sushi American Style.* New York: Clarkson Potter, 2004.

Guiry, Michael. "Seaweed as Human Food" and "Seaweed Aquaculture." *Seaweed Site.* Galway: National University of Ireland. Accessed 30 October 2006: http://www.seaweed.ie/uses_general/humanfood.lasso and http://www.seaweed.ie/aquaculture/default.lasso.

Gunther, Marc. "The MVP of Late Night." *Fortune*, 23 Feb. 2004.

Hackett, J., D. Anderson, D. Ernder, and D. Bhattacharya. "Dinoflagellates: A Remarkable Evolutionary Experiment." *American Journal of Botany* 91, no. 10 (2004).

Halkias, Maria, and Jake Batsell. "Wi-Fi and Sushi at Wal-Mart?" *Dallas Morning News*, 22 March 2006.

Hanlon, Roger, and John Messenger. *Cephalopod Behaviour.* Cambridge, UK: Cambridge University Press, 1996.

Hayakawa, Hikari, and Cozoh [Kozō] Hashimoto [早川 光 and 橋本狐蔵], *Edomae-sushi Shokunin Kirara no Shigoto* [江戸前鮨職人きららの仕事, Edomae-sushi Chef Kirara's Job], 1–12. Tokyo: Shueisha [集英社] (Super Jump Comics), 2003–2006.

Helfman, Gene, Bruce Collette, and Douglas Facey. *The Diversity of Fishes*. Malden, MA: Blackwell Publishing, 1997.

Hernen, Martin, and Wayne Hutchison. *Yellowtail Kingfish Aquaculture: Strategic Research and Development Plan, 2003–2008*. Port Adelaide, Australia: South Australian Marine Finfish Farmers Association, 2003.

"History of Japanese Foods in America." Mutual Trading Company. Accessed 27 October 2006: http://www.lamtc.com/about/history_foods.html.

"History: Pioneers." *Sushi Masters*. California Rice Commission. Accessed 27 October 2006: http://www.sushimasters.com/history-pioneers.htm.

Hites, Ronald, Jeffery Foran, David Carpenter, M. Coreen Hamilton, Barbara Knuth, and Steven Schwager. "Global Assessment of Organic Contaminants in Farmed Salmon." *Science* 303, no. 5655 (9 January 2004): 226–229.

"Hōchō-shiki" [包丁式 Knife Ceremony]. *Takabe Jinja* [高家神社 Takabe Shrine]. Chikuramachi Kankō Kyōkai [千倉町観光協会 Town of Chikura Tourism Association] Accessed 31 October 2006: http://www.chikurakankokyokai.com/kanko/takabe jinja/takabejinja.html.

Honda, Yukiko [本多由紀子]. *Sushi Neta Zukan* [寿司ネタ図鑑 Illustrated Book of Sushi Toppings]. Tokyo: Shōgakkan [小学館], 1997.

Hosking, Richard. *A Dictionary of Japanese Food: Ingredients and Culture*. Boston: Tuttle, 1995.

"Hūdo Bijinesu-kai ga Chūmoku Suru Gyaku Yunyū Gurume Shibuya de Kyūzō Suru 'Sushi Roll' Ninki no Haikei" [フードビジネス界が注目する逆輸入グルメ渋谷で急増する "Sushi Roll" 人気の背景 Behind the Scenes with the Sudden Increase in Popularity of Sushi Rolls, Which the Food Business World Is Noticing as a Reimportation in Gourmet [Shibuya]. *Shibuya Keizai Shimbun* [シブヤ経済新聞 Shibuya Economics Newspaper] 15 March 2002. Hanagata Communications. Accessed 27 October 2006: http://www.shibukei.com/special/169/index.html.

Huneven, Michelle. "A New Katsu." *LA Weekly*, 14 July 2000: 56.

Ikezawa, Yasushi [池澤康]. *Amerika Nihonshoku Wōzu* [アメリカ日本食ワォーズ Japanese Food Wars in America]. Tokyo: Asahiya Shuppan [旭屋出版], 2005.

Ishige, Naomichi. *The History and Culture of Japanese Food.* London: Kegan Paul, 2001.

Ishimure, Michiko. *Paradise in the Sea of Sorrow: Our Minamata Disease.* Translated by Livet Monnet. Ann Arbor, MI: University of Michigan, Center for Japanese Studies, 2003.

Jans, Nick. "Farmed Salmon Can't Beat Wild." *USA Today,* 6 October 2002.

Jansen, Marius. *The Making of Modern Japan.* Cambridge, MA: Harvard University Press, 2000.

Juliano, Bienvenido, ed. *Rice in Human Nutrition.* Rome: Food and Agriculture Organization of the United Nations/International Rice Research Institute, 1993. Accessed 26 October 2006: http://www.fao.org/inpho/content/documents//vlibrary/t0567e/T0567E00.htm#Contents.

"Kappa" [河童 Water Sprite]. *Gogen Yurai Jiten* [語源由来事典 Dictionary of Etymology and Origins]. Tokyo: All-Guide.com. Accessed 30 October 2006: http://gogen-allguide.com/ka/kappa.html.

Kauffman, Jonathan. "Make It Two Prozac Rolls." *East Bay Express* [Emeryville, CA], 4 May 2005.

Kelly, Leslie. "Sushi Star? From Starkville to Cooper-Young to New York, Marisa Baggett's Career Is Rolling Along." *Commercial Appeal* [Memphis, TN], 19 October 2005.

Kessler, John. "We Reel in the Sushi; But Have We Missed the Boat?" *Atlanta Journal-Constitution,* 19 June 2006.

Khan, Stephen, and Kathy Marks. "Caught in a Trap: Tuna Face a New Threat." *The Independent,* 9 June 2004.

Kim, H., C. Richardson, J. Roberts, L. Gren, and J. L. Lyon. "Cold Hands, Warm Heart." *The Lancet* 351, no. 9114 (16 May 1998): 1492.

Kiple, Kenneth, and Kriemhild Coneè Ornelas, eds. *The Cambridge World History of Food,* 2 vols. Cambridge, UK: Cambridge University Press, 2000.

Klippensteen, Kate. *Cool Tools: Cooking Utensils from the Japanese Kitchen.* Tokyo: Kodansha, 2006.

Knecht, G. Bruce. "The Raw Truth." *Wall Street Journal,* 25 March 2006: 1.

Koeller, Peter, Robert Mohn, and Marianne Etter. "Density Dependent Sex Change in Northern Shrimp, *Pandalus borealis,* on the Scotian Shelf." *Journal of Northwest Atlantic Fisheries Sciences* 27 (2000): 107–118.

Kolkovski, S., and Y. Sakakura. "Yellowtail Kingfish, from Larvae to Mature Fish: Problems and Opportunities." *VII International Symposium on Aquaculture Nutrition.* Edited by L. E. Cruz Suarez et al. 104–125. Nueva Leon, Mexico: Universidad Autonoma de Nuevo Leon, 2004.

LaMorte, Chris. "Chicago Sushi Exposed!" *Metromix.com,* 7 November 2005. Accessed 31 October 2006: http://metromix. chicagotribune.com/dining/mmx-0511108-naked-sushi-chicago,0,1974282.story.

Lie, John. *Multi-Ethnic Japan.* Cambridge, MA: Harvard University Press, 2001.

Lloyd, Christopher. "Small Size, Big Taste." *Indianapolis Star,* 14 October 2005: G41.

Louie, Elaine. "She Has a Knife and She Knows How to Use It." *New York Times,* 5 June 2002: F1.

Lozano, Rafael Antonio (a.k.a. Winter). "Starbucks in Iowa" *Starbucks Everywhere.* Accessed 31 October 2006: http://www. starbuckseverywhere.net/Iowa.htm.

Luckenbach, J. A., J. Godwin, H. V. Daniels, and R. J. Borski. "Gonadal Differentiation and Effects of Temperature on Sex Determination in Southern Flounder (*Paralichthys lethostigma*)." *Aquaculture* 216, nos. 1–4 (10 February 2003): 315–327.

"Making Food." *Kids Page.* California Department of Health Services, Food and Drug Branch. Accessed 1 November 2006: http://www.dhs.ca.gov/fdb/html/food/education%20unit/ food%20safety%20ed%20project/FSPKidsIntro.htm.

Marko, Peter, Sarah Lee, Amber Rice, Joel Gramling, Tara Fitzhenry, Justin McAlister, George Harper, and Amy Moran. "Mislabelling of a Depleted Reef Fish." *Nature* 430 (15 July 2004): 309–310.

Martinez G. M., and J. A. Bolker. "Embryonic and Larval Staging of

Summer Flounder (*Paralichthys dentatus*)." *Journal of Morphology* 255, no. 2 (February 2003): 162–176.

Matsumura, Akira [松村 明], ed. *Daijiren* [大辞林 Great Word Forest]. Tokyo: Sanseidō [三省堂], 1988.

Mattison, J. E., J. D. Trent, A. L. Shanks, T. B. Akin, and J. S. Pearse. "Movement and Feeding Activity of Red Sea Urchins (*Strongylocentrotus franciscanus*) Adjacent to a Kelp Forest." *Marine Biology* 39, no. 1 (December 1976): 25–30.

Mazzola, A., E. Favaloro, and G. Sara. "Cultivation of the Mediterranean Amberjack, *Seriola dumerili,* in Submerged Cages in the Western Mediterranean Sea." *Aquaculture* 181, no. 3 (15 January 2000): 257–268.

"McDonald's USA Ingredients Listing for Popular Menu Items." 13 October 2006. McDonald's Corporation. Accessed 25 October 2006: http://www.mcdonalds.com/app_controller.nutrition.categories.ingredients. index.html.

McGee, Harold. *On Food and Cooking: The Science and Lore of the Kitchen,* rev. ed. New York: Scribner, 2004.

Miller, Lia. "Nippon." *New York Restaurants.* New York Magazine. Accessed 27 October 2006: http://nymag.com/listings/restaurant/nippon/index.html.

"Milling Innovation." *Yamamoto Co., Ltd., Dry Polisher.* Calibration Plus. Accessed 26 October 2006: http://www.calibrationplus.com/yamadp.html.

Morgan, Diane. *Salmon: A Cookbook.* San Francisco: Chronicle Books, 2005.

Morioka, K., and Y. Itoh. "Manipulating Muscle Lipid and Collagen: A Potential Tool to Tailor the Meat Texture of Cultured Yellowtail, *Seriola quinqeraradiata.*" *World Aquaculture* 36, no. 2 (June 2005): 11–14.

Moskin, Julia. "Sushi Fresh from the Deep . . . the Deep Freeze." *New York Times,* 8 April 2004.

———. "Tuna's Red Glare? It Could be Carbon Monoxide." *New York Times,* 6 October 2004.

Moyle, Peter, and Joseph Cech. *Fishes: An Introduction to Ichthyology,* 4th ed. Upper Saddle River, NJ: Prentice-Hall, 1999.

Nagayama, Kazuo, Kazuhiko Tajima, and Hiroshi Yoda [長山一夫,

田島一彦, and 与田弘志]. *Sushi* [鮨]. Tokyo: Pie Books [ピエ•ブックス], 2003.

Nagayama, Kokan. *The Connoisseur's Book of Japanese Swords.* New York: Kodansha, 1997.

Naka, Kimiyo. "Latino Chefs Are Breaking into the Sushi Business." *Chicago Reporter,* June 2001.

Nakamura, Mitsuru [中村 満], ed. *Nihonjin wa Sushi no Koto o Nanimo Shiranai* [日本人は寿司のことを何も知らない The Japanese Know Nothing About Sushi]. Tokyo: Gakken [学習研究会], 2003.

Naruse, Uei [成瀬宇平]. *Sushi no Unchiku, Umasa no Himitsu* [すしの蘊蓄 旨さの秘密 Profound Knowledge of Sushi and the Secrets of Its Taste]. Tokyo: Kodansha [講談社], 2003.

Nelson, G., et al. "An Amino-Acid Taste Receptor." *Nature* 416, no. 6877 (14 March 2002): 199–202.

Nelson, W., J. Brodie, and M. Guiry. "Terminology Used to Describe Reproduction and Life History Stages in the Genus *Porphyra* (*Bangiales, Rhodophyta*)." *Journal of Applied Phycology* 11, no. 5 (October 1999): 407–410.

Nestle, Marion. *What to Eat.* New York: North Point Press, 2006.

Nishizawa, Kazutoshi. "Preparation and Marketing of Seaweeds as Foods." In *Production and Utilization of Products from Commercial Seaweed: FAO Fisheries Technical Paper 288.* Edited by Dennis McHugh. Rome: Food and Agriculture Organization of the United Nations, 1987.

Nomura, K., H. Nakamura, N. Suzuki. "False Fertilization in Sea Urchin Eggs Induced by Diabolin, a 120K Kelp Protein." *Biochemical and Biophysical Research Communications* 272, no. 3 (16 June 2000): 691–693.

Nybakken, James, and Mark Bertness. *Marine Biology: An Ecological Approach,* 6th ed. New York: Pearson-Benjamin Cummings, 2005.

Ōba, Hideaki, Kenji Mochitzuki, Kazuo Sakamoto, Masatsune Takeda, and Takenori Sasaki [大場秀章, 望月賢二, 坂本一男, 武田正倫, and 佐々木猛智]. *Tōdai Kōza, Sushi Neta no Shizenshi* [東大講座 すしネタの自然史 Tokyo University Lectures on the Natural History of Sushi Ingredients]. Tokyo: Nihon Hōsō Shuppan Kyōkai [日本放送出版協会], 2003.

O'Connor, John. "TV View; Why the Mini-Series Is Losing Favor." *New York Times,* 16 June 1985.

Ohno, Susumu. "Why Ontogeny Recapitulates Phylogeny." *Electrophoresis* 16, no. 1 (14 April 2005): 1782–1786.

Ohnuki-Tierney, Emiko. "The Ambivalent Self of the Contemporary Japanese." *Cultural Anthropology* 5, no. 2 (May 1990): 197–216.

Okada N., M. Tanaka, and M. Tagawa. "Bone Development During Metamorphosis of the Japanese Flounder (*Paralichthys olivaceus*): Differential Responses to Thyroid Hormone." In *The Big Fish Bang: Proceedings of the 26th Annual Larval Fish Conference.* Edited by Howard Browman and Anne Berit Skiftesvik, 177–187. Bergen, Norway: Institute of Marine Research, 2003.

Okamoto, Kanoko. *The House Spirit and Other Stories.* Translated by Kazuko Sugisaki. Santa Barbara, CA: Capra Press, 1995.

Omae, Kinjiro, and Yuzuru Tachibana. *The Book of Sushi.* Tokyo: Kodansha International, 1981.

"One Tuna Fetches 20 Million Yen at Tsukiji." *Japan Times,* 6 January 2001.

Ono, H., S. Tesaki, S. Tanabe, and M. Watanabe. "6-Methylsulfinylhexyl Isothiocyanate and its Homologues as Food-oriented Compounds with Antibacterial Activity Against *Escherichia coli* and *Staphylococcus aureus.*" *Bioscience, Biotechnology, and Biochemistry* 62, no. 2 (February 1998): 363–365.

Oshima, T. "Anisakiasis—Is the Sushi Bar Guilty?" *Parasitology Today* 3, no. 2 (1987): 44–48.

Otwell, W. S., and M. R. Marshall. "Studies on the Use of Sulfites to Control Shrimp Melanosis (Blackspot)." *Florida SeaGrant Technical Paper No. 46.* Gainesville, FL: Florida Sea Grant, 1986.

"Parasites." *Fish and Fisheries Products Hazards and Controls Guide,* 3rd ed. College Park, MD: U.S. Food and Drug Administration, Center for Food Safety and Applied Nutrition, 2001: 65–70.

"Pātonā obu za Iyā 2002: Nishimura Takumi and Nishimura Tomomi." [パートナー•オブ•ザ•イヤー：西村知美•西村知美 Partners of the Year 2002]. *Ii Fufu no Hi o Susumeru Kai* [いい夫婦の日をすすめる会 Society for the Promotion of Good Husband and Wife Day]. Accessed 5 November 2006: http://www.fufu1122.com/year/2002.html.

Pauly, Daniel. *Darwin's Fishes: An Encyclopedia of Ichthyology, Ecology, and Evolution.* Cambridge, England: Cambridge University Press, 2004.

Pennisi, Elizabeth. "Sea Urchin Genome Confirms Kinship to Humans and Other Vertebrates." *Science* 314, no. 5801 (10 Nov. 2006): 908–909.

Peters, Jenny. "Good Works with a Western Flavor." *Fashion Wire Daily,* 18 July 2005.

Platt, Adam. "Holy Mackerel." *New York,* 26 April 2004.

"The Power of Smell." Leonard Lopate, Ruth Reichl, Daniel Boulud, and Marcia Pelchat. *The Leonard Lopate Show* (radio show). WNYC, New York, 8 March 2005.

"Premium Quality Rice: Tamanishiki, Nozomi, Yume." JFC International. Accessed 26 October 2006: http://www.jfc.com/brand/threericetour.html.

Purves, William, Gordon Orians, and Craig Heller. *Life: The Science of Biology,* 4th ed. Sunderland, MA: Sinauer Associates, 1995.

"Quarterly Update June 2006." *Real Progress in Food Code Adoptions.* College Park, MD: U.S. Food and Drug Administration, Center for Food Safety and Applied Nutrition, 2002. Accessed 1 November 2006: http://www.cfsan.fda.gov/~ear/fcadopt.html.

Quinn, Thomas. *The Behavior and Ecology of Pacific Salmon and Trout.* Seattle: University of Washington Press, 2005.

Radzicka, A., and R. Wolfenden. "A Proficient Enzyme." *Science* 267, no. 5194 (6 January 1995): 90–93.

Rappoport, Leon. *How We Eat: Appetite, Culture, and the Psychology of Food.* Toronto: ECW Press, 2003.

Restaurant Supply Catalogue 7. Los Angeles: Mutual Trading Co., September 2004.

"Rice." California Rice Center. Accessed 25 October 2006: http://www.calricecenter.com/rice.htm.

"Rising Costs, Shrinking Forests Prompt Plastic Chopsticks." *Daily Yomiuri,* 24 August 2006: 2.

Roach, Mary. "Fear of Sushi." *Health,* 23 July 2001: 103–106.

Roberts, Santi. *Wild-Caught Coldwater Shrimp.* Monterey, CA: Monterey Bay Aquarium Seafood Watch, 2005.

Roe, Sam, and Michael Hawthorne. "Tribune Investigation: The

Mercury Menance." [3-article series: "Toxic Risk on Your Plate" (11 December 2005), "U.S. Safety Net in Tatters" (12 December 2005), and "How Safe Is Tuna?" (13 December 2005).] *Chicago Tribune*, 11–13 December 2005.

"Rosanzerusu de Sushi ni Jinsei o Kaketa Nihonjin" [ロサンゼルスで寿司に人生をかけた日本人 The Japanese Who Bet His Life on Sushi in Los Angeles (televison show)]. *Poka Poka Chikyū Kazoku* [ポカポカ地球家族 Global Families Under the Sun]. TV Asahi, Japan, 22 February 2003.

Ruppert, Edward, Richard Fox, and Robert Barnes. *Invertebrate Zoology*. 7th ed. Belmont, CA: Brooks/Cole, 2004.

"Saba Kaidō" [鯖街道 The Mackerel Road]. *Tabi no Techō* [旅の手帖 Travel Notebook] 29, no. 9 (September 2005): 34–37.

Safina, Carl. *Song for the Blue Ocean*. New York: Henry Holt, 1997.

Sakaguchi, Morihiko, Michiyo Murata, Satoshi Mochitzuki, and Yoshihiro Yokoyama [坂口守彦, 村田道代, 望月 聡, and 横山芳博. *Sakana Hakase ga Oshieru Sakana no Oishisa no Himitsu* [魚博士が教える魚のおいしさの秘密 Fish Experts Teach the Secrets of the Deliciousness of Fish]. Tokyo: Hamano Shuppan [はまの出版], 1999.

"Salmon at Risk in Pacific Russia." *BBC News*, 30 October 2004. Accessed 5 November 2006; http://news.bbc.co.uk/2/hi/science/nature/3964997.stm.

Sand, Jordan. "A Short History of MSG." *Gastronomica* 5, no. 4 (Fall 2005): 38–49.

Satō, Gyosui [佐藤魚水], ed. *Shokuzai Zukan: Sakana* [食材図鑑：魚 Illustrated Book of Food Ingredients: Fish]. Tokyo: Nagaoka Shoten [永岡書店], 2002.

Satomi, Shinzo [里見真三]. *Sukiyabashi Jirō, Shun o Nigiru* [すきやばし次郎 旬を握る Jirō of Sukiyabashi Makes Sushi with the Seasons]. Tokyo: Bungei Shunjū [文藝春秋], 1997.

Sbaihi, M., M. Fouchereau-Peron, F. Meunier, P. Elie, I. Mayer, E. Burzawa, B. Vidal, and S. Dufour. "Reproductive Biology of the Conger Eel from the South Coast of Brittany, France, and Comparison with the European Eel." *Journal of Fish Biology* 59 (2001): 302–318.

Schreiber, Laurie. "Elver Gold Rush of Yore Blamed for Eel Decline." *Fishermen's Voice* [Gouldsboro, ME] 10, no. 5 (May 2005).

Schweid, Richard. *Consider the Eel: A Natural and Gastronomic History.* Cambridge, MA: Da Capo Press, 2002.

Scigliano, Eric. "Viagra on the Half Shell." *Seattle Weekly,* 12 July 2000.

"Seaweed." Rebecca Sandles. *Woman's Hour* (radio show). BBC Radio, London, 31 July 2003.

Shadwick, Robert. "How Tunas and Lamnid Sharks Swim: An Evolutionary Convergence." *American Scientist* 93, no. 6 (November/December 2005): 524.

Sheff, David. "Pale Fire: Real Wasabi Doesn't Come in a Tube—and You've Probably Never Tasted It." *Saveur* 37 (September/October 1999): 43–45.

Sheraton, Mimi. "Raw Fish: How Safe Is It?" *New York Times,* 29 July 1981.

Shinmura, Izuru [新村 出], ed. *Kōjien* [広辞苑 Wide Garden of Words], 5th ed. Tokyo: Iwanami Shoten [岩波書店], 1998.

"Shufu no Ankēto Dēta 'Kaiten-zushi no Riyō ni Tsuite'" [主婦のアンケートデータ「回転寿司の利用について」 Data from Questionnaires on "Housewife Use of Conveyor-Belt Sushi"]. *Shufu, Josei Dēta Workshop* [主婦•女性データ Data Workshop on Housewives and Women]. 27 June 2005. Kaputo Burēn Torasuto [カプトブレーントラスト Caput Brain Trust]. Accessed 27 October 2006: http://soho-bank.ne.jp/work shop/news/20050627.php.

Shurtleff, William, and Akiko Aoyagi. "History of Miso and Soybean Chiang" and "History of Soy Sauce, Shoyu, and Tamari." *History of Soybeans and Soyfoods: 1100 B.C. to the 1980s.* Lafayette, CA: Soyfoods Center, 2004. Accessed 19 October 2006: http://www.thesoydailyclub.com/SFC/historyofsoyb.asp.

———. *The Book of Miso,* 2nd ed. Berkeley, CA: Ten Speed Press, 1983.

"Shusse" [出世 Success in Life]. *Gogen Yurai Jiten* [語源由来事典 Dictionary of Etymology and Origins]. Tokyo: All-Guide.com. Accessed 30 October 2006: http://gogen-allguide.com/si/syusse.html.

Sindler, Giulia. "Our History: Three Generations" and "Celebrity Sightings." Kamehachi Restaurant. Accessed 27 October 2006:

http://www.kamehachi.com/about/history.html and http://www.kamehachi.com/about/celeb_sightings.html.

Sintax [pseudonym]. "What's a Geoduck?" *Literotica.com,* n.d. Accessed 3 November 2006: http://english.literotica.com/stories/showstory.php?id=170330.

Smith, Devin. "Sushi Fans Sometimes Get More Than They Ordered." *Columbia News Service,* 7 March 2003.

Smith, W. Eugene, and Aileen M. Smith. *Minamata.* New York: Holt, Rinehart and Winston, 1975.

Snapper Aquaculture in South Australia: Fact Sheet No. 55/99. Adelaide, Australia: Primary Industries and Resources, South Australia, 2003.

Steingarten, Jeffrey. *It Must Have Been Something I Ate.* New York: Vintage, 2002.

Stern, Lisë. *How to Keep Kosher: A Comprehensive Guide to Understanding Jewish Dietary Laws.* New York: Morrow, 2004.

Stevens, Melissa. *Commercially Important Gulf of Mexico/South Atlantic Snappers.* Monterey, CA: Monterey Bay Aquarium Seafood Watch, 2005.

Strauss, Karyn. "Real Wasabi Gains Ground, Takes Root in U.S. Kitchens." *Nation's Restaurant News,* 13 March 2000: 43.

Stuertz, Mark. "Raw Clone." *Dallas Observer,* 1 August 2002.

"Suihan Kōso Kankei" [炊飯酵素関係 Related to Rice-Cooking Enzymes]. Ōtsuka Yakuhin Kōgyō Kabushiki Gaisha [大塚薬品工業株式会社 Otsuka Chemical Industry Corporation]. Accessed 26 October 2006: http://www.otuka-ci.co.jp/miora/miora1/miora1.html.

Sumbre, German, Yoram Gutfreund, Graziano Fiorito, Tamar Flash, and Binyamin Hochner. "Control of Octopus Arm Extension by a Peripheral Motor Program." *Science* 293, no. 5536 (7 September 2001): 1845–1848.

"Sushi Academy Student Data." California Sushi Academy. Accessed 18 October 2006: http://www.sushi-academy.com/pages/student_data.html.

"Sushi Masters." California Rice Commission. Accessed 5 November 2006: http://www.sushimasters.com.

"Sushi: Nihon no Kata" [鮨：日本の形 Sushi: The Japanese Tradition]. *Video Victim 2*. Directed and produced by Teevee Graphic. Performed by Jin Katagiri [片桐 仁] and Kentarō Kobayashi [小林賢太郎]. DVD. Tokyo: Kadokawa Entertainment [角川エンタテインメント], 2005.

"Sushi, Omusubi Kenyō Ohitsu-kei Robotto SSG-GTO" [寿司•おむすび兼用お櫃型ロボット Sushi and Rice Ball Dual-Use Wooden Tub-Style Robot SSG-GTO]. *Sushi, Norimaki Robotto* [寿司•のり巻きロボット Sushi and Roll Robots]. Suzumo Machinery Co. Accessed 29 October 2006: http://www.suzumo.co.jp/products/rolledsushi/index.html#.

Takaki, Ronald. *Strangers from a Different Shore: A History of Asian Americans*. Boston: Back Bay Books, 1998.

Takeuchi, Yutaka, Goro Yoshizaki, and Toshio Takeuchi. "Surrogate Broodstock Produces Salmonids." *Nature* 430, no. 5 (August 2004): 629–630.

Tamamura, Toyoo   [玉村豊男]. *Kaiten-sushi Sekai Isshū* [回転スシ世界一周 Conveyor-Belt Sushi Around the World]. Tokyo: Sekai Bunkasha [世界文化社], 2000.

Tamaru, Noriyoshi, and David Reid, eds. *Religion in Japanese Culture*. Tokyo: Kodansha International, 1996.

Tanaka, Masato [田中眞人. "Jinzō Ikura (Jinkō Ikura) no Tsukurikata" [人造イクラ（人工イクラ）の作り方 How to Make Artificial (Man-made) Salmon Eggs]. *Tanaka Kenkyūshitsu* [田中研究室 Tanaka Research Lab] Niigata University. Accessed 5 November 2006: http://capsule.eng.niigata-u.ac.jp/howto/ht_ikura/.

"Technical and Medicinal Side of Wasabi." *Information About Wasabi*. Pacific Farms. Accessed 1 November 2006: http://www.freshwasabi.com/.

Teenage Mutant Ninja Turtles III. Directed by Stuart Gillard. DVD. New Line Cinema, 1993.

"Tekka-maki" [鉄火巻き Tuna Roll]. *Gogen Yurai Jiten* [語源由来事典 Dictionary of Etymology and Origins]. Tokyo: All-Guide.com. Accessed 30 October 2006: http://gogen-allguide.com/te/tekka.html.

Thain, Michael, and Michael Hickman. *The Penguin Dictionary of Biology*, 11th ed. London: Penguin, 2004.

Thakur, Dhirendra Prasad, Katsuji Morioka, Yoshiaki Itoh, and Atsuhi Obatake. "Lipid Composition and Deposition of Cultured Yellowtail *Seriola quinqueradiata* Muscle at Different Anatomical Locations in Relation to Meat Texture." *Fisheries Science* 69 (June 2003): 487–494.

Tidwell, J. H., C. D. Webster, and S. D. Coyle. "Effects of Dietary Protein Level on Second-Year Growth and Water Quality for Largemouth Bass." *Aquaculture* 145, no. 1 (15 October 1996): 213–223.

"Trimethylaminuria." *Genetics Home Reference.* Bethesda, MD: U.S. National Library of Medicine. Accessed 5 November 2005: http://ghr.nlm.nih.gov/condition=trimethylaminuria.

Tsuji, Shizuo. *Japanese Cooking: A Simple Art.* Tokyo: Kodansha International, 1980.

Tsukamoto, K. "Oceanic Biology: Spawning of Eels Near a Seamount." *Nature* 439, no. 7079 (23 February 2006): 929.

Uchida, Eiichi [内田栄一]. *Edomae no Sushi* [江戸前の鮨 Edomae Sushi]. Tokyo: Shōbunsha [晶文社], 1989.

Uehara, Shinji, Christopher Taggart, Takumi Mitani, and Iain Suthers. "The Abundance of Juvenile Yellowtail (*Seriola quinqueradiata*) Near the Kuroshio: The Roles of Drifting Seaweed and Regional Hydrography." *Fisheries Oceanography* 15, no. 5 (September 2006): 351–362.

Uhrhammer, Jerry. "Oregon Farming Venture Succeeds in Growing Real Wasabi." *Knight Ridder,* 4 May 1999.

"Uma-yasu no Sushi [旨安のすし Delicious and Inexpensive Sushi]." *Otona no Shūmatsu* [おとなの週末 Grown-ups Weekend], no. 23 (September 2004): 8–31.

U.S. Senate Select Committee on Nutrition and Human Needs. *Dietary Goals for the United States,* 2nd edition. Washington, D.C.: U.S. Government Printing Office, 1977.

Wardle, C. S., J. J. Videler, T. Arimoto, J. M. Franco, and P. He. "The Muscle Twitch and the Maximum Swimming Speed of Giant Bluefin Tuna, *Thunnus thynnus* L." *Journal of Fish Biology* 35, no. 1 (July 1989): 129.

Watanabe, Myrna. "Generating Heat: New Twists on the Evolution of Endothermy." *BioScience,* 55, no. 6 (June 2005): 470–475.

Watanabe, Takeshi. "Broodstock Nutrition Research on Marine Finfish in Japan." *Aquaculture,* 227, nos. 1–4 (10 November 2003): 35–61.

Weber, Michael. *What Price Farmed Fish: A Review of the Environmental & Social Costs of Farming Carnivorous Fish.* Silver Spring, MD: SeaWeb Aquaculture Clearinghouse, 2003.

Weiner, Eric. "Japanese Women Are Gradually Moving into the So Far Male-Dominated Profession of Sushi Chef." *All Things Considered* (radio show). Washington, D.C.: National Public Radio, 2 March 2001.

Weir, Erica. "Sushi, Nemotodes, and Allergies." *Canadian Medical Association Journal,* 172, no. 3 (1 February 2005).

"What Is Wasaouro?" Mitsubishi-Kagaku Foods Corporation. Accessed 29 October 2006. http://www.mfc.co.jp/wasaouro/e/index.html.

Whynott, Douglas. *Giant Bluefin.* New York: North Point Press, 1995.

Worm, Boris, et al. "Impacts of Biodiversity Loss on Ocean Ecosystem Services." *Science* 314, no. 5800 (3 November 2006): 787–790.

"Yellowtail Life Cycle." Marine Harvest/Nutreco. Accessed 1 November 2006. http://www.marineharvest.com/species-products/yellowtail.html.

Yoshino, Masuo [吉野昴雄]. *Sushi, Sushi, Sushi: Sushi no Jiten* [鮓•鮨•すし：すしの事典 The Encyclopedia of Sushi]. Tokyo: Asahiya Shuppan [旭屋出版], 1990.

Yuyama, Reiko [湯山玲子]. *Onna Hitori Zushi* [女ひとり寿司 One Woman Sushi]. Tokyo: Yōsensha [洋泉社], 2004.

Zhang, Y., et al. "Coding of Sweet, Bitter, and Umami Tastes: Different Receptor Cells Sharing Similar Signaling Pathways." *Cell* 112, no. 3 (7 February 2003): 293–301.

Zhao, G. Q., et al. "The Receptors for Mammalian Sweet and Umami Taste." *Cell* 115, no. 3 (31 October 2003): 255–266.

INDEX